1981

W9-ACQ-373

Modern Nordic plays.

3 0301 00090558 4

The Library of Scandinavian Literature

MODERN NORDIC PLAYS

———

NORWAY

MODERN NORDIC PLAYS

NORWAY

LIBRARY OF SCANDINAVIAN LITERATURE

TWAYNE PUBLISHERS, INC., NEW YORK

LIBRARY
College of St. Francis
JOLIET, ILL.

The Library of Scandinavian Literature
Erik J. Friis, *General Editor*

Volume 20
Modern Nordic Plays — Norway

Copyright © 1974, by Universitetsforlaget, Oslo

Permission for all rights — professional, amateur,
motion picture, etc. — see the explanation on
copyright-page of each play

Printed in Norway by:
Aktietrykkeriet i Trondhjem

839.82
M828

Contents

96780

Introduction

NORWEGIAN DRAMA AFTER THE SECOND WORLD WAR

Drama as a slice of life, *une tranche de vie,* reached its peak with Ibsen and naturalism. The audience at a Norwegian drawing-room drama, in the 1870's and 1880's, was peeping into a — most often middle-class — parlour through the fourth wall, which had been removed for the occasion.

A great deal has been written about the kind of *illusion* this theatre created and still creates. One thing is certain, however: 'to create an illusion' has been a time-honoured phrase in Norwegian dramatic criticism, and it is still being used regularly by Norwegian drama critics, despite the fact that the history of modern drama, during the past three generations, has been a slow development away from the peep-show realism of which Ibsen has remained the most outstanding exponent.

Perhaps it is because of Ibsen's well-established position that realism in Norway has been especially hard to supplant. True enough, Ibsen himself developed away from realism: his last play, *Naar vi døde vaagner (When We Dead Awaken),* culminates in an avalanche that is as 'romantic' in its impact, and makes as unreasonable demands on the stage hands, as the final avalanche in *Brand (Brand)* from Ibsen's pre-realistic period.

But Norwegian drama did not follow the course plotted by Ibsen in his later plays. It was the Ibsen from 1877-1883, the realistic, problem dramatist, who founded the school. Ibsen's treatment of social and more personal problems, in plays like *Et Dukkehjem (A Doll's House)* and *Gengangere (Ghosts),* became the prototype for his imitators for the following generations. Gunnar Heiberg (1857-1929) and Helge Krog (1889-1962) wrote their plays in an Ibsenian style, whether or not they were treating social, moral, political, or psychological problems. And the great master's realistic form of drawing-room drama was the norm for the Norwegian dramatists who followed him.

In the inter-war years, there were those who undoubtedly felt a degree of impatience with something they regarded as an onerous tradition, a stagnated convention. As one of the first, Stein Bugge — a playwright and man of the theatre — wanted to expose the decline in the dramatic art, and create a new form of theatre — a cultic, 'ideal' theatre. For a long time, this was a voice in the wilderness. But, little by little, a growing discontent with 'Ibsen realism' began to manifest itself, also in Norway. It was maintained that the Ibsen-Heiberg-Krog tradition did more harm than good; it was a straitjacket that had to be shaken off.

But have the experiments, the attempts at renewal, resulted in anything of value? Or are the significant works still being created by the more traditional dramatists? The answer is difficult to give, but the picture presented by post-war Norwegian drama is not very impressive. Neither among the adherents of the old school, nor among the more experimental playwrights, is there a single dramatist of magnitude, even though a number of them — first and foremost Tarjei Vesaas and Johan Borgen — have won great names and reputations for themselves in other literary genres. In Ibsen's native land, the great values in post-war literature must be sought outside the drama.

Other literary genres — especially the novel — have attracted the writers. And after the Second World War, the position of the theatre in Norway has not been strong. Since the 1950's, the number of theatres has declined. The role of the old, bourgeois theatre-goers is of less importance than before, and new arrangements with organized, collective visits to the theatre have not — yet, at any rate — created a new audience that can play the same role of supporting the theatre as the old bourgeoisie did.

Few authors have had the opportunity of coming into proper contact with a theatre, of familiarizing themselves with this special medium.

The relatively weak position of drama cannot be explained, it can merely be ascertained. But it should be pointed out that there are bright spots, and that the newer media, radio and TV, are gradually providing opportunities for a new type of drama that may prove to be strong and enduring. In this introduction, a brief examination will be made of certain of the trends and some of the names that are more or less representative of the development that has been taking place, and of the position of Norwegian drama today.

It is only natural to consider the 'Ibsen' tradition first — thereafter the other trends, with emphasis on the various attempts at renewal.

'The Ibsen tradition'

In all likelihood, Helge Krog's (1889-1962) inter-war plays — especially *Underveis (In Transit)* and *Opbrudd (Break-up)* — may be characterized as the best realistic dramas that have been written in Norway during the last few generations. This is true, despite the fact that, in this Krogian theatre, the ideas are far more alive than the characters — exactly as in the plays of George Bernard

Shaw (and this is not the only feature that these two
rationalistic radicals have in common). Krog's few post-war
plays are of less significance, even though the radical
pathos is still present in his one-act play *Kom inn (Come
In)*, in which Krog is again lashing out at a sombre, nega-
tive religiosity. Even though the psychology is extreme and
one-sided, in the presentation of the helpless and perverse
fisherman and his wife, the description of a morbid, self-
delusion has a strength that is reminiscent of the intensity
of Krog's best plays.

Next to Helge Krog — and clearly inspired by him —
Alex Brinchman (b. 1888) has been the most enthusiastic harvester in the Ibsenian vineyard, and in his plays it
is possible to detect a sincerity and a genuine intonation in
the indirect preaching of radical, humanistically ethical
standpoints. But the resemblance to Ibsen's technique is
often *too* apparent, and it even happens that the theme of
the plays appears to have been borrowed directly from Ibsen
— as in *Løgnen og lykken (Happiness and the Lie)*, a particularly illustrative example of the significance of the Ibsen
tradition.

Like *Come In,* this play is about self-delusion, and all
the time, Ibsen's *Vildanden (The Wild Duck)* is lurking in
the background. After the latest in a series of miscarriages,
Dr. Storm has reluctantly agreed to let his wife keep another
woman's child, in the belief that it is her own. Everything
goes well — for four years. Little Karin has had a good
childhood with the Storms, and Mrs. Storm has had the
happiest time of her life. Then Nurse Vera appears — the
nurse who exchanged the babies four years earlier, so that
Mrs. Storm had a living child instead of her own, stillborn
baby — and she arrives like a new Gregers Werle: ' . . . he
who lives a lie, is undermining his life', she says. She does

not believe that 'a person *can* do right as long as he is living a lie.' The ensuing showdown ends with Storm and
Mrs. Storm doing away with the lie and finding each
other again. Thus, the ending is different from that of *The
Wild Duck*. These people are able to tolerate complete openness.

This particular version of the theme of self-delusion has
been quite successful. Finn Bø (1893–1962), another devotee of the traditional drama, took up the same theme in
Fordi jeg elsker deg (Because I Love You), which, in its
day, represented a typical softening up of the Ibsenian
form, with the use of flashbacks. Ibsenian in both structure
and problematics is Brinchmann's *Den som elsker sin far
(He Who Loves His Father)*, in which the protagonist —
the prime minister — neglects his family and his obligations
in favour of his political efforts. For that matter, in *Mannen
av i går* (1962; *The Man of Yesterday*), young Helge Hagerup also treats a similar theme. This play gives an interesting account of a politician, which seems to be authentic
and representative: the socialist leader who discovers that
time and progress have left him behind.

A political problem is the main theme of Hans Heiberg's (b. 1904) *Minnefesten (Commemoration)* — a realistic play in episodes about the disillusion that followed
hard on the heels of the liberation of Norway in 1945, and
in Sigbjørn Hølmebakk's *Heltedød til salgs (Heroic Death
for Sale)* — an attack on armament profiteers, German
officers in Norway, NATO, and anti-Communist agitation.
This play was written as late as 1968, but it is conventional in form and is characterized by an episodic realism,
which Hølmebakk has later practised in several film manuscripts.

Tighter in form is Axel Kielland's (1907-1963) attempt

to take up social problems as topics for discussion. His most effective play is *Herren og hans tjenere (The Lord and His Servants)*, which dramatically presents Kielland's theory about the course of events and motives in the celebrated Helander case. At the same time, it is a contribution to the intense debate about Hell that raged in Norway in the 1950's. But *Han som sa nei (He Who Said No)*, with its ingenious use of the Suez crisis, is also an effective contribution to a discussion. Here, among other things, the author implies that what the protagonist of the play is judged for (he has refused to carry out an order that is incompatible with his conscience), is the same as what German war criminals, in their day, were convicted of for *not* doing.

Kielland's *Hennes Høyhet min kone (Her Royal Highness My Wife)* is an amusing comedy in which yet another topical 'problem' is the background for the intrigue: Can a person of royal blood marry a commoner? The author derived his material from the marriage of Princess Margaret of England to Anthony Armstrong Jones. Ex-king Edward VIII also appears on the stage as a ghost of the past.

One of the most zealous adherents to the Ibsen tradition is Finn Havrevold (b. 1905). His best plays are *Uretten (The Injustice)* and *Tomannsboligen (The Two-family House)*. The first play with its presentation of the young banker who must bitterly atone for his financial rashness, is reminiscent of Ibsen's *Rosmersholm*. In *The Two-family House*, Havrevold describes two types of people: those whose only desire is to *own*, and who have no lives of their own. They are parasites, spying on the lives of others, on the family on the second floor who live a rich life without owning a thing.

Finn Havrevold is undoubtedly at his best as a writer of

radio dramas. His radio plays — collected in three volumes — have been performed in a number of countries, and have won for him several international awards. In these plays Havrevold to some extent breaks with the realistic tradition, and often reveals a ready response to the special possibilities of the radio drama.

Next to Havrevold, the best writer of radio dramas is undoubtedly Inger Hagerup (b. 1905), who is otherwise best known as a poet. The title play, in the collection *Hilsen fra Katarina (Greetings from Katarina)*, is an unpretentious and penetrating description of the inner feelings of a woman after her lover has left her – the theme and mood are not unrelated to Geraldy's *La Voix humaine*.

Comedies, revues and cabarets have probably had a greater success with the public than serious, realistic drama. Finn Bø has revealed more talent as a writer of revues than of realistic plays, and Alex Brinchmann's *Karusell (Carousel)*, from 1941, is undoubtedly his most successful work. Alf Prøysen (1914–1970) has enjoyed triumphs with his comedies in the Hedmark (Eastern Norway) dialect, partly set to music. He is the Norwegian author who has attracted the largest audiences to Norwegian theatres in the post-war period (just as he is probably the most widely-read post-war Norwegian novelist).

In his comedy *Min Kvinne (My Woman)*, Odd Eidem (b. 1913) brilliantly demonstrates how a woman can take her colours from the men who are in love with her. This is one of the few Norwegian plays that can stand mention in the same breath as plays by W. Somerset Maugham or Noel Coward.

Poetical Drama

One of the major charges against the realistic play — in

Norway as elsewhere — has been that it is trivial and un-poetical. Thus, attempts have been made to renew Norwe-gian drama by writers who have dreamed of recreating poet-ry on the stage.

Most often, these renovators have been searching for models in the theatrical poetry of earlier times, and in Nor-way the attempts have largely been lacking in originality. Shakespeare, for example, is quite discernible in Odd Ei-dem's ambitious, but undramatic, *Spillet om Bly-Petter (The Play About Lead-Peter)* — a much less successful dra-ma than *My Woman*. And a considerable part of world dra-ma — from Aeschylus onwards — stands out in the plays of the most 'literary' of all Norwegian dramatists, Tormod Skagestad: *Under treet ligg øksa (Under the Tree Lies the Axe), Flyplassen (The Airport)* and *Byen ved havet (The City by the Sea)*. In spite of their good qualities, these plays are weighed down too much by 'influences' both in details and in aspirations. His lyrical radio dramas are much less encumbered.

Tarjei Vesaas (1897-1970) is more independent — even though his dramatic production can in no way measure up to his novels and poetry. *Morgonvinden (Morning Wind),* a drama of the resistance movement, is poetic and pathetic, but undramatic and not arranged very well scenically. *Bleikeplassen (The Bleaching Yard)* has a much greater dramatic impact. Vesaas' lyrical temperament shows up to greater advantage in a series of radio plays — short stories that have been dramatized for radio.

Johan Borgen (b. 1902) has also written a play that could be called 'poetic'. *Eventyr (Fairy Tale)* is a fantasy in which human traits are embodied in animal masks and animal behaviour, and in which Borgen puts some of the speeches into verse.

Renewal?

These poetic attempts do not represent any real renewal. Have the more radical experimenters provided us with greater values? On closer inspection, it appears that they, too, are closely tied to prototypes — both older models and plays like the ones that have appeared in Europe and America in the inter- and-post-war periods.

Among the older dramatists in this category, Tore Ørjasæter (1886-1968) is the most independent. He uses the dramatic medium in an authoritative manner, especially in his two post-war plays: *Christophoros* (1948) and *Den lange bryllupsreisa* (1949; *The Long Honeymoon*). The latter is an expressionistic, topical drama, a strongly committed play about feelings of guilt and responsibility for war-time atrocities — related in many ways to the plays by Nordahl Grieg, the writer of the inter-war period, but built up of a number of realistic and symbolic characters and scenes, that do not always form a part of a harmonious union. *Christophoros,* the so-called 'dream-play', is more harmonious — a dramatic presentation of an artist at the crossroads. Ørjasæter splits the gifted painter in two: Per is the 'good half', who loves his wife and child, while Pål is the 'bad I', who tries to wrench Per out of his family ties, into an egoistic artist's life. Pål is visible only to Per (and the audience) — the other characters can only sense him, as a chill — as something dangerous, threatening. In the end, Per is saved by his love for the child.

With all his violations of realistic stage conventions, Tore Ørjasæter's plays still do not represent any radical innovation. Most of the unrealistic features — and the Strindbergian sub-title 'A Dream-play' — point backwards rather than forwards, despite the author's independent attitude to the material and the medium. But prior to Ørjasæter, Norwegian drama had been lacking in similar attempts.

In the inter-war period, Johan Borgen had already written several interesting experimental plays — especially *Mens vi venter (While We Wait)*. Since the war, he has written often highly experimental radio and TV dramas, as well as several plays for the theatre. Among these is *Akvariet (The Aquarium)*, a satire that is somewhat conventional, but unpretentious in its form, and the more ambitious *Frigjøringsdag (Day of Liberation)*, in which he presents man's futile and meaningless toil on earth, his eternal yearning for a freedom which, at bottom, he does not know how to use. It is mankind's puttering about, seen in a cosmic perspective, accompanied by the whispered comments of the Four Winds and a sound that can only be the voice of God. Here, Borgen's imagination unfolds even more freely and fertilely than in *Fairy Tale*, but he does not attain great heights. The principal lines of development are too vague, the effects too sophisticated. Borgen's sensitivity is not first and foremost scenically dramatic.

Ernst Orvil is a distinctive dramatist (and poet and novelist). Each of his dramas is characterized by his singular play upon words, his word-magic, and this, more than the dramatic structure, is what represents Orvil's unique contribution to Norwegian drama. His best play, the psychological comedy *Rødt lys (Red Light)*, is a kind of spiritual defence of our inhibitions — first and foremost, a scenically very effective pyrotechnical display of lines, the interdependence and interplay of which are very unusual, because they do not observe the customary laws of logic, but have a logic all their own and are nourished by the most remarkable associations.

Among the playwrights born in the 1920's and 1930's, there are three who stand out: Georg Johannessen (b. 1931), the youngest of these, has written only one play, *Kassandra (Cassandra)*, which, in revue and musical form, is an attack on the folly and misery of the world, and especially on Christianity. Our Lord, in the character of a 'fat man', is a recurrent figure — this is a parody of the various roles that people have assigned to their God at different times.

The structure of Johannessen's play is somewhat loose and haphazard. More integrated and promising are Finn Carling's (b. 1925) *Gitrene (The Bars)* and *Slangen (The Snake)* — especially the former. Here, the literary absurdity is in evidence: Isak, the Director of the Zoo, is dreaming of the millennium, when the lion and the lamb will lie down side by side. He ventures into the cage of the peevish old lion, Abraham, who kills him. In the meantime, Isak goes on playing as 'a dead man', until he is 'born again' by his wife Rebecca — only to go back into the cage and be killed again.

Abraham and the other beasts of prey behind the bars are able to leave their cages. Then they suddenly turn into people. Carling does not appear to operate quite logically on the two 'levels': man-animal. But with its various nuances and its scenic irony, this play throws light on human attitudes, especially to violence and war. The symbolism of the bars is significant: Man is safest behind solid fortifications, in isolation ... *The Snake,* which is a later play, deals with similar themes.

Jens Bjørneboe (b. 1920) — the *enfant terrible* of Norwegian literature during the last decade — is a polemicist and a preacher. Naturally enough, he first resorted to the realistic form: in a number of novels he attacked conditions in post-war Norway, and the world. But when it occurred to him to use the drama as a medium for preaching the gospel, he abandoned realism. The story of his dramatization of the novel *Den onde hyrde (The Bad Shepherd)* is symptomatic. An attempt to rewrite the novel in collaboration with Helge Krog, as a realistic play did not succeed. Then Bjørneboe tried — alone — following new lines, and the result was *Til lykke med dagen (Many Happy Returns of the Day),* in which a realistic illusion of reality, to some extent, has had to yield to an obviously Brecht-inspired *Verfremdung,* in a highly satirical play about the inhuman treatment of prisoners in Norwegian jails.

Bjørneboe's next attempt, *Fugleelskerne (The Bird Lovers),* has a greater unity in its tone and dramatic form. In this play, full of contrasts, the vacationing Germans — torturers from the Second World War — are lined up against the hunt-happy Italians, in the village where the Germans want to establish their vacation paradise. Bjørneboe also plays on the contrast between the cruelty of the torturers to their victims, and their sentimental love of animals and flowers, and on other contrasts between the light and dark side of people. All in all, *The Bird Lovers* is a depressing picture of two nations during and after the war, and of unpleasant aspects of human nature, characterized by Bjørneboe's deep interest in sadism, by his love/hate of the Germans, and by references directed at such phenomena as slavish discipline, eugenics, post-war German politics, NATO, tourist traffic, etc.

Later, in *Semmelweiss (Semmelweiss)* and *Amputasjon (Amputation),* Bjørneboe has continued his attacks on society — and has pursued his sadistic interest.

Next to the 'middle generation' Bjørneboe, Carling, and Johannesen, a number of very young writers have tried to renew the drama. There have been group-theatre experiments and, more than ever before, theatre directors (including those in radio and TV) are taking chances on new works — no matter how controversial they may be. Thus, the authors should be able to gain the practical theatre experience that is virtually indispensable to a playwright. The lack of theatrical experience is the very thing that has characterized most of the plays that have been written for the theatre in the post-war period — a lack of practical experience and theoretical training.

This is evident among the devotees of the Ibsen tradition. They have moved along familiar paths, writing problem plays – often with an Ibsenian theme – taking up political, moral and psychological problems as topics for discussion. If these plays have seldom been dramatic, and have seldom had any measure of success (except when a matter of very topical interest has drawn audiences to the theatres, as was the case with Axel Kielland's plays), this is largely due to the fact that, no matter how ingenious the authors may be, they have not learned *enough* from Ibsen, the great master. In most of these plays, one scene follows another without providing proper dramatic tension. The exposition is usually static, and the dramatic structure is often lacking in unity and cohesion. The authors have not mastered their trade fundamentally enough. Unlike Ibsen, they have not immersed themselves in dramaturgical handbooks, nor have they had Ibsen's practical theatre experience. More than most drama forms, the realistic drawing-room drama requires technical know-how. In Norway, very few post-war realistic plays deserve to be called, 'well-made plays'.

Another common feature is the stylistic weakness of the dialogue. There are a number of insipid, often partly or completely irrelevant speeches that reduce the excitement and

create boring passages. A comparison with Ibsen's apparently simple — but, in reality, elegant, thoroughly re-
vised, and powerful — dialogue is thought-provoking. Artistic realism is not synonymous with laxity. There is nothing
wrong with the realistic genre. It still has its great devotees, in other countries. But our practitioners have not yet
been able to develop the tradition to any appreciable extent.

The efforts to create a poetic drama have been few and
random, and do not reveal any pronounced technical skill.
And the more experimental writers do not stand on very
strong ground, as far as technical know-how is concerned.
To be sure, Ørjasæter could create a drama with inner tension. And by keeping his ears open, Ernest Orvil — who,
unlike most of his colleagues, *has* worked closely with the
theatre — has developed dialogue which, at its best, is genuinely dramatic. Johan Borgen, the dramatist who has had
the most experience in the theatre, reveals considerable
technical instinct and knowledge in his best plays. To all
appearances, however, his aspirations and poetical bent
are too subtle, too rich in nuances and associations, to find
a completely adequate expression in works for the stage.
The radio drama seems to be a more congenial medium.

The 'middle generation' — Bjørneboe, Carling and Johannessen — on the other hand, appear to lack an intimate
contact with the theatre and its techniques. This is also
why their attempts have not been very effective, theatri-
cally. Despite their absorbing content, these plays are
not as engrossing on the stage as they could have been,
if their knowledge of this special medium had been better.

The youngest group of writers have not yet had time
to profit from the experience they have begun to gain. They
have not yet begun to make their mark in a way that really
represents something new and valuable in Norwegian dra-

ma — even though writers like the Hagerup brothers, Einar Økland, and others have delivered promising works.

Our golden age of the drama was created by two poets — Henrik Ibsen and Bjørnstjerne Bjørnson — who, for long periods of time, were connected with the stage as playwrights, directors and theatre managers. The qualifications of our post-war dramatists have been flimsier. Generally speaking, the successors of Ibsen appear to have contented themselves with reading — and watching — their Ibsen and other realistic dramatists, and receiving impressions and incentives from them. Any possible theoretical studies have left few traces in the plays. And the devotees of other forms of drama have scarcely taken the technical problems any more seriously. We find impressions and reminiscences from Greek drama, from Shakespeare, Brecht, Ionesco and others, but seldom any really serious attempts to arrive at an understanding of the dramatic medium and its special conditions. To be sure, the rules of dramaturgy are by no means sacrosanct, but they cannot be neglected with impunity. And if one is to break them, one should be familiar with them, and have sound reason for doing so.

When all is said and done, the commitments that several of the later dramatic works bear witness to, hold out some promise for the future. These plays were not written because the authors wanted to write plays. They were written because the authors wanted to express something fundamental, something they felt was of current interest, new and important to say.

Even in Norway, the theatre is perhaps on the point of becoming a place in which opinions and ideals will be pitted against each other in a way that will leave a mark on society. To a much greater extent than has been the case during the past generation, it may again become a mirror of its time.

A word about the Norwegian language

The language situation in Norway is still complicated. Most authors use *riksmål* or *bokmål* (literally: 'book language') — a more advanced version of the language used, for example, by Ibsen and Bjørnson. Other writers use *nynorsk* (New Norwegian), an idiom created in the latter half of the nineteenth century on the basis of living dialects. The two languages are not very different — even though *bokmål* has been influenced by Danish much more than *nynorsk* — and they are mutually understandable. Nevertheless, the conflict between *nynorsk* adherents and (especially the more conservative) *bokmål* supporters is constantly flaring up.

Of the four Norwegian dramatists who are represented in this anthology, Johan Borgen, Finn Havrevold, and Axel Kielland wrote their plays in *bokmål,* while Tarjei Vesaas used *nynorsk.*

Eiliv Eide

The House

A Radio Drama

By Johan Borgen

Translated from the Norwegian
by Pat Shaw

All rights, including professional, amateur, motion picture, recitation, lecturing, public reading, radio broadcasting, television, reproduction by recording or any electronic or mechanical means, and the rights of translation into foreign languages are strictly reserved. Permission for any of these rights must be obtained from Johan Borgen, Akersborg Terrasse 43, Oslo 8, Norway.

Johan Borgen

Johan Borgen (b. 1902) is the most outstanding name in post-war Norwegian literature, next to Tarjei Vesaas. Throughout the whole body of his work, he has been concerned with the problems of the individual. This is apparent in his excellent short stories about children and the pressures of the compulsory world of adults under which children grow up. And in his short stories, novels, and plays, the imaginative, sensitive individual is continually being pitted against a stagnated reality, a convention-bound, bourgeois attitude to life. Of special significance is the trilogy about *Lille Lord (Little Lord)* — one of the great novels of development in Norwegian literature — and the profound novel, *Jeg (I)*. In the latter book, we encounter 'the house', which is a pronounced symbol in Johan Borgen's writing, and a protagonist of sorts in the radio drama *Huset (The House)*.

In *I*, the action begins and ends at 'the house in the forest'. It opens with 'I' standing and looking at another 'I', who is leaving the house — in reality, the two 'I's are one and the same person. Thereafter, we follow one, divided 'I', through various experiences — among others, a visit to a Kafka-like 'Nobiskro' which, in various ways, serves the theme of the book: the problem of identity. In the end, the 'I' who fled returns to the house in the forest, and is united with the 'I' who has remained there all along.

The radio drama, *The House,* is also about returning to a house: Laura and her nephew Henrik visit the house they left many years ago. The house has a distinctive atmosphere, in which its former inhabitants go on living — especially Laura's brother, Henrik's father — the man who, more than anyone, has left his mark on the house. He represents the stagnated, bourgeois person who always knows what is 'right', and is constantly saying so. They also encounter themselves, as they were then. The house becomes an ordeal which they must undergo in order to liberate — and find — themselves.

96780

LIBRARY
College of St. Francis
JOLIET, ILL.

Characters:

LAURA

HENRIK

ENEVOLD

THE FATHER'S VOICE

LAURA

Hush! I thought somebody knocked.

HENRIK

Oh. Did someone?

LAURA

It may have been the wind.

HENRIK

Yes. Or the rain. There are so many sounds in weather like this. . .

LAURA

It may have been the wind. I don't like wind.

HENRIK

No.

LAURA

I don't like something reaching after me and touching me out on the road, something that can take one by surprise at any moment. . .

HENRIK

No, but you're inside now, Aunt Laura.

LAURA

What? Yes, inside. Thank goodness. But I thought somebody knocked.

HENRIK

I can go and make sure . . . *(goes and makes sure, faint sound of door and increasing wind)*. . . No, there was nobody.

LAURA

I don't like that empty corridor either, that long hotel corridor with all the white number plates.

HENRIK
No, it's not very nice. But it's only temporary, isn't it? A few days. . . Because you don't intend to go on living here, do you?

LAURA
Have you noticed when you go out there – in the corridor — it's as if someone has just been there? And that yellow lamp at the far end of the corridor. It's blowing out there too.

HENRIK
Oh, really now. In the corridor. . .

LAURA
Well, a draught then. There's always a draught. As if someone has just gone by and left behind a gust of wind. Oh, no one's going to make me believe that someone has just gone by.

HENRIK
You seem so nervous this evening, Aunt Laura. I hardly know you.

LAURA
You don't know me at all. Fifteen years ago. You were only a boy then.

HENRIK
Well, seventeen. Remember, I'll soon be thirty-three.

LAURA
Seventeen. Thirty-three. Fifteen years ago. Those are a lot of years at that age.

HENRIK
But when one is even younger. Think of the jump from ten to twenty-five then. A whole lifetime.

LAURA

M-m. Good God! Are you already so old that it's starting to go quickly, that it's starting not to change...
Think of *later on,* then!

HENRIK

Well, what about later on?

LAURA

Later on. When it doesn't change at all. Or when you
don't notice the change. Except for the fact that time
has suddenly passed. And the memories... I distinctly
thought somebody knocked!

HENRIK

Nobody knocked. Tell me, are you expecting somebody?

LAURA

Both yes and no ... Lord, how you resemble your father in that light ... Dreadful lighting ... Can you understand where these hotels get their lampshades from?
— Sit here, so I can have a proper look at you ... Soon
thirty-three. My brother's only son.

HENRIK

Aunt Laura, if you say now that time marches on...

LAURA

Heavens, how right you are, boy! You know, I was on
the verge of saying it. Thanks for rescuing me.

HENRIK

I had to. It was sheer self-defense. You never knew,
of course, how *you* were forever rescuing *me,* at home.

LAURA

I rescued you?

HENRIK

Always. From the banalities. From everything being

said in a definite order, for a definite purpose. The way members of a family feel obliged to do with one another: 'Salt herring is good, children.' Remember that? Remember what he said afterwards?

LAURA

'Yes, and so good for you!'

HENRIK

Ugh! And: 'The water certainly was cold today . . .'

LAURA

'Yes, but that never hurt anybody!'

HENRIK

Ugh!

LAURA

Ugh! Yes, it was dreadful.

HENRIK

It *was* dreadful. Worse for me than for you, I tell you.

LAURA

Oh, it certainly was an ordeal for one and all.

HENRIK

Yes, but you were grown up, Aunt Laura. That makes a tremendous difference. You could laugh at it.

LAURA

Not out loud. Not in my brother's house. I couldn't afford to do that.

HENRIK

But alone then. On the inside.

LAURA

Oh, I've been laughing on the inside for such a long time that it has frozen up.

HENRIK

What a pity. But even so, you were out of it, above it — or what should I say. To me it was like a lid that lay over everything, over every day. 'Chin up, boy, face the facts.' . . . And then, when he slapped my back . . .

LAURA

And yet your father *wasn't* like that. My brother wasn't like that.

HENRIK

Not your brother, perhaps. But my father. Oh, I could have. . .

LAURA

No, no! Don't say it. Besides, you couldn't have at all.

HENRIK

Couldn't have what?

LAURA

Nothing. That's just the point. He felt obliged to be like that, because he didn't know any of you.

HENRIK

Perhaps. But who was to blame for that?

LAURA

Hm. You're not so old after all. Imagine asking about blame. The milieu, my boy. They've conjured up something they call 'milieu' since then. It's a useful word. It obliterates everything.

HENRIK

And what was so special about our milieu?

LAURA

Too refined to be poor, too poor to be nice, as long as it had to be refined. Do you remember the dinner service?

HENRIK:

The blue set? You bet I do... Which was never used. Except — ugh! And then it stood so high up in the cupboard. Everything stood so high up in that house.

LAURA

'In that house'... Remember, you're talking about your own home.

HENRIK

What on earth? — Why, Aunt Laura... have you also started saying that sort of thing?

LAURA

It amuses me. I've made up my mind to grow old.

Pause

HENRIK

And now the rain that never will stop. Can you understand where it all comes from?

LAURA

That belongs in the category of things that one knows without understanding. Do you know what your father would have said?

HENRIK

That it was the evaporation by the sun...

LAURA

And the condensation of the vapor...

HENRIK

And the droplets that fall.

LAURA

In short, that it was raining. He'd have said it was good for the farmer.

HENRIK

Oh Lord, that too. Don't remind me of it.

A short pause

LAURA

You asked if I were expecting somebody. Yes I am, as a matter of fact... No, no, not only in a general sense — after all, we're always doing that, we lonely ones. I'm waiting *for* somebody. Enevold. Do you remember him?

HENRIK

The real estate agent? That little pipsqueak... Oh, sorry, Aunt Laura... I forgot...

LAURA

Never mind, my dear. It was such a long time ago. An American career woman doesn't cling to a sentimental early attachment.

HENRIK

Well, ... I wouldn't know anything about that... But perhaps I should go, then?

LAURA

You dumbbell. So old Enevold and Aunt Laura can sit on the plush sofa and exchange memories? That's not why I asked you to come.

HENRIK

I would have come without a message. As soon as I saw in the newspaper that you were on the ship, I was on the look-out for you in town. Then I found out that you'd come straight up here. Strange ...

LAURA

Well, I sent a cable to Enevold from the boat. That's

probably the first time he has ever received tidings from
the sea.

HENRIK

Yes, but what do you want him for? I mean, as long as
it's not. . .

LAURA

The house, my boy. Didn't you know that the house
is for sale?

HENRIK

Our house? I had no idea! I never want to set eyes on
it again.

LAURA

Not you. But me.

HENRIK

But why on earth? I thought you hated it!

LAURA

Perhaps. I don't know. Perhaps that's why. I don't
know.

HENRIK

The garden with the overgrown lawns, the crooked
fence facing the small-town street. The iron gate with
the hinges that creaked and screeched . . .

LAURA

There you can see. You're no more than thirty-two.
And yet you're beginning to yearn already.

HENRIK

Certainly not! Yearn? . . . The stairs with the sickly-
sweet smell, as of thyme. The tall white doors that had
to be given an extra tug when one had closed them. . .
only then were they closed properly. — The green walls
in the parlor. . .

LAURA

The blue dinner service, high up in the cupboard.

HENRIK

What about the yellow service, then? The everyday service — on the white tablecloth under the lamp. The chairs with curved wickerwork in the seats and back. . . Can you tell me why it was that one always thought one had done something wrong in that house?

LAURA

Perhaps one had. . . No, no, it's not only because you were a child. It felt like that to me too.

HENRIK

And you want to see it again? Own it? Tell me: Do you want to live there?

There is a knock

HENRIK

Now there was a knock. Aren't you going to tell them to come in?

LAURA

I can't bear it. Suppose nobody was there?

There is another knock

HENRIK

I'll go and answer the door. *(as he goes)* It must be him — Enevold.

LAURA

Yes, could it be anyone else?. . .

A short pause

HENRIK

Come in, please. Hello, Mr. Enevold. Don't you recognize me?

ENEVOLD

Well, if it isn't the student. Oh, sorry, that's what we said in those days. But that's a long time ago, now.

HENRIK

Yes. Please come in, Mr. Enevold. My aunt is expecting you here... No, I'll take your coat. We'll put your umbrella in the hall.

ENEVOLD

Well, look who's here. Miss — Laura. Well, it's been a long time. Well — you haven't changed a bit! Well, hello. Well, this was a great occasion — Miss.

LAURA

Am I supposed to say *Mister* Enevold to — you? — Sit down. Changed? Let me see. You've aged, too. So you received my cable?

ENEVOLD

Yes, I should say I did. I've never been so surprised in my life. No, I haven't. Here one sits — on the edge of the world, so to speak — and then along comes a cable. What was I going to say: And how are things with you — in every respect?

LAURA

Excellent, Enevold — in every respect. Won't you have some brandy? My nephew and I were just going to have a drink ... Oh, please fetch the toothbrush glasses, Henrik. I love to drink out of toothbrush glasses when I'm in Norway.

ENEVOLD

Thanks, but I drink so little.

LAURA

That's all right, Enevold. I hadn't intended for you to

drink so much, either. . . Oh, please bring the bottle too, Henrik. It's in the suitcase — on top. That's right. Thanks. Ugh, this is hard to open.

ENEVOLD

I have a knife. . .

LAURA

Oh, it's coming. . . Why, let me see: the little pearl-handled knife with the impossible corkscrew — which at most could be used for cleaning one's nails. — There's a chip in the mother-of-pearl on the other side, if I'm not mistaken? — You see, Enevold, here's someone who remembers — little things.

ENEVOLD

Hee, hee, hee! May I be allowed to pour, perhaps?

LAURA

No, let me pour. I like to.

ENEVOLD

Oh, not so much for me . . .

LAURA

Nonsense, man. In this weather you need brandy. Why, you're soaked. Ugh! I can't stand weather like this. The rain is bad enough, but the wind. . . Skål.

ENEVOLD

Skål, Miss – Laura, I should have said. No, imagine, I remember that. You never could stand the wind.

LAURA

Could? *Can*. I'm not dead. Come and sit down, Henrik. Have a drink. You need it too. No, I can't stand the wind.

ENEVOLD

And welcome home, one might almost say.

LAURA

Thank you. *Home* — that's a good one! And things are the same as ever, here!

ENEVOLD

Yes, in a way. Although a lot has changed too.

HENRIK

Changed — here?

ENEVOLD *(slightly offended)*

Yes. Many have passed away. And others have been brought into the world.

LAURA

Oh well, I dare say that is unavoidable.

ENEVOLD

A number of new houses have been built. And others have disappeared. And still others have changed hands.

HENRIK

And you haven't lost on that? Skål, Enevold.

ENEVOLD

Skål, Henrik. Perhaps I'd better start calling you by your surname after all these years. Although I remember you best as a child, when you ran and played up by the house.

HENRIK

Ugh.

LAURA

Yes, the house, Enevold. That's what I wanted to talk about.

ENEVOLD

The house is for sale. There have been quite a few offers, because there's a housing shortage, here as everywhere else. But I'd rather see it go back to the family.

HENRIK

Did you say 'I'? Do you own it, then?

ENEVOLD

Well, in a manner of speaking. The mortgage debt . . .

LAURA

Well, well. We can come back to that. But it's fit to live in, then?

HENRIK

Aunt Laura! You're not serious, are you?

LAURA

You be quiet. Drink, I tell you.

ENEVOLD

The house is fit to live in. I was thinking of converting it into a kind of two-family house, yes I was. But that presented certain difficulties. The present owner — in name only, I might add — hasn't been too successful. He's a man who. . .

LAURA

All right, Enevold. In short, it'll be vacant?

ENEVOLD

Of course, I could have rented it out on a small scale, room by room, so to speak — thereby rendering a service to a number of people.

HENRIK

Without any appreciable loss to yourself. . .

LAURA

Henrik! Drink!

ENEVOLD

But the idea crossed my mind to put it up for sale — merely as an orientation — so to speak. And then your cable arrived saying that *you*. . .

LAURA

Thank you, Enevold. That was kind of you. The price?

ENEVOLD

The total mortgage debt, plus all the likely encumbrances. . .

LAURA

Oh, I do remember you, Enevold. You haven't changed, at any rate. . .

ENEVOLD

I'm a methodical person, Miss — Laura. Even if I do say so myself.

LAURA

My dear Enevold, I didn't mean it like that. Oh Henrik, are you sure the windows are properly closed?

HENRIK *(examining the windows)*

Of course they are, Aunt Laura.

ENEVOLD

This hotel is coming apart at the seams.

LAURA

Everything's coming apart at the seams. The wind — it eats its way in through invisible cracks — it has long hands that branch out close to one and make things unpleasant. Tell me, have you ever noticed that one can't be alone when the wind is blowing. Everything draws closer and wants something of one. . .

HENRIK

But this is absurd, Aunt Laura. There's a little wind.

ENEVOLD

I can understand Miss — Laura very well. I'm a great believer in solitude myself.

LAURA

You never spoke a truer word, Enevold. You are indeed!
But I'm not. No, I'm not. Skål ... But if one must
have solitude, one might as well go the whole hog...
Ha, ha. Do you know why everybody who's alone goes
to the movies? To see the movie — ha. No, it's because there are people around one who are *also* looking
at the movie, who are sitting in the darkness, engrossed
in the same sights and thoughts. As if they were together.

HENRIK

That was a hell-of-a note.

LAURA

And then, when the lights go on — and people gath-
er up their things and stand up and start to leave
— the lonely ones have a moment of revelation, a
flash of panic. You're right, Henrik, it is a hell-of-a
note. Skål.

ENEVOLD

I don't understand you at all, Miss Laura. I like solitude. That's why I'm alone.

LAURA

Not me. Shall we look at the house?

HENRIK

This evening? But Aunt. . .

LAURA

This evening — is there anything wrong with that?

ENEVOLD

It was intended that the workmen were to move in,
within the next few days. There are lamps missing
in some of the rooms. Otherwise. . .

LAURA

Oh, hang the lamps. Shall we go?... No, don't open the window, Henrik. Don't worry about the smoke. There's something nice about a little stale air when one comes home. Someone has been there.

ENEVOLD

Well, I'm very much obliged. This didn't take long. I have a little car downstairs.

HENRIK

Both a car and an umbrella. Nothing has changed.

ENEVOLD

When one has to get in and out of a car, one needs an umbrella.

LAURA

Enevold is right... That's fine, Henrik, if you'll help me with my coat. Yes, one can buy practical raincoats like this in America... No, not the boots. Not as long as we're driving... Well, Enevold, so you've bought yourself a car. (*They move towards the door*)

ENEVOLD

No, after you, Miss — Laura. Mind the step there. —Yes, a car. Quite small. In my profession one needs a car. When one is getting...

LAURA

On in years?... How can you say that this corridor isn't draughty? — Did you turn out the light in the room, Henrik? Oh well, I prefer to have it on when I come back ... Heavens, what a draught on these stairs ... And those potted plants in the window niches. You must admit they're touching... Porter, I will be able to get back in tonight, won't I?... Thank you (*slowly*)

Yes, I'll probably be late... For heaven's sake, Ene-vold, that's not such a small car.

A car door opens

ENEVOLD

Well, one has to have room for the customers.

Sound of car door closing

LAURA

Is the door closed properly, Henrik? — That's fine. *(car starts)* There seems to be a draught. Listen, Enevold. Can't you close that window?... Well no, I know that. I have a little car myself, over there... Heavens what a storm!... What were you saying, Henrik?

Discreet sound of driving

HENRIK *(slowly and distinctly)*

I said, it's strange to be driving here again. As if all time in the interim had vanished... Oh, what's that over by the Post Office?

ENEVOLD

Oh yes, that's right. You haven't been here for quite some time... No, the Post Office isn't there any longer... They've moved to a brand new building down on the square.

LAURA

The square. Downtown. You can almost feel it stealing over you.

HENRIK

The panic...

LAURA

The memories. Lord knows what. After all, it's no more than fifteen years. No time...

HENRIK

No time.

ENEVOLD

A long time. And a short time. So to speak. And here
— hee hee, yes, here I dare say the illustrious visitors
hardly recognize where they are... You see, perhaps,
that Molde's Paddock...

HENRIK

Molde's Paddock...

ENEVOLD

Molde's Paddock — hee hee — has disappeared. Pure and
simple. Did you see that modern new building?

LAURA

I dare say you have a finger in the pie, Enevold?

ENEVOLD

One might as well admit it. A finger, Miss.

HENRIK

Did he have much to drink?

LAURA

You be quiet! The hills start here.

HENRIK

Yes, The hills start here.

Shifting of gears

LAURA

The school, Henrik?

HENRIK

Good Lord, the school...

LAURA

But Lover's Lane is gone completely... Or is it just the
darkness?

ENEVOLD

Lover's Lane, as it was called, is almost gone, so to speak. The new construction company. . .

LAURA

In other words you, Enevold?

ENEVOLD

Hee hee hee! Hee hee hee!

HENRIK

Did he say 'hee hee' before, Aunt Laura?

LAURA

Yes. He never did say much. . . You always said 'hee hee', didn't you, Enevold?

ENEVOLD

Hee hee. And now here's the Prefect's Curve? You remember that?

LAURA

I remember everything.

HENRIK

Everything.

LAURA

We went sledding here as children, Enevold. You and I, I did the steering.

ENEVOLD

It *is* a long time ago.

LAURA

Henrik, don't you think that window there is open a crack?

HENRIK

Well, I'll. . .

ENEVOLD

Only a moment now. Oh, look at *the house* in the moon-light. It has stopped raining. No, it went behind a cloud again. Oh yes, it's still raining a bit.

A short pause

LAURA

I saw it. Did you see the house, Henrik?

HENRIK

I saw it.

LAURA

Can you still see it?

ENEVOLD

We'll be there in a minute.

A short pause. They arrive. They get out of the car

ENEVOLD

Well, now I just have to find the keys.

LAURA

Don't bother about that, Enevold. I have the other set.

HENRIK

You don't mean to say that you have. . .

LAURA

I've had them all the time.

HENRIK

Well, I never. . . Here, take my arm. . . that's right. . . to the left here. Then you won't step in the puddle.

ENEVOLD

Hee hee. No, that has been filled in. Certain improvements.

LAURA

You remembered the puddle?

HENRIK

Didn't you?

LAURA

I'll say like Enevold: Hee hee ... And now the key.

Key in the lock

HENRIK

Lord. I could hardly wait to see if you remembered that the key turned the wrong way.

LAURA

Do you think I'm dimwitted, boy?... But what's this strange smell in the hall? Ugh!

ENEVOLD

There's been some dried fish hanging here.

HENRIK

What a disgusting smell. Is it still hanging here?

ENEVOLD

It has been removed now. I'll turn on the light.

HENRIK

You're going the wrong way, Enevold. The switch is here. *(turns on the light)*

A short pause

LAURA

Yes, *that's* how it was... It was bigger than I thought.

ENEVOLD

It is quite empty here...

ENEVOLD

It's smaller than I thought. – That was really a disgusting smell.

ENEVOLD

As I said before, it has been removed now. Well, the source, so to speak.

HENRIK

Did he also say 'So to speak' before, Aunt Laura?

LAURA

This chest of drawers here. . .

ENEVOLD

Remember, there have been people living here, yes, if I may say so — strangers, here for — some time. Oh, sorry, I'll lead the way.

Starts to go upstairs

HENRIK

Aunt Laura — do you remember father's feet ahead of you on the stairs? *(follows)*

LAURA

Take it easy, boy — Do you notice. . . *(follows)*

HENRIK

The smell of thyme. *The house,* Aunt Laura.

LAURA

Well. . . what about the house?

HENRIK

It's incredible. It's as if we're reliving it even more intensely, now that it's empty.

ENEVOLD

And here is the sitting room.

A pause

LAURA

Why are you looking at me like that, Henrik. . . Henrik!

A sudden gust of wind

ENEVOLD

The wind is increasing. Driving away the rain.

LAURA

Henrik. . .

HENRIK

The spinet. Is that still here?

ENEVOLD

The house was sold furnished — with some of the furnishings, at any rate. The spinet has probably been here all the time.

HENRIK

All the time —! So have we, as a matter of fact. *(Sits down and plays Schumann's 'Kinderscenen' no. 1: 'An fremden Ländern und Menschen'. Talks as he plays)* Yes, the house is sold with its furnishings and everything. With the smell in the stairway and the creak in the steps. With the living and the dead — with us. . . Is there a mortgage on that too, Enevold?. . . And when the last note was played on the spinet here, it too was included in the sale and continued to go with the house. . . We're the only ones who can continue to hear it, Enevold. Not you, for example. . . Just us. . . But it will continue to live when it's absolutely quiet. *(The music, which has grown fainter and fainter, stops on exactly his last word)*

ENEVOLD

Perhaps I'd better show you what's in here—?

4 — Modern Nordic Plays: Norway

LAURA

He wants to show us. Do you hear, Henrik, he wants to show us —!

HENRIK

It's like a dream. It *is* a dream. — The tassel on the window shade is missing, it has been replaced by a knot. Why did they paint the pantry pink? — One Sunday we ate ptarmigan. Do you know what he said? — 'They cost a crown-and-a-half apiece now'. It was a reproach, to make them taste better. Do you see those holes there in the door frame? They're from my trapeze. The first time I managed to hang by my knees, you stood watching, Aunt Laura. That was why I managed to hang by my knees, you stood watching, Aunt Laura. That was why I managed to do it.

LAURA

Henrik —!

HENRIK

Father got to know about it. He asked how many inhabitants there were in Valparaiso. – That was the first time I struck him.

LAURA

You struck him? I thought he struck *you*... All right, Enevold, we're coming...

HENRIK

Is that what you thought? No, he made me do it. I fooled you that time, Aunt Laura.

LAURA

You never fooled me —!

HENRIK

I thought I had. That's the main thing.

LAURA

That one isn't alone —?

HENRIK

That one doesn't think one is alone —?

ENEVOLD *(outside)*

Shall we have a look at the bedrooms?

LAURA

All right, Enevold — !

HENRIK

But he made you believe that he struck me. Pretending to be a tyrant.

LAURA

Then he wasn't —?

HENRIK

Yes, that's just it. But he was a humanist, you see. Remember, he was a pedagogue. He was modern. A modern sadist.

LAURA

You have no right! He helped me for many years. I ran the house . . .

HENRIK

You never ran anything, Aunt Laura. The house ran you. Father ran you. I. . . I know that now.

LAURA

Now — ?

HENRIK

Yes now. Only now.

LAURA

You're maligning your father. Your mother . . .

HENRIK

She has always been dead, you know.

LAURA

Oh —!

HENRIK

And I who thought you always understood. . . Have I been alone all the time, then?

LAURA

No more than I have. I also thought I'd understood.

HENRIK

Understood what?

LAURA

Why he was alone when he died.

A pause

HENRIK

There was a storm that evening. (*a sudden gust of wind*)

ENEVOLD *(outside)*

Are you coming?

HENRIK

It lashed against the windowpane. The old maple tree which he was always going to cut down, it stood lashing against the pane in a way that irritated him.

LAURA

Me too. But, you see, he had a prior claim — to be irritated.

HENRIK

Did you hate him so?

LAURA

You sat playing when he died. . . All right, Enevold!

ENEVOLD *(coming back)*

> I just wanted to show the family that the blue china-
> ware is intact, so to speak. Here... it's on the top
> shelves... No, I'll get a chair...

HENRIK

> The blue china —! The gravy boat. The soup tureen
> *(very faint sound of dishes being taken down one at a*
> *time — a sudden gust of wind)* Your fair weather is
> going to the dogs, Enevold — ?... But what's become
> of him?... Enevold!

ENEVOLD

> My illustrious visitors — hee hee...

LAURA

> He's deserting us... Enevold — !... No, I'm not going
> to stand here with plates in my hands. That's not why I
> came.

HENRIK

> Why did you come, then?

LAURA

> Enevold — !

Faint sound of music. Same melody. Fades away abruptly

HENRIK

> What did I say — ? The last note. We're the only
> ones who can hear it.

LAURA

> Enevold — ! Aren't you going to show us the house,
> then —? You are going to lead us — out of this, aren't
> you?

ENEVOLD

> You're far away now.. The mortgage debt...

HENRIK
You see, he wants to show us the liabilities. The blame. You didn't want to hear about that at the hotel.

The same music. Very faint. Dies at once

LAURA
He's not in the kitchen. . . Someone is always deserting us.

HENRIK
First father.

LAURA
You sat playing. You didn't hear him calling for you.

Same music. Faint

THE FATHER'S VOICE
Hen-rik —!

THE FATHER'S VOICE *(fainter)*
Hen-rik —!

Music stops

HENRIK
When I came out, you were sitting on the stairs in a kind of house coat. You hadn't heard him, either.

Music swells

THE FATHER'S VOICE
Hen — rik — ! Lau — ra — ! There's something I have to explain to you. . .

HENRIK *(inasmuch as he is repeating aloud what he was thinking at the time)*
There's always someone who has to explain something.

The music stops abruptly on 'something'. A short pause

LAURA

And then — Enevold. One is always being deserted by someone.

HENRIK

You were quite young at the time — ? Wasn't there something about a boating trip?

A sudden gust of wind

LAURA

We were in a sailboat. We couldn't see land. Enevold couldn't manage the sails any longer. His hands were wizened. He folded them and acted as if he were praying. The water was churning. Do you know what he said? — 'Your brother, the headmaster, also prays in critical situations?' He yelled that into my ear. From then on I was lonely.

A sudden gust of wind

HENRIK

But afterwards, then?

LAURA

I caught sight of land. It lasted for a moment. A darker streak in the fog, close by. I realized at once where we were. I know the waters around here.

ENEVOLD *(over the storm)*

Pray, Laura —! The headmaster. . .

LAURA

I managed to bring the boat in while he was praying. I didn't notice the storm until we were on land and the boat was saved. Our hands touched along the gunwale. His were blue. Did you notice this evening that his hands were blue?

HENRIK

Aunt Laura, were you really in love with him?

LAURA
I was alone.

HENRIK
And father — ?

LAURA
He was my brother?

HENRIK
And — me —?

LAURA
Hee, hee —! As Enevold said . . . Enevold —! . . . Why,
the house is empty, boy.

HENRIK
Empty — ? Are there only memories —?

The music

LAURA *(over the music)*
Oh, there are quite a few memories. Enough to make
life unendurable, if one doesn't protect oneself against
them.

The music stops

HENRIK
It was you who wanted to come out here. Live —!

Music, faint

LAURA
In order to see it through, at last. — Are you afraid.

HENRIK *(from the outside)*
There are no lamps in the kitchen.

LAURA
You're going the wrong way. It was to the left. . .
(exclaiming) But isn't there a light here — !

HENRIK

Are you afraid? Everything's the same. I know the way.

LAURA

Where?

HENRIK

Didn't you want to see it through — ?

LAURA

Enevold — ! *(fainter)* Enevold —!

Faint sound of a car starting

LAURA

Did he go — ? We're alone now, Henrik.

HENRIK

Do you think so — ? Come : on — !

LAURA

Where are you going — ?

HENRIK

Straight through.

LAURA

But it's dark everywhere. . . Henrik — !

HENRIK

We must go on. Do you remember the smell? Listen to the maple tree against the windowpane.

LAURA

This is where he was lying. . . Henrik —!

HENRIK *(outside)*

On —!

LAURA

But we're here by the spinet again. Did he call? *(the music)* You were playing while he was calling.

HENRIK

   I didn't kill him.

LAURA

   You said you could have. . . down at the hotel. . .

HENRIK

   That was a long time ago.

LAURA

   It was this evening. Did somebody knock?

HENRIK

   It's the tree in the wind. Well, here we are again — !

LAURA

   That damned wind. So, open the door then —! Let
   them come in, as long as we can't get out — ! All the
   doors — ! Let them come — !

HENRIK

   They *are* here. All the doors are open. See how they fill
   the rooms —!

LAURA

   Yes, do you see them: Humiliation. Unkindness. Jealousy.
   Suspicion. Look at Effacement lurking silently in the
   corner. The Unspoken Word . . .

HENRIK

   And the one in the red cloak?

LAURA

   The stiff upper lip. The interrupted embrace. The dry
   kiss. The inability to give of oneself. Oh yes. I've met
   you before.

HENRIK

   Here— !

LAURA

Everywhere — ! A sunny day on the shore. In the thick of the traffic on a pearl-gray morning. Like a dagger through the heart. A cloud across the sky. The cloud of unimaginativeness and avarice that blots out every sun.

HENRIK

This is the way we kill. . .

LAURA

And the blackest shadow falls on those who are closest to us . .

HENRIK

We envelop them completely. . .

LAURA

Envelop them as we ourselves are enveloped. A procession of families, of classes, generations. — There they are again. . .!

HENRIK

Everywhere. Everywhere.

Music, faintly

THE FATHER'S VOICE

There was something I wanted to explain.

HENRIK

Always something to explain. The spinet. (*music increases*) We're here again —!

LAURA

Again and again. Year after year. Put off making a stand against them . . . Come, then!

HENRIK

They're coming — ! It's dark — ! We must escape — ! I can't find the way out — !

LAURA

Stop, boy —! There is no way out. *(the music stops abruptly)* Let them come — !

Curtain

The Injustice

By Finn Havrevold

Translated from the Norwegian
by James Wesley Brown

All rights, including professional, amateur, motion picture, recitation, lecturing, public reading, radio broadcasting, television, reproduction by recording or any electronic or mechanical means, and the rights of translation into foreign languages are strictly reserved. Permission for any of these rights must be obtained from Finn Havrevold, Thomas Heftyes gt. 64 C, Oslo 2, Norway.

Finn Havrevold

Finn Havrevold (b. 1905) made his debut shortly before the out-break of the Second World War, with a well-written collection of short stories, and wrote his best novels in the years after the war. Like many of his colleagues, he analyses the causes of fascism and the mentality of violence, and, among other things, he questions the ideals that are characteristic of the male-dominated society: 'manliness' the competitive mentality, the desire to *possess,* to possess things *and* people.

These themes also recur in his later novels, in his numerous radio dramas, and in his handful of realistic plays — especially in two of his best: *Uretten (The Injustice)* (1955) and *Tomannsboligen (The Two-Family House)* (1959).

The title theme recurs in several variations in *The Injustice:* Åke Vendel, the young bank director, has done Ulf Gram an injustice. Ulf has avenged himself by employing unscrupulous methods to set a trap for the bank director. Åke Vendel ponders over this injustice. He is up to his eyes in self-pity, and reveals his despicable character. With the money gone, his self-respect has vanished. Previously he went about *possessing,* he was what he possessed. Even Helle, his wife, was merely a piece of property on which he spent large sums for maintenance and to increase her value — in order to possess her even more, and to possess more.

Now, Helle is about to become the manager and creative director of Ulf Gram's fashion house — independent, economically independent.

The play reveals Helle between the two men — and the injustice perpetrated by them on her: Both men regard her as a piece of property or an erotic object. It is first and foremost *this* injustice that is implied by the title.

Helle escapes — like Nora in Ibsen, and Vibecke in Helge Krog's *Break-up.* But, unlike her predecessors, she throws herself into the arms of a third man — a colourless person who, in his weakness, is less inclined to regard her with feelings of masculine superiority.

The play gave rise to considerable discussion when it was performed at the National Theatre in Oslo. With its clear delineation of characters, and its interesting approach to the problem, it is one of the most vigorous shoots on the Ibsen trunk.

Characters

ÅKE VENDEL

HELLE VENDEL

ERIK JØRN

ULF GRAM

Place:

A garret studio

Time:

A spring evening

ACT ONE

The studio is a furnished garret with a skylight. There are three doors in the room: one on the left, leading to the bedroom, and two at the rear, one opening onto the landing at the top of the stairs, the other leading to a vacant attic room where the telephone is located. A low table and chairs at stage front. At the rear an open closet with dresses hanging in it. A drawing board, covered with sketches, scraps of cloth, drawing materials, etc. A desk. It is afternoon and an intense spring light fills the room.

HELLE

Just look at the light. . .

ÅKE

Reminds you of something, doesn't it?

HELLE

No, please don't say it.

ÅKE

You miss it, don't you, Helle?

HELLE

Our drawing-room. . .? No, not the room, but the light in it perhaps. The morning light. How bright the morning sun was in that room on a spring day like today; bright, but never white or glaring. Freshly cut branches of cherry blossoms on the window sill, and the carpet covering that enormous floor like deep, golden moss. Erik's painting on the wall behind the sofa. *(soberly)* Marie would already have cleaned and vacuumed and straightened up the room and wheeled my breakfast in front of the window.

ÅKE

There, you see?

HELLE

I haven't missed it for a second.

ÅKE

That's my brave little girl!

HELLE

Oh, I'm not like you. You're the one who misses our drawing-room at Solhaug.

ÅKE

I miss a lot of things.

HELLE

But more now than you did in the beginning, right?

ÅKE

You get used to a lot of things in the course of four years. But it hurts every now and then. It hurts every now and then.

HELLE

It's so unfair you know? Because I've become so wonderfully free from all that these past four years. I wish you could've done the same.

ÅKE *(teasing)*

'Marie', you said, 'already would have vacuumed,' you said. 'And your breakfast in place by the window . . .'

HELLE

But all that doesn't mean anything! Just things that I can savour in my memory and then realize that I don't really care for the taste any more. Solhaug and all that were there and everything else we no longer own has simply ceased to exist. They no longer concern me. Not now.

ÅKE

Pardon me, madam. I had forgotten about your success.

HELLE

No, please don't mention that. Help me to straighten up the place, will you?

ÅKE

What was it they wrote . . . ? *(Reads)* 'The new designs from the House of Andrienne created the sensation of the evening's fashion show. Helle Vendel's creations have attracted attention far and wide. It is rumoured that Andrienne's energetic head, Mr. Ulf Gram, will employ this talented fashion designer in his firm as manager and artistic director. We congratulate both the head of the House of Andrienne and its new manager and predict . . .'

HELLE

Please, don't. Why don't you help me instead?

ÅKE *(continues reading)*

'and predict that our leading fashion house will soon achieve a world-wide reputation. We award yesterday's prize to Helle Vendel's evening dress in white and grey brocade with its profusion of black lace, so exquisitely dignified, yet boldly provocative . . .' *(Change of tone)* When are you supposed to meet him?

HELLE

I'm meeting Ulf Gram at seven o'clock. Erik's coming by here to pick me up.

ÅKE

Erik! Your faithful galley slave!

HELLE

Well, you won't take me. What am I supposed to do when you refuse to have anything to do with the business arrangements between Gram and me?

ÅKE

Aw, I have a little to do with it, don't you think?

HELLE

Yes, that's exactly it. You help me. Advise me. Inspire and criticise. And there are all the sketches you have made and all the work you've put into the whole thing. And Ulf Gram knows it, too. He would really like to meet you.

ÅKE

I've already met Mr. Gram.

HELLE

Yes, at Easter four years ago. By chance. And you had met him before at board meetings at the bank. But everything was so different then, quite different from the way things are now. . . and that's exactly why he would like to meet you.

ÅKE

By chance? Yes, perhaps it was. . .

HELLE (eagerly)

Well, wasn't it? That's why he wants to meet you this evening.

ÅKE

Yes, perhaps it was by chance.

HELLE

You don't have anything against all this, do you? Because if you do, I won't go. But I think it's a bit hard,
Åke. After all, you and I have worked and created
together for four hard, difficult and happy years in
this old garret of ours. Setbacks and disappointments
and our first modest successes. . . we shared them all.
And finally I'm offered this position as manager and
artistic director of our most important fashion house.

ÅKE

Splendid. And I set the conditions. You've been shame-
lessly exploited. But now we've got him, my dear, now
we've got him. He's launched your name, and he's going
to pay for it. What's the House of Andrienne without
Helle Vendel? So he's going to pay through the nose
for you. Art is expensive.

HELLE

Does our success have to be so bitter?

ÅKE

Wonderful, my dear.

HELLE

But you were the one who wanted things this way. I
said that we should be in on this together. Both of us.
Completely. In name as well. Åke and Helle Vendel.
And Ulf Gram realizes this and that's why he'd like
to talk with you before we. . .

ÅKE

There's only one stipulation that you're interested in
making, Helle, before accepting Gram's offer: That I

am to be raised from the dead, resurrected for the whole world. Åke Vendel. Fashion designer and bankrupt bank manager. Ha ha.

HELLE

No!

ÅKE

No... because the offer is to come from our friend, Mr. Gram. It will be said that I am indispensable to the firm. Åke Vendel, fashion aesthete and bankrupt banker, inspires, criticises and sketches from nine to four in my honourable firm. With regards, Ulf Gram. No, thank you.

HELLE

During these four years since... since *that* happened... you've devoted all your time and energy to this. I wasn't the only one who created the glamorous Helle Vendel designs, it was both of us. You haven't tried to get other work during this time. You rejected all outside help. We'd manage all right. Oh, that was our daily battle cry and clarion call: We'd manage all right!

ÅKE

Yes, and we did manage, didn't we?

HELLE

And now, on the day of our victory, you give up.

ÅKE

You simply don't understand. As far as I'm concerned, this has just been a game. An amusement... nothing else. Well, we've lived off of it, of course... almost.

HELLE

You don't realise how much you're hurting me. The joy and pride over doing something together with you.

Fighting and losing or fighting and winning together ...
with you. And you call it an amusement, nothing but
an amusement.

ÅKE

I said, as far as I'm concerned it has been an amusement.
I played around with fabrics and colours, with pencils
and brushes. Perhaps to comfort myself for all that
happened four years ago. A childish game, a rather childish comfort. But you don't believe, do you, Helle,
that this obliges me to wade about publicly in your
wake?

HELLE

No, that's not what I want you to do either.

ÅKE

No, but that's precisely what you're asking me to do,
my dear.

HELLE

I'm fighting for something that means something to me.
I may be fighting with the wrong words. You're betraying us this evening.

ÅKE

You mean I'm letting you down, don't you? On your
day of victory.

HELLE

I mean exactly what I say: you're betraying us.

ÅKE

Helle, my sweet, you simply don't understand.

HELLE

How happy we've been, and we've grown closer together than we've ever been before. How free I've felt.
I felt we both became so doing this work.

ÅKE *(towards her)*

Helle, my dear, you shall be happy. . .

HELLE

Do you really mean that?

ÅKE

You shall be happy. Proud. Free.

HELLE

But together with you.

ÅKE

You didn't need my help. I just joined in, scribbling a drawing as best I could. This is your victory. Your evening.

HELLE

But I'm interested in *us,* don't you understand?

ÅKE

You'd better get dressed, Helle. Erik'll be here at any moment. What dress are you going to wear?

HELLE

I don't know. . . the blue one?

ÅKE

Always the little girl. Why don't you wear your sailor outfit with the whistle?

HELLE

The blue's fairly sober. I want to be business-like this evening.

ÅKE

You. . .!

HELLE

Well, look business-like then.

ÅKE

As far as your own self's concerned, you humbly heed fashion's second commandment: Hide thy weaknesses. But you ignore the first: Accentuate thy strong points! What on earth are you doing in the fashion business anyway?

HELLE *(somewhat coquettish)*

All I want to do is. . . to please you. Understand? Just please you. But I guess I'm going to have to straighten up the place all by myself. . .

ÅKE

No, go and get dressed. I'll straighten up. And wear your red dress.

HELLE *(examining the dress)*

I'm not so sure. This dress ought to be worn by a queen.

ÅKE

That's precisely my point. You all are going to the theatre first, aren't you? An operetta? When people look at you, they'll regard you as their High Priestess of Vanity. I think the business-like thing to do, my dear, would be to display your sex. *(Clearing things away)* Put on the red dress.

HELLE *(thinking)*

Perhaps it's the light in here that frightens me. This spring light. It makes me feel so naked.

ÅKE *(stops cleaning up, looks at her)*

Do you like Ulf Gram?

HELLE

Sure.

ÅKE
  A lot?

HELLE
  Sure.

ÅKE
  So much that. . .?

HELLE
  Wrong question. You've been asking a lot of wrong
  questions lately.

ÅKE
  You said that I was betraying you. On your day of
  victory, you said.

HELLE
  You said it, not I.

ÅKE
  One doesn't say such things casually, Helle. Your accusation gives you away.

HELLE
  Do you really think so. . .? Is that really what you want?

ÅKE
  I think you'd better get dressed. I don't want you to
  be late. Come on. Hurry up. Get dressed. I'll tidy
  up before your galley slave arrives.

HELLE (*holding the dress, near the bedroom door*)
  Åke.

ÅKE
  Hmm. . .?

HELLE
  Do you think I ought to wear the red dress after all?

ÅKE *(absentmindedly)*
Yes, perhaps you ought to, dear.

HELLE
After all, I think it's about time I displayed my sex.

ÅKE *(feigning dismay, without looking up)*
Why, Helle, really . . .

HELLE
I do so want to please you, Åke. *(Stands still a mo-ment, expectantly)* Do you hear? Please you. *(Pause)*
You!

Exit

As Helle leaves, Åke looks up and watches her, shakes his head and then returns to his tidying up. The bedroom door remains half open.

ÅKE *(after a pause)*
You are probably right about the light in here, Helle.

HELLE
What did you say?

ÅKE *(a bit louder)*
I said that you are all wrong about the light in here.

HELLE
In what way?

ÅKE *(takes a large bunch of keys on a ring out of his pocket and plays with it)*
It hasn't the slightest resemblance to the light in our drawing-room at Solhaug, dear. It's nothing but a rotten, naked, spring light penetrating a dirty sky-light. *(In a lower voice)* No, Solhaug was a palace. The bank manager's little royal residence. The bank manager's wife's little paradise. *(Throwing the keys*

up into the air and catching them) Mine. Mine. Mine.
(Louder) We had awnings in front of the windows
at Solhaug. I said that we had awnings in front of
the windows at. . .!

HELLE
Ye—es!

ÅKE
You almost need to wear sunglasses all day long with
this Easter glare in here. *(Louder)* Do you remember
the Easter we spent four years ago, Helle? Up at our
cabin?

HELLE *(entering from the bedroom in a negligee and robe,
cleansing cream on her face)*
Our last Easter in our cabin up in the mountains. Yes.
At any rate, I remember at least one thing from that
Easter vacation.

ÅKE
Ulf Gram.

HELLE
You and your Ulf Gram! Oh, no, the tracks he left behind him were soon wiped out. I was thinking about
our ski trip. Just the two of us alone on our way up to
the top of the mountain. The sunshine. The peace and
quiet. We stopped to take it all in. Don't you remember. . .?

ÅKE
You were quite taken by him. You two danced together
all evening.

HELLE
Yes, but don't you remember. . .?

ÅKE

A fortnight later and my game was up. I had to sell everything. And I think he must have known about it the whole time he was up there. And that's not all, my dear. Maybe he even knew more ... you clever little devil.

HELLE (*massaging her face, absentmindedly*)

But did he... Gram... know about your speculations then?

ÅKE

To hell with my speculations. They had nothing to do with my fall. It was the bank. My bank. My own bank!

HELLE (*as before*)

But you submitted... your resignation... as bank manager... didn't you?

ÅKE

Yes, I did, fancy that! After a reprimand from the board. My own board!

HELLE (*as before*)

Hmm... well, did you have to?

ÅKE (*bitterly*)

After that reprimand! (*Silent, deeply offended*) The board accepted my resignation. Unanimously. Immediately.

HELLE (*with naive surprise*)

Well, didn't they have to? After all, you submitted it, didn't you?

ÅKE

Don't you understand anything?

HELLE

Well, how am I supposed to since you've never wanted to talk about the whole thing.

ÅKE *(walks excitedly back and forth)*

No, no. Maybe you're right.

HELLE

You think Ulf Gram should have warned you . . . that time at Easter. . . being a member of the board?

ÅKE

Ulf Gram. . .! Warn me? Him!

HELLE

But don't forget all that he has done for us since, Åke. Do you remember the first time I went around with my fashion designs. And you sat up here waiting. I would come home disappointed and discouraged every single day. Until I went to Ulf Gram and he saw at once that they were good. Don't you remember? We were stony broke. I came back home with an advance and we had a party.

ÅKE

Sure, sure. *(Changing the subject)* My dear, of course I remember our trip to the top of the mountain. It was Holy Saturday. Four years ago.

HELLE

What?

ÅKE

Our ski trip. You asked me if I remembered it.

HELLE

Oh, yes. You remember it, don't you?

ÅKE

All that sunshine, and the snow was just like silk. You

were wearing a new ski outfit. And I remember
how the grey hood framed your face. How beautiful
you were. And so happy.

HELLE

No.

ÅKE

You weren't happy?

HELLE

No.

ÅKE

No? At any rate, we stopped and looked at some —
some trees, didn't we?

HELLE

My, my, do you remember that? Do you remember
the birches?

ÅKE

And the fir tree, Helle. The fir tree.

HELLE

I was thinking of those birches and that light when I
designed the dress that made such a hit yesterday. A
black veil draped over birch branches ready to burst into
leaf. Silver trunks, the branches forming a wild pattern
against the sky and ... (Soberly) That black veil-like
stuff that hangs from the branches, do you think that's
some sort of parasite, some sort of lichen that con-
sumes the tree, perhaps destroying everything that's
going to... (Stops and stares at Åke)

ÅKE (stands in a stiff, unnatural position. His face is
distorted when he speaks. His hands illustrate his speech)
The fir tree... towering above the stunted growth of
the scrub birch. It stood alone. A dead arm: like this!

Erect, split by lightning, calling out, grey and silent,
to empty space. Another branch: like this. Knotty, living
knuckles. The will to live for a thousand years. To
live — and eventually triumph. And the roots — mad-
ly clinging to the bare stones in order to survive — to
survive the storm. Until the day of victory. Resurrection.
The sun. (*Very agitated. Plays nervously with the keys*)

HELLE
Give them to me.

ÅKE
What? Like hell I will.

HELLE
Give me those keys.

ÅKE
There, there, my dear.

HELLE
Give them to me!

ÅKE
I'm putting them into my pocket, Helle. See? I'm putting them into my pocket. I'm going to lock them up
inside the desk and never take them out again. No,
never take them out again. Never again.

HELLE (*close to him*)
You frighten me.

ÅKE
My dear girl, you're so quick to misunderstand. You
mustn't misunderstand so easily. . .

HELLE
Kiss me.

ÅKE

You mustn't. . .

HELLE

Kiss me.

ÅKE

You oughtn't take it like that. On the contrary. After all, you were the one who brought up that trip of ours, and then, well. . .

HELLE *(laughs nervously)*

You looked just like that fir tree.

ÅKE

I did? Well, a fir tree can be a useful thing to have around. It's good to have a little fir tree in the house. *A bell rings*

HELLE

There he is.

ÅKE

It's only Erik. Your galley slave. Humble, ever-loving Erik, who always leaves his galley empty-handed.

Åke walks out to open the door. Helle goes into the bedroom and closes the door before Åke and Erik enter.

ÅKE *(carrying a painting)*

How very nice. How very nice of you. Helle will be simply delighted.

ERIK

I wanted to please Helle. After all, I know how much she liked this painting of mine.

ÅKE

Splendid. Where shall we hang it? How about here for the time being, so she'll see it the moment she comes

in. *(Hangs up the painting)* Drat this light. Your painting hung better at Solhaug, Erik. Do you remember?
Above the sofa in the drawing-room? Lovely room. Lovely picture, I mean.

ERIK

I think it's one of the best things I've ever done.
There's joy in it... and freedom.

ÅKE

And now this dirty hay loft. After the rooms at Solhaug.

ERIK *(to himself)*

Helle has always emitted a kind of radiance. Yes, that's
what she's like: a pure, white flame on the path in front
of you. That's why I so want to... *(Coming down
to earth)* I think you two get along all right up here.

ÅKE

Sure. We get along. We work and slave away. We have
our small joys and a lousy economy. But I'm going to
see to it that Mr. So-and-so coughs up from now on.
Do you know what that swine used to pay Helle for her
designs?

ERIK

I've never had anything to do with fashion design, so I
have no idea what prices are like. But that part of the
business is in order now, isn't it?

ÅKE

I'll see to that. I'll see to that. Helle, poor thing, isn't
interested in such things. She thinks it's just a lot of
fun. Her so-called 'creations' are nothing but a game
as far as she's concerned. Something to bide the time
with while we... while we wait.

ERIK

Wait?

ÅKE

Exactly.

ERIK

Oh, you mean the contract. Waiting for Helle to begin her new job as manager.

ÅKE

I've got my plans. I've got some very definite plans. But I also have my suspicions, my dear chap. Do sit down.

ERIK

I've wanted to visit you before, but I had the impression that you preferred being left alone and that you didn't want to be. . . well, disturbed.

ÅKE

Of course, of course. The fact is that Ulf Gram is a pest. Not just a slippery customer, but a pest. But he can be crushed between the nails like this. Just like a louse. He's a cousin of yours, isn't he?

ERIK

Yes, in a way. But. . . what do you have against Ulf Gram?

ÅKE

Nothing other than the fact that he makes you feel dirty. Like a long train ride. *(Gesticulates with his hands)* It simply can't be avoided.

ERIK

I thought that you two owed Ulf Gram quite a lot. Would Helle's career have been at all possible with-

out. . .? And Helle has nothing but good to say. . .?
Why do you hate him?

ÅKE

Me? Hate Ulf Gram? I don't hate travelling by train,
even though I know very well how dirty I get.

ERIK (*staring hard at Åke, suspiciously*)

How well do you know Ulf Gram?

ÅKE

Very little. Very little.

ERIK

Well, for heaven's sake, how can you stand there
and. . .! Look here, Åke, why don't we talk this over.
I realise that these years have been pretty hard for you.

ÅKE

Splendid! Wonderful! What in the world are we
standing for? Sit down! (*Sits down*) It's really nice
to see you again, Erik, old chum. It's been a long time.
And thanks again for the painting. It was very touching
of you to give it back to me.

ERIK (*sits*)

I knew how fond Helle was of this particular picture.
I didn't like the idea of anybody else owning it but
her.

ÅKE (*taking out the bunch of keys*)

No, of course not. I assure you, Erik, nothing hurt me
more that time than having to give up your painting.
Absolutely nothing! It was the last article at Solhaug
to be auctioned off. But I had to do it. I simply had to,
Erik, in order to meet the claims of those damned
creditors of mine. Do you understand now how happy
you've made me by returning this little masterpiece to
me?

ERIK

The success that Helle has had is going to be the turning point for both of you. You'll see. For you too. You've got to get out of this . . . out of this . . .

ÅKE

Ha, her success. Isn't it completely idiotic? *(Gets up)* Imagine this happening four, I mean five years ago, Erik. The celebration we would have had at Solhaug. Champagne. Candles. Music. Happy people. Beautiful ladies seated at my table. And then a nice little after-dinner speech, cheerful and elegant, teasing but sincere . . . in honour of my wife. *(Sits down)* What have you got to do with this lousy fashion crook?

ERIK

Well, you see. . . You're referring to Ulf Gram, aren't you?

ÅKE

Of course. Yes, I mean your cousin.

ERIK

Well, you see, he's doing very well now as a result of all the good fortune he's had for the past couple of years. He's obviously in a very sound financial position and wants to push Andrienne up into the international class if he can. With Helle as his collaborator, he's surely counting on. . .

ÅKE

I know. Answer the question I asked you.

ERIK

But my dear Åke? Well, I've been commissioned to decorate Andrienne's premises. I haven't done murals for several years now, so when Ulf asked me if I was interested in the job, well. . .

ÅKE *(jingling the keys)*
    Splendid. That's what I wanted to know. That's what
    I wanted to know.

ERIK
    And this is how I came to see a good deal of Helle
    down there, you see. And when she asked me to join
    her and Ulf for dinner this evening to celebrate...
    What an enormous key ring!

ÅKE *(looking towards the bedroom, puts the keys back
    into his pocket)*
    So you think so too?

ERIK
    I've been sitting here, saying to myself: he can't need
    those many keys any more, can he? Oh, I'm sorry.

ÅKE
    You're perfectly right, Erik, my boy. She oughtn't be
    alone with that chap. Do me a favour, will you? Try
    not to get as drunk as you usually do.

ERIK *(with forced calm)*
    These have been difficult years for you. But both you
    and Helle are over the biggest hump now. Things are
    looking up, Åke. And what you need right now, what
    you both need, is to get away from here and rest, make
    plans, and get used to the fact that things are going to
    be different from now on. Better. Less insecure!

ÅKE *(calling)*
    Are you ready, Helle?

HELLE
    Be with you in a little while.

ÅKE
    You're a riddle to me, Erik.

ERIK

Me?

ÅKE

Yes, you. Erik Jørn. The painter, Erik Jørn. Yes, you, and nobody else.

ERIK

Why, Åke, I don't think that there's anything strange about me.

ÅKE

But there is about me, is that what you mean?

ERIK

I don't want you to think that I believe for a minute that you've become what one can call ... You've changed, you know. You seem a bit nervous, perhaps. I don't know if you understand what I mean, Åke, but I think that maybe you're a bit. . .

ÅKE

Do you know what you lack?

ERIK

Who? Me? No?

ÅKE

You're a great painter. In my opinion you're one of the most important artists we have. A master. *(Pointing)* There he sits: Master Erik.

ERIK

Thanks a lot, but. . .

ÅKE

Yet you're almost devoid of self-awareness. *(Bangs on the table)* Where's your self-awareness, Erik? It's a mystery to me that you, with your name, your career,

your artistic triumphs, still act as though you completely lack normal self-awareness. And I deliberately said:
normal self-awareness, mind you.

ERIK

I don't quite understand. . . Do you mean self-respect?

ÅKE

When I say self-awareness, I mean self-awareness. Never
mind: call it self-respect if you like. Perhaps it'll be
easier.

ERIK

I think I understand you better now. But I've been
sitting here, feeling a bit uncertain about you. You've
become a different person during these past four years.
It's your character, I think . . . but maybe that's where
I can help you.

ÅKE *(irritated)*

What are you talking about?

ERIK *(unperturbed)*

After all, you know that I've gone through much the
same thing as you. Financially, I mean. I too had money,
remember, and became poor . . . and I remember what
hurt me then. *(Earnestly)* It wasn't the money. I didn't
miss my possessions or my luxurious, comfortable habits.
Oh! . . . but there was one thing that I felt was irre-
trievably lost when the money was gone: my self-
respect! It was as if the person that I thought I had
been, had been dissolved in the caustic acid of poverty and had become. . . what shall I say? An amorphous
mass of shyness and cowardice and discouragement.
(With disgust) Like jelly, Åke. Like jelly!

ÅKE *(with a gesture towards Erik)*

That's exactly what I mean. Like jelly.

ERIK

Yes, isn't it? But the self-esteem that comes from money is false. (*Comforting*) You see, financial security is the poorest lie a man can cling to.

ÅKE (*raising his hands to the ceiling*)

Oh, Lord, have mercy on us!

ERIK (*perplexed*)

Are you all right?

ÅKE

Blockhead!

ERIK

What. . .?

ÅKE

So you inherited a fortune. You used up the fortune. (*Angry*) Did that take any talent?

ERIK

What do you mean? Talent?

ÅKE

You're not going to call it a tragedy, are you? I don't think that it's tragic or that it takes any talent to squander money away like that. After all, you didn't know what to do with it anyway. What did you get out of all that money, you chump? Nothing. Absolutely nothing.

ERIK (*shaken*)

You seem to have lost your sense of proportion as well as all feelings for other people during these last years.

ÅKE (*pained*)

I wanted to do something! You can't understand that.

ERIK *(sits for a while, looking carefully at Åke, measuring him)*

You were a very competent bank manager... somewhat daring, so they say, but competent. People really wondered why you resigned, in spite of the fact that you had overspeculated. Was that necessary? You didn't do anything dishonourable... there's no blot on the name of Vendel. Why did you hide yourself away like a condemned animal, leading a shadow of a life up here for all these years?

ÅKE

You're an artist. You don't understand.

ERIK

You, too, are an artist.

ÅKE

It's not the same. For me it's just ... it's simply not my function.

ERIK

You mean you'll never take it seriously. But Helle has shown me some of your sketches. She has told me about how you two have worked together.

ÅKE *(lecturing)*

There's a wide-spread misconception, Erik, that people want to possess things because property implies, well ... power, strength, security, material comfort, and all the good things in life.

ERIK

Do you call that a misconception?

ÅKE

It implies such a superficial understanding of the real purpose of property that I think that we can safely characterise it as a misconception.

ERIK

Are you sure it's not you who, well, in your loneliness, have come to certain conclusions which in turn have affected your views about. . .

ÅKE *(pointing)*

Look at a child.

ERIK *(annoyed)*

Now wait a minute, my dear Åke . . .

ÅKE

I said: Look at a child — the first time it dawns on him that he owns the things that he's got in his hands. The doll, the wooden horse. At that moment the first little spark of humanity is kindled . . . in the child! The seed of his self-awareness is there. *(Stronger))* If people didn't own things, they would be animals. Just the fact that I can say: this is mine . . . makes it possible for me to say: this is me!

ERIK

But I don't want to possess things. I hate it. I repudiate it. Your form of self-awareness disgusts me.

ÅKE

You're an artist. Don't you understand what I'm getting at? The artistic function alone has become your property. Just as science is for the scientist. But this in no way alters the truth of what I'm saying. There are no exceptions to the rule, Erik, merely divergences. Merely divergences.

ERIK

You've lost contact with life. Why did you hide yourself? Fleeing from a defeat you didn't suffer? It's all in your imagination. You sit up here dreaming up things and believing that. . .

ÅKE

You're the artist. You're supposed to create. I'm supposed to own what you create. Only by owning things
can I become a human being. I can grow, act... be
myself... only through the things I own. *(With increasing force)* And I can't share my self-awareness with
anybody else. This is why collectivism, all this talk about
joint ownership in its widest meaning is nothing but a
hair-raising bit of naiveté. It's more than that. It's a
complete surrender of human values. Collectivism breeds
beasts. Collectivism requires beasts.

ERIK

You're fighting the battle of the dead against life, and
you're going to lose. Why, you've already lost! Why
did you hide yourself?

ÅKE

You ask me that? Don't you understand that I stopped
existing when they took my things away from me?
I didn't lose my job, my basis for existence... I lost
myself! I got hold of a revolver then and I still have
it. I hid myself because I felt that I had become a
beast. A dumb beast. *(Rises, not seeing Helle standing
in the bedroom door)* Do you understand now what
I've gone through? Do realize the injustice, Erik?

ERIK

Pull yourself together, man!

ÅKE *(shaking the keys in his raised hand)*

But I see my release. A blazing, white autumn morning. A storm has ravaged through the forest. But I
held myself erect! ... because I've clung by the very
roots of my heart to cold, naked stones for four years!
To the stones, Erik, for four long... long years.

HELLE *(numbed)*

And me? What am I to... The stones, what do the stones cling to?

ÅKE *(putting the keys in his pocket)*

I didn't mean you, Helle. You misunderstand, dear. Doesn't she, Erik? We were talking about something ...something else.

ERIK *(rising)*

Yes, Helle, I think you're making more of this than...

HELLE

Give them to me, please!

ÅKE

Shall I ring for a taxi?

HELLE

Those keys. Give them to me!

ÅKE *(nervously explaining)*

The telephone's in another room up here in the garret. It's all so idiotic. You see, we'd thought of furnishing that room as well, but we couldn't afford it... well, we'll probably be moving anyway. Right, my dear? This place no longer suits you now.

HELLE

Why are you going just as soon as I come in?

ÅKE

I'm going to telephone for a taxi for you and Erik. Ah, you did put on the red dress, didn't you? Isn't she lovely, Erik? Isn't she lovely? *(In the doorway)* Everything's so awkward here. So idiotic. So stupid. *(Exit)*

ERIK *(leads Helle to a chair, where she sits with her back to his painting)*

Sit down... I'm sorry about all this, but, then, you

ought to know him by now. Åke must have been
going around in circles all these years with this story
about the bank and his bankruptcy. But you two have
got to get away from here, Helle. . . both of you.

HELLE

Do you think he's mad?

ERIK

Do you mean 'insane'?

HELLE

Yes, I mean insane.

ERIK

No, that thought never occurred to me.

HELLE

If I could only get him to give me those keys to Solhaug. I mean if he would give them to me voluntarily.

ERIK

Are those the keys to. . . Solhaug, which you two sold
four years ago?

HELLE

To every single door, every closet, every drawer, every
cubbyhole from the cellar to the attic. He's got the
keys to them all. Even the garage. The toolsheds. Every
single padlock! (*Laughs quietly, but tense*)

ERIK

Helle, really! Damn it, you wouldn't happen to have
a drop of brandy up here, would you?

HELLE (*shaking her head*)

There were just those padlocks. You know, he even
had a padlock on the croquet box!

ERIK

But Åke's not miserly, is he?

HELLE *(with more calm)*

No, not at all. He's really awfully kind. That's just it. That's precisely what. . . frightens me so.

ERIK

I remember the way Åke acted that time I was down and out. Good Lord, what he didn't do for me! Commissioned paintings. Got others interested. Portraits. And he did it all in that way of his, you know, so naturally, without the slightest suggestion of charity. So I have no idea where he's got this from. . .

HELLE

You mean the keys?

ERIK

The whole works. The padlocks. These theories of his. And he's so excitable!

HELLE

I don't know . . . Perhaps his dream of owning Solhaug again has got such a hold on him that he's no longer able to see things clearly any more. He just thinks that Solhaug is standing there waiting for us . . . for him . . . for him to return to it.

ERIK

Do you think that if you got him to give you that keyring, that these thoughts would. . .

HELLE

I don't know. I thought so. Maybe I hoped. . .?

ERIK

My dear girl. No, please don't, Helle. You've become too wrapped up in these whims of his. Åke's an only child, remember. And you two have been living too much to yourselves these past four years. . . especially Åke.

HELLE

Yes, I know that it's stupid of me, but... He's only been like this for the last half year, as if the whole thing has somehow completely possessed him. *(Changing)* My dear Erik. Always my friend.

ERIK

I jolly well have to be. Because I can't entirely forget or wipe out or escape from... *(In confusion, toward the painting)* Well, I thought that I'd make you happy today.

HELLE *(thoughtfully)*

Oh, it's been such a disappointment. Because we've been so happy during these four years. At least I thought so. I believed right up to the last six months, perhaps... and now I'm no longer sure.

ERIK

Happy? Yes. Haven't you and Åke always been happy together?

HELLE

No. No, we haven't. In the very beginning, why, yes. And I thought we had strong, genuine feelings for each other during the past four years. But everything in between. Those years at Solhaug, no! I would have left him. I had made up my mind to do so... when the crash came. *(Changing)* His blessed bankruptcy. Our sweet little bankruptcy. If we could just keep on going bankrupt. Over and over again.

ERIK

Is it as wonderful as all that?

HELLE

Not the bankruptcy. That's nothing but tears and sleepless nights. Suicidal thoughts. No, it's what follows it. The battle. The furious, desperate struggle to survive. Living from day to day. Struggle and live! I found it wonderful, Erik.

ERIK

But I don't think Åke found it so wonderful, did he? It wasn't exactly the bank manager's cup of tea.

HELLE

He was very brave. It was worse for him than it was for me, and yet he strove to keep both our spirits up. *(Changing)* Erik, you're not bitter about Åke, are you? After all these years?

ERIK

No, I'm not bitter about Åke.

HELLE

But. . .?

ERIK

I'm bitter about you! You, the woman who. . . made the choice. *(Changing)* Why did you choose Åke? You could have gone bankrupt twelve times a year with me.

HELLE

My sweet Erik.

ERIK

My sweet Erik. My kind Erik. Always my friend. *(Rising)* Damn it!

HELLE

Do you find me so dreadful?

ERIK

Yes, I'm afraid I do.

HELLE

And yet. . .?

ERIK

Yes, I'm afraid I do. I fight against it, but I come just
the same. I wrestle with it, but I lose every time. And
the more awful you are, the lovelier you become, and
the worse time I have of it. *(Stops)* You've changed,
Helle . . . since that delightful bankruptcy of yours.

HELLE

I've become more dreadful.

ERIK

Yes, from my point of view you've changed for the
worse. I noticed it when we met every now and then,
and most recently at Andrienne's. You've become so,
well, so tall and thin, in a way. It's as if some of your
girlish frills have been blown away by the storm. So
very beautiful. . . but in a different, more orderly way
. . . that I thought when I met you once, I mean, the
thought struck me. . . I mean. . . that. . .

HELLE

. . . That I had met another man besides Åke?

ERIK

Yes. . .?

HELLE

Well, I haven't.

ERIK

No, no. So it was nothing but the raptures of bankruptcy,
then?

HELLE

You see, it all became so important to me: the ideas,
the sketches, the dress designs that we worked on together, Åke and I. Every day meant something. We were
going to create, bring it off.

ERIK (*sits*)

Yes, I understand what you mean.

HELLE

But I'm not quite sure that I mean the joy of work exactly. . .

ERIK

Oh, yes, you do. It may be a weak phrase, but it implies a lot: the struggle, the pain, the devotion, the rapture and the despair. Everything!

HELLE

But I don't mean the joy of work.

ERIK

Yes, you do. That's exactly what you *do* mean, only you don't know it yourself.

HELLE (*smiling*)

You mean that I don't know how much you enjoy your work when you're painting. . . but *you* do!

ERIK (*uneasy*)

I beg your pardon. You see, I simply thought . . .

HELLE

Yes, of course there was, as you say, the struggle and the joy and the despair, but there was something else as well. These past four years have meant something else for me. It can be a great and wonderful feeling for a woman, a married woman, to grow out of the feeling of inferiority that marriage usually brings. Imagine me? A somebody! 'There goes Helle Vendel . . .' (*Tenderly*) But it wasn't really that, Erik. It wasn't the pride and the self-assurance that made me happy.

ERIK

No. . .?

HELLE

No! It was my becoming strong enough to be able to save Åke from his despair. Yes, I thought that I'd made him live again. It was so wonderful. All that peculiar pent-up despair of Åke's . . . was simply washed away.

ERIK (*smiling*)

The bank manager was able to get along without his self-awareness.

HELLE (*laughs*)

So you've heard about that too. (*With warmth*) Oh, I've come back from town, tired and perhaps disappointed because my sketches had been rejected. Poor Åke'd been sitting here all day drawing. The place would be one hell of a mess. His hair sticking up, pencil smudges all over his face, the floor covered with sketches, his head full of ideas. And his heart . . .! (*Pauses, then softly*) I'd thought that it was all over between us, but it wasn't. It seemed as if we two, he and I, shared everything.

ERIK (*stands up, walks uneasily back and forth*)

I understand all of this, of course, Helle. But . . . couldn't things go on like this?

HELLE (*flatly*)

You saw him today, didn't you?

ERIK

Yes. No. But what made him like that?

HELLE (*uneasily*)

I've been asking myself over and over again lately whether I began neglecting Åke once we were successful. Did I simply just not have enough time to look after

him properly these past six months? I don't understand... Two people who were so very close to each
other... and it seemed to me that we were until day
before yesterday. But today? It's as if he blew out a
light inside me ... an easy thing for him to do... but
I'm the one in the dark.

ERIK

Well, then, you'll just have to go on alone.

HELLE

I don't know... Nothing but an amusement, he said.
A childish game.

ERIK

Are you uncertain about your partnership with Ulf
Gram?

HELLE

I've become uncertain about it today. Uncertain about
Åke. Uncertain about everything. *(Thoughtfully)* It's
difficult to decide, Erik. It can be terribly painful having to make a choice.

ERIK *(bitterly)*
So you've discovered that at last!

HELLE *(in a low voice)*
Do you think it was easy for me to choose when I
married Åke?

ERIK

Easy? No. Every serious decision involves pain... otherwise there'd be no choice to make. Am I bitter because you married Åke? Yes!... but the only thing I
reproach you for is for what you just said: *(slowly)* 'I
chose.'

HELLE

But. . .

ERIK *(vehemently)*

Has it never occurred to you that whenever you're bothered by a choice, it's because, deep down, you'd rather
reject both possibilities the choice offers you. You don't
want to say: yes. . . to one of the possibilities and: no
. . . to the other. You'd much rather be allowed to be
silent, Helle, and wait.

HELLE *(defiant)*

Either I accept Gram's offer of a partnership or I reject
it.

ERIK

You mean: Either you'll choose a safe, secure existence
at the cost of a happy relationship with your husband,
or you'll reject Gram's offer and try to straighten out
your relationship with Åke . . . and start all over again
from scratch *(with a sweep of the hand)* up here in
this messy garret.

HELLE

No! It can't be like that.

ERIK

No? Why do you make yourself a victim of this choice?
(Earnestly) A choice, Helle, in which others, Åke and
Ulf Gram, set the terms.

HELLE *(after a pause, low and slow)*

And you believe that had I waited. . . that time. . . I
wouldn't have had to make a choice. That I would have
gone to you. Of my own desire and free will.

ERIK

Yes!

Tense silence in which both hesitate. . . for a long time

ERIK *(with an effort)*

I've been very interested in this question of choice.

HELLE *(nods, flatly)*

Yes. . .

ERIK

Because it's tormented me. Because I've had to fight with it — for my brief moments of happiness, of freedom, of . . . I didn't understand that if a person dares wait until he grabs spontaneously for something he wants, grabs from desire — he needn't choose out of fear. Do you know when I realized this?

HELLE *(as before)*

No, Erik, I don't know.

ERIK

When I inherited a handsome sum of money once. Suddenly the choice was there, smothering me, crushing me, filling me with fear: What are you going to do with the money? How are you going to invest it? Are you going to save it or use it, waste or increase it? Hell. I just did *one* thing, Helle.

HELLE *(smiling)*

Got rid of it.

ERIK

Yes.

HELLE

And afterwards. . .?

ERIK

Afterwards I began to realize what freedom was. *(Intensely)* Live or possess, Helle! There's no middle way. There's no bridge across.

HELLE

Freedom... Happiness...?

ERIK *(soberly)*

Just understanding this doesn't immediately make you free. And I'm still far from being a happy man... *(Smiles quickly)* Except every now and then.

HELLE *(slowly)*

And that's when you paint... or love?

ERIK

There's something strange about critics... Oh, there's nothing strange about the fact that the critic and the artist have different ideas about things. On the contrary. But that the critic can turn the artist upside-down, simply hold him there and cry out triumphantly: This is what he's like! Well, I just don't understand it. Take me, for example. They say I've become so constructive. So perceptive. So calculating. *(With growing excitement)* But they don't realize that I paint like a blind man! In a kind of ecstasy! I mean, of course, when I turn out something good. Let's not talk about my bad stuff. But when I'm successful, do they really believe that I stand there consciously choosing? No! No!... But that's the moment you can be pierced by happiness.

HELLE *(afire)*

Yes.

ERIK *(intense)*

And all walls inside me and outside me cease to exist and I'm flooded with ... light!

HELLE

Yes!

ERIK

Ah. That's ecstasy. A kind of happiness which *(involuntarily raising his hands)* if I dared approach you right now and... *(Stops, points to the painting and says with effort)* There hangs proof — that I'm telling the truth.

HELLE *(not understanding)*

What...?

ERIK

The proof is behind you.

HELLE *(turns around, entranced)*

The most beautiful...!

ERIK

It's yours, Helle. To you — from me.

HELLE *(rises slowly, happy, with open arms)*

No one could have made me as happy as you do now. Nothing could have made me as happy as this. Oh, Erik. My friend ...

They embrace. Erik takes her face between his hands and kisses her passionately ... as Åke comes in the door.

HELLE *(tearing herself away)*

Oh, Erik. Yes. No, Erik...!

ÅKE *(with difficulty)*

I couldn't get a cab. I've been sitting in there ringing and ringing. Now I'm going to go down to the taxi stand on the corner to see whether I can find a cab...

ERIK

A cab...? *(Paralysed, with increasing resentment)* Taxi stand? What the hell, I'll get a cab. *(Moves toward door)*

ÅKE *(as before)*

Wouldn't you rather stay here — with Helle?

ERIK *(in anger)*
> Don't you think *you* ought to stay here? With Helle?

ÅKE *(as before)*
> So if you two'll just watch out — when I ring three
> times — from below — I'll be there — with a taxi.

ERIK
> Watch out. . .? *(Angrily)* Are we supposed to watch
> out now as well? You'd better watch your. . .! Watch
> your own. . . *(Gropes after words)*

HELLE *(with assumed gravity)*
> Self-awareness, Erik.

ERIK *(looks desperately at Helle, nods. Says to Åke, on
> the verge of tears)*
> Watch your own self-awareness, my man.

Goes out quickly

Helle and Åke look silently at one another without moving

HELLE
> Well?

ÅKE
> Yes?

HELLE
> What were you thinking?

ÅKE
> No. . . Thinking. . .?

Starts to circle round her, observing her

HELLE *(in nervous irritation)*
> What's the matter? Is there anything wrong?

*With the exception of the last words at the end of the act,
Åke delivers the following lines in more or less the same
tone of voice: monotonously. . . as if he were talking in his
sleep. . . sometimes with a slightly childish tone*

ÅKE

Anything wrong? Of course not.

HELLE

Why are you staring at me like that?

ÅKE

Hmm. . .? Your dress is lovely.

HELLE

Why are you walking around like that?

ÅKE

Does it bother you?

HELLE

I'm cold. . . I think I'll take my coat.

ÅKE

I'll get it. Sit down, Helle, my dear. I'm afraid you'll have to wait a while before Erik comes. (*Åke gets her coat. Helle sits down on the arm of one of the chairs downstage*)

HELLE (*with a repressed earnestness*)

Come with me, Åke. Come just as you are, but come. Be with me this evening. I need you. Do you hear? I beseech you!

ÅKE (*stops with the coat in his hands, smiles a distant smile*)

Helle, do you remember. . . our first long trip together? That spring in Paris. . .?

HELLE (*tiredly*)

Yes, of course, I remember that spring.

ÅKE

We were so young.

HELLE

It was a long time ago, you mean.

ÅKE

I saw nothing but you... Every morning you were
new to me. Every day you were a different person
from the one you had been the day before. And the
nights were such that...

HELLE *(coldly)*

Did you think that you had seen who I was — all of a
sudden?

ÅKE *(quickly)*

But the days. The days, Helle! Do you remember the
dresses I bought for you? Just about every other day
we made the rounds of the shops and bought — new
things — expensive things. *(Laughs softly, happily)* I
had money then. Had begun speculating. Yes, I had lots
of money then...

HELLE *(unpleasantly agitated)*

Far too much... far too expensive things. I was never
used to such.

ÅKE

But you liked the dresses I bought for you, didn't you?

HELLE

I remember that even then I didn't really like it. It was
all so terribly unnecessary. I believe I thought that
you hurt me — although I didn't understand why...
· then.

ÅKE

You have such a strange way of remembering things.
Do you always remember things the wrong way?

HELLE *(in growing rebellion)*

Wasn't I good enough for you naked? Did you have to
renew your woman every other day with those dresses of
yours?

ÅKE *(putting the coat over Helle's shoulders, remains standing behind her)*
Perhaps it was my way of thanking you for your caresses, Helle.

HELLE *(as before)*
I was hungry for life. For days with your hand in mine. Nights with you inside me.

ÅKE *(lost in memories)*
I remember one dress in particular... A red evening dress. You seemed so delightfully shameless in that dress. Like a scream. A cry after crime and violence. I noticed how they turned their heads. I laughed when they envied me ... But it was expensive. My, oh, my, that dress cost a lot of money.

HELLE *(nervously irritated)*
Why are you standing like that? Why are you standing behind me the whole time? Do you hear me, Åke. Do you hear?

ÅKE *(moves and says to calm her)*
I'm just standing here looking at you. Looking at you and thinking about the good old days. *(Laughs)* Did you think that some criminal stood behind your back threatening: *(laughs, teasing)* Your money or your life. Your money or your life.

HELLE
Yes! You heard it too, didn't you? But I want you to answer this question behind my back: *(whispers)* live or possess? Live or possess?

During the following Åke paces back and forth

HELLE *(half to herself)*
I don't know.... Here I sit talking about life and you

walk about thinking of your money. But if you won't choose life, and choose it with me, well, we've reached a parting of the ways. I'm so afraid. Alone. I'm so afraid of the dark.

ÅKE *(stops, feigning despair)*
And we weren't even newly-weds.

HELLE
What. . . Who?

ÅKE
In Paris. People thought that we were newly-weds, you know.

HELLE *(dryly)*
We had been married for over two years when we were in Paris that spring.

ÅKE
Just the same, people thought that. . .? We must have looked extremely happy.

HELLE
Are you coming? Are you coming with me now?

ÅKE
It's a matter of business, Helle, between Gram and you. You have to choose. It's up to you whether you want or don't want to join the house of Andrienne.

HELLE
It's our choice. It concerns us both.

ÅKE *(with one of Helle's dresses)*
Have you seen anything more like it? It's almost exactly the same dress I bought for you that time. The pastel blue. Remember? *(Laughs)* I don't think that you realize how unconsciously you copy my, no, I mean your

dresses from Paris. People turned round to look at you, that's how beautiful you were. Everybody had to smile. Everybody had to nod. . .

HELLE

. . . at the new dresses. . . that Åke had bought.

ÅKE (*continuing*)

Why, Helle, really? (*With another dress*) Or this one. Do you remember that time at Montparnasse in that little dive where the students formed a ring around you?

HELLE

No, around your dress. That was your padlock on me. Your little padlock on something you thought you owned. (*Stands up, strong, defiant*) Don't you see who I am! Don't you see that I'm wearing my red dress! (*The bell rings three times*)

ÅKE (*flatly*)

Erik. . . the cab. . .

HELLE (*with sad encouragement*)

Poor little Åke. Did I frighten you?

Helle kisses him lightly on the cheek, walks toward the door, turns quickly. . . on a playful impulse. . . and points at Åke with her hand raised as if she were aiming at him with a revolver.

HELLE

Your money or your life, Åke Vendel! Your money or your life!

Exit quickly

Åke laughs, almost silently at first, but with increasing volume once Helle has gone. . . while staring at the closed door. The laughter suddenly stops. He becomes aware of the dress he is crushing in his hands and flings it against the door in impotent hate and anger.

ÅKE *(screams out as curtain falls)*
   You slut. . .!

ACT TWO

The scene is the same, a couple of hours later. A reading lamp is on the table as well as an open book. The stage is empty a moment before Ulf Gram and Åke Vendel enter. They are both slightly out of breath.

ULF
   That really takes it out of you.

ÅKE
   After six flights you begin to feel the effects of all those cigarettes. . . and your age.

ULF
   Imagine . . . an old sportsman like me, oarsman, gymnast, wheezing like a whale by the time I've reached the third floor.

ÅKE
   Must be rather disappointing wasting your youth on boring sports — only to wind up with palpitations of the heart on the third floor.

ULF
   Oh, no, you're all wrong, Vendel, old chap. This ship's in fine shape. Heart, lungs, guts and temper. Both my internal and external machinery are in the best possible working condition. That's right, chap. And as for my blood pressure. . .

ÅKE

You must have come to the wrong place. I'm not a doctor.

ULF

Little low in spirits this evening, chief? *(Pause)* By the way, we dropped titles, didn't we, that Easter four years ago — remember Vendel? Up in the mountains — at your cabin? That was really a nice Saturday we had. Yes, a most enjoyable evening. *(Pauses. Smiles)* I've never had a chance to thank you for your hospitality. We've hardly seen one another since.

ÅKE *(with forced calm)*

I told you when I opened the door for you, you've come to the wrong place, Mr. Gram. So if you'd be so kind as to take your internal and external machinery — your athletic guts and all — you may begin your retreat. You'll find that going down is easier than coming up. If, however, you feel the need for assistance, I shall be delighted to help you!

ULF *(with a hearty laugh, sits down)*

I really think you're funny, chief. I like you. I see you've been sitting here reading.

ÅKE

Yes. . . books!

ULF

Hah! That was aimed at me. Me, Ulf Gram, a man of little formal education, free from the burdens of book learning. But we're doing all right, Vendel, old chap — we're doing just fine.

ÅKE

We? Who's we?

ULF

Your talented little wife and myself. (*Pauses, smiles*) I like your wife too, Vendel, my chap. A delightful person.

ÅKE

Would you mind leaving?

ULF

Are you coming along?

ÅKE (*sitting down*)

No, I said. I made that quite clear downstairs when I opened the door for you, but you insisted on coming up here. Under no circumstances will I go with you to that restaurant. I'm staying right here. I'm waiting for my wife.

ULF

But, don't you see, she's the reason I'm here. She begs you to join us. Poor little thing. She's obviously upset. We've called and called, God knows how many times, but there was no answer. Is your phone out of order? Or didn't you want to answer it?

ÅKE (*calmer*)

I've just come back in. I've been out for a little walk. A short evening stroll.

ULF

I see, so you've got to go out and air it every now and then, do you?

ÅKE

What do you mean . . . 'air it'? What's 'it'?

ULF

Oh, don't pay any attention to a simple, vulgar chap like me. (*Pause*) Come on, Vendel. We've just been served coffee and liqueur, and the restaurant's right around the corner, man. I didn't even put on my coat to walk the few steps here. Within three minutes, you're in the presence of your sweet little lady — wife, I mean.

ÅKE

I said no!

ULF

But she wants you to come so terribly, chief. Don't be unreasonable. How can you resist such a delightful little delicate creature like your wife, chief?

ÅKE

I'm not your chief.

ULF

She's been nervous and distracted all evening. Silent as well. Not even an old sportsman like myself has been able to get to first base with her. Not to mention Erik, that sourpuss. He just sits there stuffing himself with caviar and champagne... looking as if I was treating him to nothing but black bread and skimmed milk! That's artists for you, goddamn'em.

ÅKE

Aha... your machinery is out of order.

ULF

What did you say, chief?

ÅKE

Your spirits are sinking in spite of your increasing outlay for caviar and champagne. Most depressing. Extremely painful. Good night, Mr. Fashion Designer.

ULF

Be a nice guy, chief.

ÅKE *(half rises, shouts)*

I'm not your chief! Get out of here! Get out! *(Falls back into his chair)*

ULF *(smiling after a pause)*

There, you see! We're getting there. We're getting there.

ÅKE *(after a pause, with uncontrollable curiosity)*

Getting there. . .? What are you babbling about now? We're getting where?

ULF

We're getting close to you, my dear Åke Vendel. You! Personally.

ÅKE

For the last time, are you going to get out of here of your own free will?

ULF

We are of slightly different mould, we two. There's coarser stuff in me, you see. Ulf Gram doesn't move on of his own free will — no, not like a certain little cowardly bankrupt bank manager I know.

ÅKE

You'd better watch your step.

ULF

You're nothing but an infected little boil, you know that? Full of a conscious-stricken itching and a soulful yellow pus. And this wife of yours, this delightful female body goes around wasting her energy applying hot comforting compresses on her bankrupt spouse. But I'm afraid her treatment's all wrong. Hot compresses are used for colic pains.

ÅKE *(trembling)*

I've got a revolver somewhere. . .

ULF

My, my, you don't say! No, my dear Bank Manager,

boils like you have to be squeezed so that the whole rotten mess can come out.

ÅKE *(stands up holding his keys in his hand, says numbly)*
Helle thinks it's wrong for me to keep everything locked up. She also thinks it's wrong for me to go around with these keys. But I keep this one *(holding the key ring by a particular key)*, the key to my desk, because my revolver's loaded. It's loaded.

ULF
Have you got a permit to keep a revolver? What does your wife say to that?

ÅKE *(curt)*
She doesn't know anything about it. *(Threatening)* Now you've got to choose.

ULF
Your money or your life, what?

ÅKE *(hoarse)*
Say that again. Say that again, you dirty little fashion slob.

ULF *(drumming on the table, sizing Åke up)*
That affair with the bank did you in. Jesus, some people don't last long. Perhaps you gave suicide as a reason when — when you applied for your gun permit. But, as the old lady said: The good thing about suicide and salvation is that they can be postponed.

Åke walks slowly over to his desk, like a sleepwalker. Ulf sits immobile at the table, observing him, alert and tense, yet calm and cold.

ULF
Come here and sit down, Vendel. Let's talk first — you can shoot me afterwards.

ÅKE *(stops, flat)*

 Talk . . . about what?

ULF *(warmly, almost tenderly)*

 About the injustice that's been done to you, my friend.
 And I'm sure we can air it out better than you did on
 your little walk this evening.

ÅKE *(reluctantly returning)*

 Be careful, Ulf Gram. I have some idea as to the role
 you played that time.

ULF

 All the same you resigned. Of your own free will. Four
 years ago.

ÅKE *(sitting down)*

 I lacked the confidence of the board, wasn't that it?

ULF

 Yes, you resigned as bank manager after receiving a
 reprimand from the board — phrased so carefully and
 so vaguely—*(excited)* that not a soul would have dared
 demand your resignation then. No! But a hint was more
 than enough for our spoiled, sulky Åke Vendel. He took
 his hat and coat and walking stick and left — for his
 attic — in order to feel sorry for himself.

ÅKE

 And that surprised Board Member Gram.

ULF

 On the contrary! That was exactly what Board Member Gram had counted on. No, sir, it was somebody
 else who was surprised — wasn't it? When the board
 accepted your resignation *(triumphantly)* without a
 murmur! *(Teasing)* You hadn't counted on that, had
 you, my friend?

ÅKE *(bitterly)*

No, I hadn't expected that. *(Painful)* The reprimand had hurt me deeply. But I thought that my threatening to leave would fall like a bomb on . . . *(gesticulating)* but the roof fell in on my head instead.

ULF *(yawning)*

That was exactly what was supposed to happen. The roof was supposed to fall in.

ÅKE *(tense)*

You admit, then, that you were responsible for the board's decision?

ULF

In a tête-à-tête with the bank manager — yes, I think I can admit that.

ÅKE

And the plan was already ripe when you 'accidentally' dropped by my cabin in the mountains on that Saturday afternoon four years ago.

ULF

Right you are, Vendel. I wanted to study my victim one last time. I wanted to make sure that the spoiled boy would react as he should. . . when I came forward with my proposal of non-confidence.

ÅKE

And the victim reacted to your satisfaction?

ULF

Completely! I tested my plan out by flirting a little with his wife. A delightful woman, simply delightful — but the main thing was that the bank manager reacted as I had hoped. Ashamed on behalf of me and his wife, he discreetly withdrew, pretending that he

hadn't noticed my advances. He behaved most politely
towards the scoundrel Ulf Gram. I then said to myself: *(chuckling)* at the first board meeting after Easter,
you're going to lay that fellow flat.

ÅKE *(smiling palely)*

Wasn't there something rather uncertain about that plan
of yours? After all, I hadn't done anything dishonourable.

ULF

Honourable? Dishonourable? That's a matter of opinion.
No, I always place my stakes on people... whenever
there's something I want to achieve. *(Slyly)* You see,
there's a dirty under-current in people, and you've got to
be sure that you get down to it, if you really want to
be something in this world, Vendel.

ÅKE

So you mean that your dirty surface is what makes for
success, do you?

ULF

I said: dirty under-current — in people.

ÅKE

Well, it seems that there's something wrong with your
drainage, Mr. Gram.

ULF *(angrily)*

Easy, easy! ... *(Forcefully)* You were favouring a firm
in which two of your highly distinguished friends
were partners, Vendel, my boy. You took advantage of
our position in order to give this firm credit without
bringing the matter to the attention of the board. Do
you call that honourable? *(Thoughtfully)* At the same
time, you privately invested all that you owned in
a short-term but daring — and very, very promising —

gamble. *(Reprimanding)* You know very well that the board would never have approved the securities placed by that firm. *(Pauses, then says softly)* And there you sit, you well-drained son-of-a-bitch.

ÅKE *(crushed)*

It was my letter of resignation that did me in. I lost all my credit when I resigned as bank manager. I ought to have waited. Three more months of credit — and I would have won the battle.

ULF *(reproachfully)*

Don't be so egotistical, Vendel. You're quite welcome to give people a good story, call it a circus number if you like: a bank manager privately mobilizes all the credit he can muster in his position. He then makes investments and jumps. . . at the great dividends hanging there three months in the future. He sends in his resignation, and it is accepted. He then loses his credit. He lands on his ass with a loud crash. Can it be more simple than that, Vendel?

ÅKE *(with disgust)*

Filthy! Filthy! All about you is filthy. . . Yes, even your very presence is contaminating.

ULF

Well, you've managed to accept my money these past four years. That was clean enough for you, you weakling. *(Changing the subject)* Come on down and say hello to your wife, Bank Manager.

ÅKE *(with forced calm)*

Why did you do it?

ULF

Do what, chief?

ÅKE

Why did you do it, man?

ULF

Do what?

ÅKE

I was desperate. I'd been speculating for a long time, but I had had nothing but losses — losses. It was then that I saw my way out and invested everything. That was before that Easter vacation when Helle and I went up into the mountains. At last I felt safe. I could finally breathe freely and relax.

ULF

Bosh!

ÅKE

You dropped by my cabin that afternoon. Did you know then how much I'd invested?

ULF

Not exactly — but I had some idea.

ÅKE

Did you know that I, out of pure kindness on my part — had stretched myself quite far for that firm? Had given it extensive credit in the bank?

ULF (poohpoohing)

Out of kindness?

ÅKE

Did you know that I had strained my own credit to the utmost, but that I would be a rich man after three months — if nothing unforeseen happened.

ULF

Humph! That's the trouble with the unforeseen, chief. You've always got to take it into consideration.

ÅKE

And you gambled on my sense of honour and my pride.

ULF *(heartily)*

I think you're very funny, Vendel.

ÅKE

You coldly and cynically figured out that an unexpected reprimand from the board would cause me to lose my bearings. Well, you reasoned correctly. I did lose my bearings. I sent in my resignation. But, Christ, it never dawned on me that the board of my own bank would accept . . .! *(Changing the subject)* Why did you do it, Gram? Why did you do it?

ULF

It was a rather serious affair, that. Giving credit without sufficient securities, wasn't it, old man?

ÅKE

Nonsense! That company was solid enough. But what was it you wanted to achieve? Such baseness requires both time and energy. Where was the profit in it for you?

ULF

Drop that tone, Vendel. It doesn't at all suit a jerk who's being supported by his wife.

ÅKE

You don't even dare reveal your motives. Not even four years later. Not even during a tête-à-tête with your victim.

ULF

Not dare! Just you wait and see! *(Low and threatening)* So, my fine, conceited, unapproachable Åke Vendel, you think I'm still afraid of you today, do you? No, old chap, you're dreadfully mistaken.

ÅKE

Still as afraid of me as. . . as you were then. . . you mean?

ULF

Don't pretend that you've forgotten the whole affair.

ÅKE

No, of course not. . . And you thought that I was — conceited?

ULF *(full of hate)*

Oh!. . . Splendid! *(Pauses, then says cuttingly)* But I wasn't good enough. By no means.

ÅKE

Yes, of course! Yes, now I'm beginning to. . . Ah, yes, I remember that affair. *(Smiles)* You were offended, weren't you?

ULF

What do you think? I finally had a chance at a decent job — in a steamship line — a real good job! . . . after having crawled around in shit all my life.

ÅKE

And you didn't get the job?

ULF *(almost speechless at Åke's matter-of-factness)*

Didn't get that job? You mean you didn't even bother to find out whether I. . .!

ÅKE

I don't seem to have followed your career as closely as you seem to have followed mine.

ULF *(moved as he recalls the situation)*

I was completely qualified for the job. The whole thing

was just about in the bag — but then: 'What about your references, my young man.' 'Naturally. You can just refer to Vendel.' 'Vendel? Oh, you mean Åke Vendel, the bank manager! In that case, my young man . . .'!

ÅKE *(involuntarily becoming the bank manager once again)*
The point is that you were in such a hurry that you apparently forgot to ask me whether I was willing to give you a recommendation. Unforgivably naive of you. Unforgivably impudent. Did you think that the steamship line wouldn't contact me to verify? Or did you think that I'd just say 'Hmm' and 'Ha' and 'yes' and let the whole thing ride?

ULF *(sullen)*
You knew who I was. We had met before at the Rowing Club.

ÅKE *(coolly)*
Were you applying for a job as seaman first class?

ULF *(rising, angrily)*
Oh, hell . . . ! I didn't dare ask. I didn't dare ask for an audience with our fine bank manager, Mr. Vendel. *(Walking back and forth)* The fop! Rich, fashionable and newly-wed. Even dropped by the Rowing Club every now and then, but stopped the first time he got blisters on his hands. *(More calmly)* And such fine hands, too. How easily and matter-of-factly they brushed that upstart Gram from off his jacket lapel. It cost me four years. I was on the verge of giving up and going under for good. *(Mimicking)* 'You mean you didn't get the job . . .?'

ÅKE *(absentmindedly)*
Eleven years ago. Yes — we had just married, Helle and

I. The youngest bank manager in the country... *(Sighs, changes the subject)* Four years, did you say? We two ought to be quits soon, don't you think, Ulf Gram?

ULF *(mockingly)*
Sure, sure.

ÅKE *(surprised)*
You've had your revenge, haven't you?

ULF *(as before)*
Sure, sure.

ÅKE
That reprimand. *(With ironic admiration)* That was really a stroke of genius — in all its simplicity.

ULF *(stops walking, elated)*
Yes, wasn't it!

ÅKE *(as before)*
Absolutely. Undoubtedly a stroke of genius — *(With great self-control)* My dear Ulf.

ULF *(begins walking again, lost in memories)*
The strange thing about it all was that there was really nothing else I could put my finger on. As far as your running of the bank was concerned, that was faultless... that was what made the whole thing so difficult. Therefore I had to go to work with a certain delicacy, you understand, preparing each member of the board one by one. Cajoling them. Pampering them. And do you know what I played on?

ÅKE *(as before)*
On their dirty under-currents, my dear Ulf.

ULF *(slyly)*
On the fact that you were so different! No one could ever really make you out. They thought you were con-

ceited. Arrogant. You spent a lot of money, living on a
level far above that your salary permitted or your position as bank manager required. You had a lovely wife.
And you kept everybody at such a distance! The moment he came near you, you could make the most newly-
shaven, well-scrubbed guy feel as if he had just gotten
off the train. But that's the sort of thing that makes
hate grow quietly among men, chief, a silent hate.
(Bright and happy) And that's the sort of stuff one can
take advantage of when you know people and have
figured out both parties. And that's exactly what I
did.

ÅKE

Are you so sure about that?

ULF

Of course. Oh, yes, I knew that you were, hmm, how
shall I put it? An artistic type. Over-sensitive. Priggish
and shy. Very full of soul! And when I found out that
the studs on the board sat around the table glower-
ring at the sophisticated gentleman they thought just sat
there despising them . . . *(Frankly)* Well, I thought it was
perfect stuff to work with, chief.

ÅKE

And they had their revenge.

ULF

Yes, don't you think so? I, at any rate, think I got mine
all right.

ÅKE *(dryly)*

No, you don't really think you have. *(After a pause,
calm and controlled)* You've revealed enough about
yourself this evening so that the whole thing is quite
clear: it wasn't that false reference of yours that you

wanted revenge for, Mr. Gram. No. It was 'the sophisticated gentleman' that was the thorn in the cad's eye.
(Beating his forehead, says softly) Deep down, I knew
it all the time. There was something revolting associated
with your name. *(Loud, mocking)* Oh, no, it wasn't
the board members who hated me, my friend. It was
you. But board members also become dirty when they
have — ha, travelled by train long enough.

ULF

You were the engine driver — until the rest of us
kicked you off the train.

ÅKE

Do you want to know why you hate me? All right, I'll
tell you. Because you're a swine, Ulf Gram, and know
it as well. I've met your type before, but never such
an extreme case. You're nothing but dregs, do you know
that? Almost as perfectly base in your actions, I think,
as you are in your dreams and desires. And you think
there's something bloody unfair in the fact that you have
to be like this! . . . while other people *(pointing to himself)* are allowed to walk around and be 'gentlemen.' And even in our rags, Gram, even in our rags,
we're still 'gentlemen' . . . but we'll pay for it, won't
we? Pay until it hurts. That's it, isn't it? Pay until
it hurts.

ULF

Ugh. . . I could crack that pride of yours between my
fingernails, chief. Like this! Just as I can crack a louse
when I want to.

ÅKE

There's just one form for revenge that can satisfy you —
for a short time: *(slowly)* Contamination! But you

didn't manage to bring it off that time. *(Secretive)* But what about now? Yes, maybe you'll manage it very soon, very soon, indeed! *(With emphasis)* If you can contaminate my wife. She's the one who's got to go down into the dirt. Because if you can possess her, if you can walk over her... Well, then you've got *me*, right? Then your revenge will be complete.

ULF *(thickly)*

I honour and respect your little lady... your wife, I mean... A delightful little creature.

ÅKE *(dryly)*

Yes, she'd have to be, otherwise there'd be nothing to contaminate, you jerk.

ULF *(stamping on the floor)*

You devil, you!

ÅKE *(rising)*

Yes! And your plans are always very simple. By launching Helle, you'll be able to take advantage of her rich artistic talent, while at the same time manage to separate her from her husband. You want to associate her honesty and self-esteem with your name, with your person. After a while, I'll become superfluous. A bit despicable. A nobody. A hanger-on. *(Changing)* But Helle, the child, must have told you about how proud she was of me... who helped her with sketches and ideas. Splendid! All you have to do then is make the bank manager and husband part of your firm. The fashion-fop could make himself useful, while the husband side of him daily went through a hell of jealousy whenever the House's head and his beautiful manager 'conferred' in the inner office. And then, when the time was ripe... *(Harshly)* But you're not going to have her.

(Walks to the door) I'm going down to the restaurant and bring back those two. We've got to talk about all this and get it over with. Helle and I have other possibilities. She can get other offers. At any rate. She's not going to become manager for the House of Andrienne. *(Opens the door, smiles, and says quietly)* And she's not going to become your mistress, Ulf Gram.

Exit

ULF *(stands still, strikes his forehead)*

Idiot! *(Paces a little)* How stupid! How stupid of me! *(Takes the book from off the table, shakes his head, puts the book back down. Says softly)* Fashion slob. Isn't that what he called me? Fashion-slob? And filthy? *(Examines his hands, puts them in his jacket pockets and continues to walk. He opens the door to the bedroom, detecting a female aroma. Says softly, tentatively)* Helle? Helle Vendel? *(Picks up her housecoat and presses it against his face)* Helle? Will you be mine? Will you be mine? Hmm? *(Listens, puts the housecoat down and walks toward the middle of the room. Sound of quick steps, and a key in the lock. Helle enters with her coat loosely thrown over her shoulders)*

HELLE *(out of breath, excited)*

Åke? *(To Ulf)* Where is he? *(Pointing to the bedroom)* Is he in there?

Ulf's behaviour is noticeably different when Helle is present: polite, respectful, almost chivalrous in an old-fashioned way.

ULF

He went down to fetch Erik and you. Just now — about two minutes ago.

HELLE *(disappointed)*

Oh. . .!

ULF

It's strange you didn't run into each other on the stairs.

HELLE

I met Iversen, the caretaker. He brought me up in the elevator.

ULF

What a shame, Mrs. Vendel.

HELLE *(sitting down)*

How stupid of me. I'm always doing spontaneous things like this. . . I suddenly felt so afraid. I had to see him. He's been so. . . I don't know. . . lately. So I got my wrap and ran. *(Laughs)* Without even saying goodbye to Erik. Poor Erik.

ULF

Oh, Erik can take care of himself. But Mrs. Vendel, you worry me. It's not quite safe for a woman like you to be running around in the city at night.

HELLE

Oh, it wasn't very far.

ULF

I sincerely hope that you and your husband will move once you and I come to an agreement concerning our contract, which I hope will be soon. Once that's in order, it'll be in the firm's interest, of course, to put up securities for. . . *(Jovially)* I think you two ought to build, Mrs. Vendel. A little nest, what? With a small garden. That's the life, you know. It's then that you begin to feel alive.

HELLE

Yes, maybe... although I really don't know... (*Impulsively*) Do you think Andrienne could take over this place? Two large attic rooms. And we need another sewing room. It's so crowded where we are now.

ULF

Did you hear what you said, Mrs. Vendel? (*Smiling when Helle doesn't understand*) You said: '*We* need ...' (*With warmth*) I'm very glad you said that.

HELLE (*uneasy*)

It just dropped out. But, after all, this place is very centrally located. There's lots of room, and... (*Somewhat uneasy because of Ulf's gaze*) Have you been up here very long? Erik and I started to wonder... (*Laughs nervously*) I suddenly became so frightened. I don't know...

ULF (*mischievously*)

You didn't think that your husband and I had been falling out with each other, did you, Mrs. Vendel?

HELLE (*confused*)

Heavens, no. That would have been... What on earth should you two fight about?

ULF (*laughing*)

It would have had to have been about you... ahem, Mrs. Vendel.

HELLE (*with a forced laugh*)

No, that wasn't what I was thinking as I ran over here.

ULF (*bowing slightly*)

I hope I didn't offend you, just now. I was only joking.

HELLE *(unpleasantly embarrassed)*

What? Oh, by no means. That would be ridiculous of me. *(Tries to straighten up the situation)* What must you be thinking of me? I haven't even asked you to sit down. I've made no attempt to... *(With clumsy heartiness)* And shouldn't we soon be calling each other by our Christian names? Otherwise things become so stiff and *(laughs)* silly.

Ulf makes a gesture with his hand as if to signify that it's all up to her.

HELLE *(laughs more freely)*

How utterly absurd. We've been sitting drinking champagne together, but as soon as we come up here in this messy garret ...

ULF *(laughing heartily)*

...You suggest that we call each other by our first names. *(Offering her his hand as he sits down.)* That would be very nice, Helle. I really appreciate this. *(Sits a while, then says cautiously)* I was wondering... since we two are sitting here in your *(laughs)* messy garret, why don't we take a look at our contract? Perhaps we can come to an agreement. At least get rid of the minor snags. What do you think? *(Takes out two documents)*

HELLE

I would rather that Åke also...

ULF

Dependency! Thy name is woman!

HELLE

Yes, but... I'd prefer to wait.

ULF *(placing the documents before Helle)*

As you wish. But you know we've worked so well together before — and I hope we'll continue to do so.
This paper is nothing but a confirmation of a relationship that has already existed — though in more modest
forms.

HELLE *(trying to be business-like)*

Yes, I know. Nothing will be different, really

ULF   *(close to Helle, bending over the documents)*

Oh, is that what you think, do you? Well, what about
your salary, for example. . .? Let's see, where is it
now. . .

HELLE

Gracious! What a lot of money.

ULF

Naturally, Mrs. Vendel. After all, we're hiring an
expert. And now look here . . . *(Mumbles, then says
aloud)* Yes, here we are. Five years. Maybe you think
that's a long time — but I feel that I'm investing in
you. Quite a lot too — so, you see, I've got to make sure
that you don't suddenly fall into the arms of my competitors and — desert me.

HELLE

Oh, no, Ulf, I'll certainly not desert you.

ULF

Of course not, my dear! I was only joking. But otherwise you find the conditions reasonable, don't you?
Hmm?

HELLE

I think you're just wonderful. You've been so dreadfully kind — to us both. Åke and me, I mean.

ULF *(slightly embarrassed)*

My dear. . . you mustn't look at it like that. . . This is business. I'm paying you for your artistic talent. It has nothing at all to do with kindness.

HELLE *(confidently)*

Oh, yes, it does too. *(Naively)* After all, you could have cheated me, you know.

ULF

What are you saying. . .!

HELLE

You could have cheated me. Tricked me into signing.

ULF

No, Helle. No, I couldn't do that. People just don't do things like that. *(Takes out a fountain pen and offers it to Helle)*

HELLE *(taking the pen)*

Yes. No. Where do I sign?

ULF

Just look here. You see? I felt so confident that I've signed already! In duplicate, you see. You'll keep one copy and I'll keep the other. In this way we're both safe, understand? Both of us. Aha. On the dotted line. . . there. Yes, your name. . . next to mine.

HELLE *(about to sign, but hesitates)*

I'd rather that Åke read through everything first.

ULF

But *you*'ve already read it.

HELLE

I so much want Åke and me to do everything together. *(Explaining)* Then it would be both of us.

ULF

You mustn't be so dependent. This position will make
you independent, Helle. You'll have financial security.
A prominent position. A career!

HELLE *(with dignity)*

I am independent. I feel completely free.

ULF

But you've been an ordinary free-lancer. A designer
paid for piece-work. You can't help but see the difference.

HELLE

There's no difference. I carry my freedom inside me.
I've been independent for a long time.

ULF

But, Christ . . . Why do you want Åke to look at this,
if, as you say. . . you've been free. . . for a long time?

HELLE *(calmly explaining)*

But it's my feeling of solidarity with Åke that makes me
free. It's my concern for him that gives me my inde-
pendence.

ULF *(quietly sinks down in his chair, appalled)*

Christ, give me strength. . .!

HELLE *(screws the top back on the pen and returns it to
Ulf)*

I think the contract's very fine. You've been wonderful
to both Åke and me . . . so I'm really looking forward to
signing as soon as Åke has looked at it. After all,
there's no rush, is there? I'm not going to desert you,
you know that.

ULF *(with a forced smile)*

Of course not, Mrs. Vendel. No, there's no hurry at all.

I just thought... that since we two were sitting here...
that it would be practical for us to... But as you
wish. As you wish. *(Short, painful pause)*

HELLE

Did you say that Åke went out to fetch Erik? ...
And me too? Well, they should be here soon, then. I
mean...

ULF

We won't be left alone much longer, my dear. There's
no need for you to worry about Åke. They'll be here
any minute now.

HELLE *(quickly laying her hand on Ulf's)*
Excuse me. I didn't mean to be impolite. It's just that
I'm so... *(Changing)* I'm sorry I can't offer you any-
thing. I don't think we've got a drop in the house.

ULF

Thanks, but I'm driving, so I keep my drinking down to
a minimum. Why can't we just sit here — and then
the four of us can drive over to my place.

HELLE *(happy)*
Yes, let's. That would be very nice. Åke is by himself
too much. I'd really like to see him let himself go for
an evening. Maybe even get slightly intoxicated?

ULF

I think we can manage that, Helle. The two of us.
(Changing) You worry about Åke.

HELLE

Worry?... Oh, I don't know. Not really. But he's gone
through so much the past few years. He hasn't found
anything to build on... the way I have. I do so much
want to help him find something.

ULF

Åke Vendel is a most exceptional man. Quite unique.

HELLE (*tenderly*)

Hmm. He often seems to me to be a forlorn little child who's had his toys taken away from him.

ULF

Hah...! (*Checking himself, says quickly*) I mean... Well, isn't he basically...

HELLE (*uncertain*)

What?

ULF

Well, with the exception of his purely professional qualifications as a banker, Åke is pretty much of an artist. In temperament. I mean. Sensitive. Nervous. The whole man.

HELLE (*nods*)

Yes, he is.

ULF

The sort of person who's deeply hurt by any kind of insult or injustice or grossness.

HELLE

Precisely.

ULF (*stands up, paces a little*)

These past few years must have been pretty hard — for Åke. A person like him must have suffered more than — almost more than — well, than he had the strength to bear.

HELLE (*uneasy*)

Has he mentioned anything to you about...

ULF (*quickly*)

... about the revolver, you mean?

HELLE *(dumbstruck)*
What. . . did you say?

ULF *(pretending not to notice Helle's reaction)*
The loaded gun he keeps in his desk. Yes, he kept bringing the subject up the whole time we sat here talking
— a bit too often, I thought. Rather strange. . . *(Acting as if dismayed)* I hope I haven't been so foolish
as to give away something you didn't. . .

HELLE *(as before)*
I had no idea.

ULF
Perhaps I'm making a mountain out of a molehill,
and reading things into what Åke said that weren't
there . . . *(To Helle)* Listen to me. You've got to keep
yourself under control, Helle. Be brave. We'll manage
this all right — the two of us.

HELLE *(helpless)*
Do you really think that. . .?

ULF *(seriously)*
Frankly, there's no doubt in my mind that your husband is going through a serious crisis. But please don't
say a word to him about that revolver. . . this evening.
We're going to have a lot of fun. Åke's going to drink
and drown his sorrows.

HELLE
You talk about him as if he were your patient.

ULF
Don't you trust me?

HELLE
I don't know. . . *(Quickly)* Of course, I trust you. *(Un
sure)* I have to, don't I. . .

ULF *(wandering around)*
   Well, that's that. *(Changing subject)* That wasn't a
   bad idea you had about that sewing room up here. Do
   you always have such good ideas?

HELLE *(rising)*
   And there's such wonderful light up here. *(Pointing)*
   Easter light.

ULF *(turning towards her)*
   What kind of light?

HELLE
   Åke calls it Easter light. He says we ought to wear
   sunglasses.

ULF *(appalled)*
   Sunglasses for the dressmakers? That'll mean additional
   expenses for the firm, madam.

*Åke and Erik enter. Helle and Ulf stand with their backs to
them laughing. They turn and laugh even louder when
they see the serious expressions on their faces... Erik is
carrying Ulf's overcoat, which he places on a chair. The
laughter stops suddenly, followed by an awkward pause.*

ERIK *(awkwardly)*
   Whew! Those stairs are deadly! *(Pause)* Lovely moonlight tonight. *(Pause. Says helplessly)* Outside, I mean.

HELLE
   We've been waiting for you two.

ÅKE *(sarcastically)*
   I hope we haven't come too late.

HELLE *(unsuspecting)*
   For what. . .?

ERIK *(to Ulf, trying to change the situation)*

I brought along your coat to be on the safe side. The head waiter sends you his compliments and says that your bill's in order. We were bowed out. But I'm afraid you're going to have to take care of your car yourself. It's standing outside the hotel entrance... *(To Helle)* What happened to you?

ULF

Thanks a lot, Erik. I'd better ring the doorman about the car. I doubt if it can stay there much longer.

ERIK *(repeats)*

What happened to you?

Ulf saunters over to the bedroom door and remains standing there during the following. Åke stands immobile near the front door. Helle walks down to the table at the front of the stage. Erik starts to follow her, but stops for a moment in the middle of the room not quite knowing what to do.

HELLE

You'll just have to excuse me, Erik, but I ran. I had to come up here. I can't explain it to you now, but... I simply had to. *(Sits)*

ÅKE

This business partnership is taking a rather piquant turn. Be careful, little girl. Remember: unwanted 'creations' are conceived in dark attics.

ULF

You're not being just.

ÅKE

I wasn't speaking to you. 'Just'! How dare you use that word!

HELLE

Åke. . .!

ULF

I can see that you're all worked up. But you're not being fair to me now — and you're insulting your wife for no good reason. I, for my part, am willing to forget this injustice.

ÅKE

Do you hear that, Erik. Just listen to the gentleman: Mr. Ulf Gram. That chimpanzee has acquired manners.

HELLE

I think it was nice of Ulf to say what he did.

ÅKE

Oh, you do, do you? Ulf! Yes, Ulf and Helle Ltd., that's the idea, isn't it?

ULF

But my dear man . . . your wife has been here harmlessly talking business. You don't mean to say that you suspect. . .

HELLE (*flaring up at Åke*)

You don't think that I have to account to you, do you?

ULF

Pardon my clumsiness, madam.

ERIK   (*quietly, to Helle*)

What's got into you, Helle?

HELLE (*subdued*)

Don't you start too.

if my car can stay where it is a little while longer.
The phone's in here, isn't it?

HELLE

I don't think the light's on. You'll find the switch on
the right.

ULF

On the right. Thank you, my dear. *(Exit)*

*Tense pause. Helle wanders restlessly back and forth.
Erik sits uneasily, watching her.*

ERIK

Do you like Ulf Gram?

HELLE

Why, yes.

ERIK

A lot?

HELLE

Why, yes.

ERIK

So much that. . .?

HELLE *(with sad bitterness)*

You too. . . The same question from you as well.

ERIK

I'd have thought that you were above this sort of thing.

HELLE

You've become rather moral since you were up here
last.

ERIK

All this here is nothing but nonsense on your part.
You've got no business being up here alone with Ulf —
like that. You're just being foolish.

HELLE *(with increasing good spirits)*
Am I to understand that you put your mark of ownership on me when you kissed me today?

ERIK
What do you mean by that remark?

HELLE *(as before)*
... Just that Åke's not the only one who likes to put
padlocks on croquet boxes.

ERIK
Helle, you don't mean that you can fall for a guy like
that who ...! A vulgar old money-bag. A rake who ..

HELLE
Ulf happens to be my employer. Yours too for the time
being. *I've* got no complaints. Have you?

ERIK *(miserable)*
So you don't want to talk any more about all this. *(Bitterly)* And how I looked up to you all these years. You
were a pure, white flame lighting up my path.   Something unobtainable for me. A dream I could walk towards with outstretched hands. A bitter-sweet joy I felt
in my heart. *(With disgust)* And now this with Ulf
Gram.

HELLE *(trembling with indignation and defiance)*
Ulf Gram brings out the woman in me. He makes me
realize that I'm in the same room with a man. I like
that. I find it flattering and have no objections to a man
finding me desirable.

ERIK *(naively shocked)*
Helle...! How can you say this to me? You know how
much Åke loves you as well, and he's a thousand times
better person than him in there.

HELLE *(half-mocking, half-crying)*
Since I'm yours and Åke's common property, I apologize for my erotic solvency. *(Bitterly, crying)* You'll just have to devaluate me. Write me off as a loss. *(Sits down and cries, silently and bitterly)*

ERIK *(after a pause, hoarse)*
What's become of Åke? *(Pause)* I thought I heard him say something about some whisky.

HELLE *(remains silent)*

ERIK
Åke did say something about whisky, didn't he?

HELLE
I heard you!

ERIK *(standing up)*
I think I'll go and see if I can find him.

HELLE
Please do.

ERIK
What did you say?

HELLE
I said: Please do!

ERIK
Do you think I could borrow your keys... in case the gate is locked down there... *(Pause, change in tone)* Every now and then I don't express myself very clearly.

HELLE *(rummaging in her purse after her keys)*
I don't think so.

ERIK
I don't always mean what I... I mean, it's not always what I say that...

HELLE

You express yourself very clearly. (*Giving him the keys*)
Here you are.

ERIK (*hesitates*)

You've changed, Helle.

HELLE (*muffled*)

What again?

ERIK

I said: You've changed, Helle.

HELLE (*furious*)

I heard you! For the better or the worse — this time?

ERIK (*snorting*)

For the better. . . from my point of view.

*Erik walks back and forth. Helle sits down in a chair,
proud, defiant, tiny and very unhappy.*

HELLE (*after a pause*)

So you're through with me now, are you?

ERIK

Huh?

HELLE

The flame's gone out. The pure, white flame lighting
up your path.

ERIK

Flame? What. . .?

HELLE

Yes. . .? That's what you said.

ERIK (*shaking his fist at the ceiling*)

Ugh!

HELLE (*after a pause*)

I suppose you'd like your painting back now.

ERIK

I don't prostitute my feelings.

HELLE

The way I do, you mean? That's what you mean, don't you? The way I do!

ERIK

I'm not accusing you of anything. I'm not even talking about you at all. I haven't uttered a word about you since I came up here.

HELLE

It seems to me that you've been talking about me the entire time.

ERIK

Oh, you're so self-centred. So very, very self-centred.

HELLE

Go on, abuse me. Run me down. Destroy everything that was fine and good and... *(bursting into tears)* between us.

ERIK *(crushed)*

Why, Helle! My sweet, dear, little... Don't you realize that it's simply because I'm so...

Clumsily pets Helle

HELLE *(shaking him off)*

Get away from me. Go find yourself another flame to trot after. Down your path.

ERIK *(paces, insulted once again)*

As you wish. As you wish.

HELLE *(in a low voice)*

And you're supposed to be an artist.

ERIK *(alert, says sharply)*

Did you say: *supposed to be* an artist?

HELLE *(flaring up)*

That's right! Because there are some things you ought to understand. For you, at any rate, a woman ought to be a human being. First and foremost a human being. Your equal. And not a package or parcel. Not some sort of beauty cow fitted out in pretty underwear for you men to grin and laugh at, you bulls.

ERIK *(with forced calm)*

So you mean that artists are responsible for the degradation of your sex.

HELLE

I never said that. That's never been my meaning.

ERIK *(with rising indignation)*

But it fits, doesn't it? The weak ones only kick those who are down. You let the tyrant you've got on your back just stay there, but if you find some poor soul who's weaker than you, you give him a kick in the face. You step all over him.

HELLE

I've never kicked anybody. *(Snorting with rage)* At least not in the face.

ERIK *(low, on the point of exploding)*

Can't you think about anything other than yourself? Your own private, self-centred self? Not even for a second? A single second?

HELLE *(hurt, childishly)*

If you say so. You've already said that.

ERIK

I'm trying to look objectively at things. You always want to drag the discussion down to one thing: yourself. Nothing else but yourself.

HELLE

That's what drags things down, is it? *I* drag things down!

ERIK

Not things. The discussion!

HELLE

Why I thought we were having a good old-fashioned quarrel. But go right ahead. Look objectively at things, if you like.

ERIK

Can't you ever discuss anything in a peaceful, calm, dignified manner? Hmm?

HELLE

Go right ahead. Discuss in as dignified a manner as you like.

ERIK *(with forced calm)*

Well, you said that for an artist a woman ought to be a human being. All right. But let's look at your sex's degradation: from human beings: to beauty cows — to domestic slaves. *(Demonstrating with hands)* On the one hand, we have the result of slavery: a shocking, worn-out old hag — to hell with her! On the other hand, there's the imbecilic triumph of today's Venus — peppermint-flavoured sex. *(Furious)* But has it never occurred to you that *(pointing)* the dirty, lecherous swine that you run up to attics with have ten fat fingers ready to take part in the woman game?

HELLE *(sits quietly for a while)*

It's strange how quickly one man's woman is degraded by another man's desire. What have I done? What's different about me now from what I was when you came today? What did I have then — that I no longer have?

ERIK

Hah. . .! It's mighty strange indeed. He who runs towards the beautiful lands in the gutter. He who worships
the light is cast out into darkness. I hate the word.
I hate the term which betrays my sin, like a caste mark
I can't hide: ARTIST.

HELLE

No, you don't. . . A thing that's receptive to light can't
be destructive. (*Laughs quietly*) You know you can't
hate, Erik. When you're angry and hurt — you don't
think that's hatred, do you?

ERIK

The artist's a pariah. It doesn't matter whether he's
in rags or in silks. He's a pariah. I hate him. I loathe
being one.

HELLE

But that's not hate. Hate's different. Hate's pale and
damp, with the smell of mouldy earth. You don't know
what it's like. But I've had a glimpse of it. I caught
sight of it today!

ERIK

Then look at the artist — look at him with other people's eyes. Join them and point at him and snicker when
you hear them whisper: there goes the man who wrings
his soul. There goes the man who sells his love and
displays his naked pain for public contemplation. (*Gri-
macing*) Artist! ! (*Stops, says threateningly*) I'm ashamed
of it. It's something I have to be. Something I don't
want to be — but have to. Do you think I'm one by
choice? Do you hear me, woman! Do you think I'm one
by choice?

Ulf enters quietly from the left, remains standing, silent, in the half-open door.

HELLE *(rising)*
All I know is that without artists the world would be a place of darkness.

ERIK *(doesn't see Ulf, says, hurt and angry)*
Oh, no, you don't. That won't work. Because I no longer believe in you. You're going to make a career, Helle. Rake in lots of money. Forge ahead! With him in there.

Helle stiffens as if expecting a blow, and quickly turns her back to Erik who stands benumbed for a moment before dashing out the door in the rear.

ULF *(discreetly clearing his throat)*
Thanks for letting me use your telephone. I've got to go fetch the car, but it'll only take a few minutes. Where did Erik go?

HELLE *(tonelessly)*
To the caretaker's.

ULF
And your husband?

HELLE *(as before)*
The caretaker's.

ULF
We're a fine bunch of cavaliers, Mrs. Vendel.

HELLE *(smiles faintly.)*
Well, you haven't gone to the caretaker's.

ULF
Would you like for me to wait here — until the others come back?

HELLE

No. Please, go. You too.

ULF

My dear, dear Helle. I do so much want you to be happy. It hurts me to see you like this.

HELLE

Really? I'm very grateful for that.

ULF

Everything's gone wrong this evening. But we still have the night ahead of us, my dear. I promise you it's going to be a pleasant one. Just you rely on your friend Ulf.

HELLE

I don't seem to have anybody else.

ULF *(alert, cautiously)*

Shall we go then. . .? To my place?

HELLE *(nods mechanically)*

Yes. Let's go.

ULF *(as before)*

The two of us? Right away?

HELLE

We've nothing to wait for.

ULF *(undecided whether to make his move now or wait, loses self-control)*

Oh, Helle. Yes, yes! Come on, the two of us. . . alone.

Kisses Helle, who is pressed back up against the drawing board. Ulf holds her tightly.

HELLE *(in quiet panic)*

No, no. I thought you meant. . . You didn't mean. . .? Let me go! Let go!

ULF

I've longed for you so, Helle. You mustn't let me down now. That would be bloody unjust — to me. Come on. The two of us. Tonight. . . and for always.

HELLE

You're disgusting! Disgusting!

ULF *(releasing her, stamps on the floor)*

You she-devil!

Helle walks stiffly to the middle of the stage, raises her hands to her face and remains motionless. Ulf slings his coat on and stands for a while, his hat on the back of his head, his coat unbuttoned. . . sizing up the woman in front of him. He then walks quietly over to her, sticks his hands in under her arms from behind, clutches her breasts, holding her close up to him for a moment.

ULF *(tenderly persuasive, with his lips against her neck)*

Helle, please!

Lets go of her and exit quickly

HELLE *(filled with horror, disgust and rising anger)*

What kind of man are you? What are you trying to do to me? What are you trying to make of me?

Curtain

ACT THREE

The scene is the same, a few minutes later. Åke is sitting stage-front. Helle is pacing uneasily back and forth. A bottle and glasses are on the table.

ÅKE

Why don't you sit down, Helle?

HELLE

But did he say that he was coming back up here? Here?

ÅKE

That's what I understood.

HELLE

What's his game? Who does he think I am?

ÅKE

Shall I mix you a drink, Helle?

HELLE

Did he mention the party as well? The four of us. . . at his place?

ÅKE

For the tenth time: I didn't talk to Ulf Gram.

HELLE (*nervously resigned*)

I don't understand a thing.

ÅKE (*very slowly and clearly*)

Erik said that they were just going to get the car. . . (*Points*) To park it outside and then come up here.

HELLE

Well, they can just stand down there and ring. I'm not going to let them in. He's not coming back in here any more.

ÅKE (*pouring himself a drink*)

You've given Erik your keys so they won't have to ring the bell downstairs. Shall I pour you out a drink?

HELLE

Erik! Why did Ulf Gram want Erik with him?

ÅKE (*putting the bottle on the table*)

For the eleventh time: I didn't talk to Ulf Gram.

HELLE

But why did Erik go with him? I just don't understand.

ÅKE *(lifting his glass)*

Skoal!

HELLE

But why. . .?

ÅKE

If someone asks Erik to come along and fetch a car, well Erik goes along and fetches that car.

ḤELLE

I don't think Erik should've gone with Ulf Gram.

ÅKE

Galley slaves always do what people ask them to. That's what makes them galley slaves.

HELLE

I don't like that nick-name. Erik's a great artist.

ÅKE

Yes, so he is. And a first-rate galley slave as well.

HELLE

Don't call him that!

ÅKE *(unmoved)*

Constantly running around looking for things he can do for people. Carrying packages. Running errands. Lending money to needy friends, begging them not to pay him back. Making himself useful! *(Thoughtfully)* What a nice dog Erik would have made. Always on guard. His front paw raised, his tail wagging expectantly, he waits day and night hoping for new tasks to do for his lord and master — the more difficult and dangerous the better. A magnificent animal. Had I a dog

like that I wouldn't part with him for... for...!
(Changing) But he's mad, you know. There's something called rabies. Canine madness.

HELLE

Erik's my friend.

ÅKE *(dryly)*

So I've noticed.

HELLE

He's a man who's alive! In mind and body. He doesn't
just walk around like a living wax doll.

ÅKE

There's no need for you to praise Erik for my sake. He
and I are old friends. I have great appreciation of
'Master' Erik.

HELLE

Appreciation! *(Pause)* Do you appreciate me as well?

ÅKE

I appreciate both you and Erik. Individually and *(smiling)* together.

HELLE

So you think that Erik and I are a suitable pair?

ÅKE *(as before)*

Shall I pour you a little drink? *(Slowly)* For the little
girl who 'put her red dress on.'

HELLE *(desperate, crying)*

Erik! I believe in Erik! I have to believe in someone
in this world.

ÅKE

Why my dear...

HELLE *(more calm and sober)*

I can rely on Erik.

ÅKE *(in a convincing tone)*
You sure can, Helle.

HELLE
Erik will never let me down.

ÅKE
There's not a woman in the world Erik would let down. . . if he could help it. If he could manage not to let the whole lot down.

HELLE
Nonsense. Erik's no lady's man. Erik never tries to play Don Juan.

ÅKE
Heaven's sake, no. What a horrible thought.

HELLE
Are you so sure about that? I'm sure Erik's not a bad lover.

ÅKE
I see you're possessed by this delusion of yours. Let me pour you a drink.

HELLE
He's warm. He's tender. He's. . .*(groping for words)*

ÅKE
Just eager to serve, my dear. An indication of our galley slave's inexhaustible generosity. Tenderness, warmth, heroism, ambition and generosity — nothing but the symptoms of his incurable rabies. Why don't you sit down?

HELLE
Do you consider loving a woman an indication of generosity? Or of ambition?

ÅKE

We're talking about Erik now, aren't we. One thing at
a time, madam. Shall I. . .? Why don't you. . .?

HELLE

No, thank you. I don't want to sit down. I don't want
a drink.

ÅKE

As you like. As I said: I believe I'm going to have to
disappoint you by pointing out to you that Erik's
infatuation is nothing but an indication of his desperate need to carry all the burdens of the world on
his shoulders — the burdens of husbands as well. It won't
be the first time it's happened, and you're not going to
be the last. Skoal. What dreadful whisky! Wouldn't
you like a little glass?

HELLE

You're not going to be able to lower my opinion of
Erik. No! Not of Erik.

ÅKE

But, my dear child, he's the last person in the world
I'd want to lower in anybody's estimation. Imagine,
Erik! A little lady of my acquaintance once told me —
in strictest confidence — how she and Erik — *(Changing)* Pardon my asking, but are you Erik's flame for the
time being? . . . Pure and white . . . on the path . . . in
front of him?

HELLE

Agh!

Suddenly bites her hand and turns half away

ÅKE

Aha! I see. Splendid. The point is: so was this lady

acquaintance of mine. She managed to play the role of the great artist's pure, white flame so well that she fell for the unfortunate idea that she wanted to ignite more than his artistic soul — in the privacy of her marriage bed. *(Mock dismay)* Just imagine. The flame went out. She said herself that if all the fire brigades in town had been hiding in her bedroom, they couldn't have done a better job of putting it out. *(Smiling)* Come on and sit down here beside me and be a little bit nice, Helle, my dear.

HELLE *(walks a little, forced)*

Yes... I guess I'll soon be able to sit down beside you and share your low-mindedness. Share the filth! And the hate, the envy and self-contempt . . . with you.

Continues pacing

ÅKE

Why, Helle, sweet . . . Is this our new 'manager' and 'artistic director'?

HELLE *(whirls around, furious)*

Careful now! You'd better watch what you say. Yes, you... *(pointing)* the little man in the chair there.

Paces again

ÅKE *(hesitantly, after a pause)*

I won't understand a single thing soon... We've been struggling for four years now — hard, happy years — in order to reach our goal. You weren't the only one who made a name for Helle Vendel's designs. It was both of us. I refused help. I used all my time and all my energy . . . *(Changing)* What happened to the contract?

HELLE *(both hands over her ears, trembling)*

Oh . . .! Oh . . .!

Heavy pause. Both look away

HELLE *(soberly)*

Whatever's happened to those two with the car?

ÅKE

You said you didn't want them up here. *(Low, tense)* Did you sign the contract?

HELLE

I want to get the whole thing over with. I want peace. I want to sleep.

ÅKE *(hesitantly, after a pause)*

Don't you think it's rather... *(groping for words)* thoughtless perhaps... to throw him out — just like that?

HELLE

I'd never throw Erik out.

ÅKE *(carefully, clearing his throat)*

I wasn't talking about Erik.

HELLE *(aghast)*

You mean ...! And after everything I've told you about him! About him and me! Up here?

ÅKE

I only thought that we — maybe...?

HELLE *(as before)*

You're thinking of selling me to Ulf Gram?

ÅKE *(raising his hand towards the ceiling, resigned)*

Oh, God, have mercy on your poor servant.

HELLE

And what's the price? How much do you want to get rid of your wife?

ÅKE

This can't be Helle. Not my little Helle! *(Shaken)*
Good God, look at how independent work and a certain
amount of freedom can destroy all the fine, inexpressible,
attractive. . .

HELLE *(mocking)*

Yes. I have changed, haven't I? For the better. . . or for
the worse . . . *(On verge of tears)* I can't remember
which.

ÅKE *(patronizingly)*

Helle, my dear . . . try to think for a change. *(Gesticulating)* Put your feelings in one drawer and your
thoughts in another. Let's pull out the drawer with your
thoughts and see if we can find something . . .

HELLE *(struck by Åke's metaphor, says quickly)*

The revolver. You shouldn't have loaded weapons lying
about. I want you to throw it into the sea.

ÅKE *(leaning back in his chair, stares resignedly at Helle)*

Skoal. *(Tempting her with the bottle)* A little drink'll
make you feel better, my friend.

HELLE

I thought you despised Ulf Gram. I thought you were
just awful to him — just now, when you and Erik came
in. But in a way you were right. Disgusting. Ulf Gram
is disgusting.

ÅKE

Of course, Helle dear. Of course. I'm always right.
And I've seen through every little prank that guy's
been up to during the past — eleven years. Completely.
The question now is: are we going to play our cards.

HELLE *(unmoved)*

   ... But we can't work together with a person we both despise, can we?

ÅKE

   I agree completely. Splendid. *(Demonstrating with his hands)* Well, we'll push that drawer in and pull out the drawer with your thoughts. There! What's happened lately? Ah, yes. Ulf has been rather vulgar. To another man's wife, right? Not quite the thing. The baboon loses his head for a minute, forgets all his training, revealing the wild beast inside and — tableau. *(Uneasy because of Helle's stare)* Don't you think it would be easier for us to talk if. . .?

Gestures towards the bottle on the table

HELLE *(in a low voice, at a loss)*

   Oh, no. . . you don't really mean. . .?

ÅKE *(with raised forefinger)*

   The drawer with your thoughts, Helle! We've locked up your feelings for the time being. *(Eager and gay)* Well, you're offended by the animal's behaviour. Splendid. But the question then arises: what has gone on inside the orangutang's own breast? Aha! *(Slyly)* It's possible, isn't it, that his muddled mind is being ravaged this minute by the angry storms of regret, embarrassment and a bad conscience?. *(With raised forefinger)* Precisely! The chimpanzee has gone soft. Our hairy brother from the communal jungle is willing to make concessions, my dear. *(Enthusiastic, with open arms)* Voilà! See, our hands are loaded with trumps, Helle, my dear. *(In a low, secretive voice)* But the cards have to be played, my friend. We can't simply throw them on the floor. The cards have to be played,

Helle. We've got to play them well. . . and we've got to play them tonight!

HELLE *(trembling, in a whisper)*
I think you've lost your mind. You don't mean what you're saying, do you?

ÅKE *(holding the bottle, disappointed)*
Ah . . . Is there anything more elusive and impregnable than the madness of a woman's emotions. *(Outraged)* I haven't thought of carrying on white slave trade up here in the garret!

HELLE *(tired, softly)*
From now on I don't care at all what you think. You've betrayed us for good, Åke Vendel. That's all. *(Walks restlessly back and forth)*

ÅKE
Humph!

HELLE
If only they'd come soon — those two, then we could get the whole thing over with. I can't stand it any more.

ÅKE
Can't you stop tramping back and forth like that. . .? It makes me nervous. *(Pauses, coaxingly)* Just a half a glass, hmm?

HELLE
The car was right around the corner. I don't understand what's keeping them.

ÅKE
What time is it?

HELLE

Almost half past one. They've been gone more than twenty minutes.

ÅKE

Hm... *(After a pause, annoyed)* You don't like Ulf Gram, do you?

HELLE *(stops, laughs silently, then says with conviction)*

No.

ÅKE

You can't stand him. Not at all?

HELLE *(bothered)*

No.

ÅKE

But do you think he's so repulsive that...? That you couldn't even imagine sitting here with him and...?

HELLE *(sitting down, says after a pause, in a calm voice)*

Have you never loved me?

ÅKE *(resigned)*

Oh, God!

HELLE *(as before)*

I mean, have you never loved? Have you any idea what it is? What it feels like?

ÅKE *(after a pause, in a low voice)*

I remember my mother. Now *there* was a woman...!

HELLE

But what about later. Other women. I'm not thinking about myself, but other women you've met who ...

ÅKE

I said: my mother — there was a woman. *(Pauses, half to himself, in a frozen tone)* But I didn't even let

her. . . I didn't like it, I mean. I remember that even
as a little boy how much I disliked being touched.
Physical contact with another person. I've chaste feelings inside me that you're scarcely aware of. Hand-
shakes. Caresses. *(Shudders)* I can't stand having people
take hold of me and slap me on the shoulders.

HELLE *(looking down, says cautiously)*

Have you never been happy these past four years —
with me?

ÅKE

I've always appre. . . *(Checking himself)* Of course, Helle.
Why, yes, my dear. I'm very fond of you. You know
I'm very fond of you, don't you? *(Dreamily)* And what
a wonderful hostess you were at Solhaug in the good
old days. So distinguished. So fine. Yet at the same
time so simple and unaffected.

HELLE

Thanks. *(In a small voice)* And the past four years?

ÅKE

I haven't complained, have I?

HELLE *(with difficulty)*

But what about our work and. . . your sketches and. . .?
Don't you feel that all that brought us closer together?

ÅKE *(in a friendly tone)*

On the whole, nothing but the dregs of society work,
my dear. You're so naive. Don't you realize that work,
toil, drudgery are just about the crudest means one has
to channel one's energy?

HELLE *(examining the palms of her hands, says in a low, trembling voice)*

Have I been blind for nearly twelve years? For how

many days of my life? What have I believed in? What have I hoped for — and felt — and desired?? Wanted so much... that I believed in my own lies. *(With rising indignation and anger)* My God. What have I done to myself? A little girl who grew up with a dream, longing for love. What have I dared give her? What have I dared offer my own heart?

ÅKE *(suddenly stands up, walks a little, then says in an insulted and mocking voice)*

Poor thing... one really feels sorry for you. Oh, the emotional egotism of the female sex. This eternal howling of the female to be loved, loved. They expect a hell of a lot from a man. Oh, pardon, me.

HELLE

Hadn't we better talk about something else? Or just keep quiet?

ÅKE

Now take Ulf Gram, for instance... Granted that the man has insulted you. That's all well and good! But frankly speaking, in such situations it usually takes two to tango. I'm not at all convinced by that conventional assertion women come with that the man made a sexual move without the least encouragement on her part.

HELLE *(trembling, but still under control)*

Do you mean to say that I tried to seduce Ulf Gram?

ÅKE

I'm not trying to say anything. I'm trying to look objectively at things.

HELLE *(with rising emotion)*

And all the filth you've poured over me during the course of the evening, that was being objective, was it?

ÅKE *(stopping in front of Helle's chair)*
    Shut up. Don't be impudent!

HELLE
    And the lies about our friend Erik! Was that being
    objective? Because you did lie about him. I know you
    did! I feel that . . . you're lying.

ÅKE *(screaming)*
    None of your bitchy ways! I forbid it!

HELLE *(wild, violent)*
    A fool. . . A childish old weakling. . . whom I, a young
    woman, suckled at my breast, giving it my warmth
    and strength. *(Standing up)* A spineless creature who
    froze at the sight of his wife's flesh and shuddered at
    her outstretched hand. You couldn't stand my being your
    equal. Because you've nothing without your pride,
    man! And your pride's nothing unless you can walk
    over a woman every single day.

ÅKE *(cries out, sharply — as if giving a military command)*
    The devil's in my house!

*Åke throws himself over Helle, who falls back into her
chair.*
Åke tries to strangle her

ÅKE *(with clenched teeth)*
    You devil! You devil! You devil!

*Erik and Ulf, having heard Åke's cry, enter breathlessly,
backstage. Erik tears Åke away. Ulf follows Erik half-way
across the floor, then turns. . . and calmly puts his overcoat over a chair near the hall door.*

ERIK
    I'll kill you. . . If you touch her. . . I'll kill you.

ÅKE *(convulsively)*
> The devil. In my house. I forbid it.

*Helle stands up and walks back slowly holding one hand
against her throat.*

ERIK *(as before)*
> Not a word. . . I'll kill you. Not a word.

ÅKE *(coming to his senses, in an injured tone)*
> You should have heard her!

ERIK *(shoving Åke so that he falls back into his chair
again)*
> Shut up. Shut up.

*Erik holds Åke down in his chair and the two stare silent-
ly and desperately at each other. . . while Ulf walks quickly and silently over to Helle. He stands behind her and
the ensuing dialogue between them is intense, quick but
muted.*

ULF
> Any regrets? The car's outside.

HELLE
> Disgusting.

ULF
> But what about your future, Helle? I'm offering you
> everything. It's all yours, woman!

HELLE
> Disgusting.

ULF
> You know that I'm more of a *man*. . . than those two
> poodles of yours over there.

HELLE *(raising her hands in disgust, shuddering)*
> Oh. . .!

ULF

Ugh! *(Moves quickly in front)*

ÅKE *(whining, to Erik)*

You should have seen her. I think then that. . . I think then. . . that even you. . .!

Erik lets go of Åke and turns away in contempt

ULF *(in a jovial, pacifying tone)*

Gentlemen! Gentlemen! What must Mrs. Vendel think of us? *(Sits down at the table, calm and non-plussed)* May I, chief? A little drink helps steady the nerves.

Erik cautiously approaches Helle.

HELLE *(in a hoarse, almost whispering voice)*

Just leave me alone. I'd rather you'd just. . .

Nods in the direction of the table

Erik remains standing where he is for a moment, uncertain.

HELLE *(as before)*

Just go. . . Just sit down. . .

Erik sits down at the table, involuntarily.

ÅKE *(heartfelt)*

You misunderstood, Erik. Old pal. It wasn't what it looked like when you came in.

HELLE *(standing with her eyes closed, says slowly)*

. . .And the lie a person has inside him — it just goes on spinning around, never slowing down, never stopping.

ERIK *(to Åke)*

What made you do such a thing? And to Helle, too! And what's become of you? You . . . a friend I could trust . . .

ULF

I understand you very well, Vendel. One doesn't have to take anything from anybody. Skoal!

ÅKE (*as before*)

You misunderstand me, Erik. Do you think I'm a brute? Do you think I lose control of myself for no reason whatsoever? It hurts me, Erik, to see you sitting there judging me — unjustly.

ULF (*quietly*)

Suppose the lady asked to be raped.

ERIK (*half-rising, to Ulf*)

Do you want me to knock you down? Is that what you want? Blood? Broken glass?

HELLE (*as before*)

You're a sewer, that's what you are. All this has run out of you . . . and has washed over us.

ÅKE (*raising his hand to calm Erik. Says slowly, in a friendly tone to Ulf*)

But now our sewer baron's going to keep quiet. We've had more than enough stench out of him. And since it has dawned on me that invective runs off him like water off a duck's ass — that's the expression, isn't it? — well, then, my friend and I are going to go to the trouble of throwing him from the sixth floor down to the cellar. But before we do that, my friend and I have to sit here for a while and rest. Your company is rather exhausting, you know. Sit down, Erik. Have a drink. It'll just make the bad worse or the good better — depending upon how you feel.

The reading lamp flickers and slowly goes out. Simultaneously the moonlight increases in intensity, transforming the interior into a greenish-white, phosphorescent dream set. After the first trivial remarks, their voices gradually become more and more monotonous and their movements slow and mechanical.

ERIK

Has the current failed?

ÅKE

What else do you think it could be?

Helle flicks a wall switch.

ÅKE

Don't bother. It'll come on again.

ULF

We can still see our glasses, that's the main thing. Why don't you come and sit down, madam?

HELLE

No.

ÅKE

Your business partner's calling, madam. Come and sit down.

HELLE

No.

ERIK

Just look at the moon.

HELLE

Just look at the light . . .

ÅKE

Reminds you of something, doesn't it?

HELLE

No . . . Never again. Never again.

*The three at the table sit motionless, staring darkly at
Helle, who stands stiffly, as if frozen, radiant in the
moonlight streaming through the window.*

ULF

A dirty little fashion-slob – that's what I am, aren't I?
And I can't clean my hands by washing them in soft,
silky velvety materials. I like fabrics like that. They're
so delicate. And when they cling like skin to a woman's
body, they fill me with awe. There's nothing higher in
my estimation than the body of a lovely woman dressed
in beautiful clothes. I want to reach up to it or bring it
down to me. It's unjust — that's what it is — to a swine
like me. And these damned women are going to pay for
this injustice, because they could've raised the beast up.

ÅKE

Belated self-recognition has nothing but a shabby effect.
Root around in your sty, swine, so we can hear whether
you're enjoying yourself.

ULF

Aren't you a bit shabby, yourself, you little suicide?
There's room for more here in the sty.

ERIK

You were my liberator. Only when your light flowed
through me did I have any idea of what absolute freedom was. You are my dream of freedom from the
burden of things.

ULF

Whenever painters fall in love, they become just as
crazy as their own paintings. Drink some whisky. Alco-
hol has singed the wings of many a dreamer before you.

ÅKE

Mother . . .

HELLE

Yes.

ÅKE

I reject you.

HELLE

I know.

ÅKE

You're no longer mine. *(Tossing his key ring at Helle)* Here! Take the key ring to my kingdom of dreams. *(The keys fall to the floor with a rattle)*

ULF

And to a drawer in the desk, madam, where you'll find a present for you. Use it!

ÅKE

You're no longer a part of my body and my soul. If I cease to own you, I'm free.

HELLE

And I . . . ?

ÅKE

You're betraying us. You should have stroked our insults with a gentle hand, holding before us every day the grave injustice the world has done to us.

HELLE

That's a heavy burden for a woman to bear, especially when the injustice against the man is that not every man is every one else's superior.

ULF

You betrayed us!

ÅKE

And now we're the ones who are betraying you.

HELLE *(to Erik)*

And you . . .?

ERIK

I refuse to choose. I want to walk toward the light. *The ceiling light and the reading lamp begin to glow, flutter for a moment, and then grow to full intensity.*

ULF

Ugh. Switch off that light.

ÅKE

Who switched on the ceiling light?

ERIK *(half-rising)*

What an awful . . .?

HELLE

I'll do it. *(Switches off the ceiling light and walks towards the bedroom)* But none of you were hidden by the darkness. I saw you all well enough. I've never seen you so clearly. *(Exit)*

ULF *(hoarsely)*

Now let's you and I Indian wrestle, chief.

ÅKE

You're inexhaustible. How deep in the dust do you want to drag me?

ULF

You don't dare, you rotten little bankrupt.

ÅKE

And all of this because eleven years ago I didn't wangle a deformed oarsman out of his rowlocks and set him down behind a desk in a steamship line, shouting 'Congratulations' . . . to the new apprentice. Oh, Nemesis, you're too hard on me!

ULF *(viciously)*

You talk too much. Use too many words. Far too many big words.

ÅKE

You had a difficult time keeping up at school too, didn't you? Egad! All those letters in the alphabet — those strange symbols that mean: A-B-D. It was much easier for you to shove around boys who were weaker than you. Or peek at small girls sitting on the toilet: then you were the best in your class, little Ulf. The best in your class.

Erik, who has been sitting immobile staring at the table, rises in annoyance and quietly walks towards the back. Every now and then he approaches the door to the bedroom as if to call for Helle.

ULF

Go on preaching. You've already talked the wit and the vitality and the sexual desire out of your wife. In a couple of years there's going to be nothing left of her get-up-and-go but tears and bones.

ÅKE

This has been a bitter evening for you, brother Ulf. The operetta. Caviar. Champagne. And then the 'nach-spiel,' ha! The dead-drunk husband falls asleep, the galley slave shuffles off home empty-handed. And then . . .? *(Full of bitter longing)* Then the night lamp's pale glow interrupts the moonlight and a white, white and trembling bird of the night is a guest in your room. *(With disgust)* The gorilla loosens his garters . . . *(Soberly)* What a world we're living in, my friend. Such boyish tricks don't always work out as planned any more.

ULF *(muffled)*
Now we're going to Indian wrestle, chief.

ÅKE
The steamship line's discarded head apprentice demands revenge.

ULF
Did you say discarded? You who have been up here in this trash bin for four years. And as far as our success with the wife goes — I think our contest is still undecided: the score remains nothing-nothing. You're going to be sleeping on the doormat as far as the rest of this marriage is concerned. Believe you me!

ERIK *(subdued)*
Helle . . . . Helle . . .? It's me, Erik.

ULF *(teasing Åke)*
Just listen to your little successor. His flute's got a seductive sound.

ÅKE *(stands up, takes off his jacket and rolls up the sleeve on his right arm. Says between his teeth)*
We'll see. We'll see.

ULF
Going bathing, chief?

ÅKE
Come on, you old wreck of an athlete.

ULF *(stands up smiling, throws off his jacket and rolls up his shirtsleeves)*
I hope the oarsman's blisters have healed? This is dangerous business, you know.

ÅKE *(sitting down, ready for the contest)*
I find the confidence you place in that revolting shell of fat and varicose veins rather touching.

ULF *(sitting down opposite Åke)*
Been training regularly with your eraser all winter, I see. It might result in biceps on the upper part of your arm, you know — if that's not just a wart growing there.

Ulf and Åke grasp each other's hand, warming up preliminaries.

ÅKE
Erik, you're the referee.

ULF *(to Erik)*
We've wasted enough sugar on the ladies this evening, you know. Life has become serious over here.

ERIK *(as before)*
Helle . . . ! Have you gone to bed?

ULF *(to Åke, pointing at Erik)*
Have you seen a more tiring suitor? There's much more action with us! Almost a matter of life and death.

ÅKE *(sternly to Erik)*
My wife's asleep. You'd better come over here and bury your cousin.

ERIK *(towards the table)*
The muscle eroticism between you two doesn't interest me in the least. What am I supposed to do?

ULF
Be the judge. Douse water on the bank director afterwards and splint up his arm.

ÅKE *(to Ulf)*
Just look at the son-of-a-bitch! Will you keep your elbow on the line!

ERIK *(towards the bedroom door)*
Helle . . .!

ULF *(annoyed, to Erik)*

Little Red Riding Hood's gone to bed, understand? Come on over here, you big bad wolf, and get this game going.

ERIK *(in the direction of the table)*

Oh . . .! Go on and break each other's arms! That, at least, would turn this into an enjoyable evening.

ULF

Not as funny as you think, cousin Erik. That wouldn't stop us from putting you in your place, if need be.

As if in tacit agreement, Åke and Ulf begin to Indian wrestle. The contest is fought in silence, broken only by groans, muffled oaths and cries. The exertion causes Åke's voice to become high and squeaky, while Ulf's voice descends into a low gurgle.

ERIK *(in the direction of the table)*

Åke, the fine gentleman, versus Ulf, the upstart. But who's who? Both clowns are painted alike in this circus. There's every indication that you're going to die of suffocation. If only you'd hurry up and burst! Burst a blood vessel, go ahead! I'm not going to wipe you up. *(Turning away)* Ugh, the male sex . . . you can really make a person sick. *(Near the door to the bedroom)* Are you awake, Helle? Come on out and watch. The circus has come to town. Two impotent violent criminals are looking for comfort and are falling into one another's muscles. Come on out and say goodbye to the bridal couple, Helle. You're never going to see them again. They're so happy with one another . . . *(Leans up against the back wall and remains there, immobile, like a shadow in the twilight, during the following)* Get out of your bed, woman. If you want a future, you're going to have to go it alone. Your two fellows from the circus are completely wrapped up in one another.

The contest's outcome has been wavering back and forth during Erik's monologue. Åke eventually wins, and the two contestants throw themselves back into their chairs with a groan. They immediately lean forward again, fumbling after their glasses with one hand and each other's heroic shoulder with the other. Both have a hard time breathing in the beginning.

ULF

Well, I'll be damned . . .!

ÅKE

I beat you . . . Did you see it . . . I beat you, all right.

ULF

Never would've believed it . . . You're pretty strong, old man.

ÅKE

I almost didn't pull it off . . . Almost didn't pull it off.

ULF

Well, I'm not exactly a baby, you know.

ÅKE

You put up a good fight. You put up a good fight, you old goat.

ULF

I gave you a hard time, didn't I?

ÅKE

Oh . . . I really had to work at it.

ULF

Skoal, for the winner and my friend.

ÅKE

Skoal, Brother Wolf. God help me, but I think I almost like you.

They raise their glasses with trembling hands.

ÅKE *(philosophical)*

... And why shouldn't I? We've got something in common, my friend: lonely hearts. Contempt for the weak, contempt for people who cling together out of fear and say they're doing it out of love, solidarity and fellowship. *(With self-pity)* But you're free, you know, Brother Wolf. But I'm locked up here in my cage. *(Gloomy)* I've been locked up here too long — impotent — in my rusty old cage.

ULF *(moved)*

Much too long, dear Åke. Much, much too ... *(Raising the bottle, matter-of-factly)* Not a drop left of your dishwater. There's so much I want to talk with you about. I don't know ...?

ÅKE

Do you regret having asked us over to your place?

ULF

On the contrary! I was just sitting here thinking about your wife.

ÅKE

You'd like to have her come along?

ULF

No, on the contrary ... *(Quickly)* What I mean is, you know how much I respect her. A fine, good woman. Cultivated. Kind-hearted. In short, everything. On the other hand I have to say that — well, you understand, don't you?

ÅKE

Absolutely. Absolutely . . . Poor thing, I think she's over-worked. Slightly hysterical. You know women. It's been a big day for her, hasn't it? Manager. Artistic director. But she's really not quite in her line, I mean. A woman like Helle – well, she's simply too nice to have to shuffle about like a sexless, sour career woman.

ULF

Exactly, Åke. Exactly! And that's what I really want to . . . (*Searching for words*)

ÅKE

Air?

ULF

Precisely. Air. Just the two of us.

During the following, the opponents roll down their shirt-sleeves, stand up, put on their jackets, straighten their ties, hair, etc. . . and at the same time are very considerate and helpful towards each other . . . as they prepare for their departure.

ÅKE (*with an air of assumed indifference*)

Did you sign the contract?

ULF

What was that?

ÅKE

Did you two sign a contract this evening? You and Helle?

ULF (*moved*)

My God, she was sweet, believe you me. And a bit frightened, you understand. . .? Not having her spouse safely by her side.

ÅKE (*with a slow laugh*)

Overwhelmed by the seriousness of the occasion, huh?

ULF

Oh, like a child . . .! After all, it's quite an enormous business deal for a little lady like your wife. (*Teasing*) Becoming an independent woman. Not being responsible to anybody.

ÅKE (*with a forced smile*)

Did you sign it down there, during supper, or . . .

ULF (*chuckling*)

You're afraid now, aren't you?

ÅKE (*coldly*)

What do you mean?

ULF (*as before*)

It was really too bad, you know. While I'm up here arranging the contract with your wife, you're dashing around the corner trying to mess up the whole thing. It was a nice try.

ÅKE

I'm not begrudging Helle a living.

ULF

Really? But you'd rather have a better one yourself, wouldn't you? And even then . . .?

ÅKE

What do you mean?

ULF

Just that your wife'll no longer be *yours* any longer . . . once she's backed up by a managerial job. You know that, don't you, my boy? There's nothing more to talk about. (*Slaps Åke jovially on the shoulder*)

ÅKE *(sharply)*

> You've recovered your strength since your defeat in wrestling.

ULF *(unhappy)*

> Oh, I've recovered from more than that, you know. I've had an even worse defeat this evening. *(Extending his hand)* Give me your paw, old foe. Shall we call it quits?

ÅKE *(suspicious)*

> I'll be damned if I can figure you out. I don't know what you're up to.

Ulf and Åke involuntarily fumble towards one another and meet in a long, heart-felt handshake.

ULF

> Of course I didn't sign that contract, Åke! I'm afraid I disappointed your wife, you know — but, well, I'm against it on principle. A personality like yours. Superior intelligence. Brilliantly gifted. A born leader ... stashed away up in the corner of a garret. While a very ordinary female is going to be allowed to run around, slamming doors, giving orders all over the place, as she settles her fat behind down in a director's chair. *(Shocked)* You don't think I'm talking about your wife, do you?

ÅKE *(absentmindedly)*

> Why, no .... After all, Helle's slender, isn't she?

ULF

> It's the principle of the thing, understand? A matter of principle. If you let the ladies take as much of the cake as they like, well, how much do you think they'll leave behind on the plate?

Ulf and Åke reluctantly let go of each other's hand.

ULF *(relieved)*

You're still interested in your old bank, I believe?

ÅKE

Oh, you know: 'An old love . . .'

ULF

The point is this: I was elected chairman of the board after you . . . after you . . . *(Coughs in embarrassment)*.

ÅKE *(helpfully)*

You don't say? Were you really?

ULF

Quite a large stockholder. Quite a lot of influence. I'm sure to have other offers for you, that is, if you find them suitable.

ÅKE

I guess I'm not quite as choosy as I was when we last met.

ULF *(disappointed and annoyed)*

Oh . . .? It's the fine, proud, discriminating Åke Vendel I have use f . . . whom people are interested in. *(Brutally)* That's the way you've got to be. If you remain modest, you'll have to sit up here in your attic.

ÅKE *(perplexed)*

But of course, Ulf. Of course, I'm not — modest.

ULF *(curt)*

Well, let's go, then.

ERIK *(to Åke, quiet but intense)*

You can't mean this. You can't leave Helle like this!

ULF *(sharply)*

You sure take charge of things, Erik. I guess a man can do exactly as he pleases. *(Thumbs expectantly through a pile of sketches)*

ULF *(to Åke)*

Talk to her. You've got to go in to Helle, and — explain.
At any rate, you can't walk out without saying a word.

ÅKE

I have talked to Helle. Enough for today — and for a
long time to come.

ERIK

You're not drunk, are you? You're not mad? You're a
human being, aren't you?

ÅKE

How nervous you've become, Master Erik. The game's
no longer funny, eh?

ERIK *(sits down alone at the table, bitter)*

Well, I guess I'll have to talk to Helle alone, then.
You two can wait. In the car. *(With his head in his
hands)* What a bunch of cowards we are. My God,
what a bunch of cowards!

ERIK *(to Åke)*

This sketch is signed ÅKE V. You draw well, you old fox.

ÅKE *(to Ulf)*

Pshaw, just for the fun of it. Nothing but amusement.

ULF

Really . . .? Just for the fun of it, eh? *(Pointing at Åke)*
So this is the source of Helle Vendel's creations.

ÅKE *(curt)*

By no means. They were Helle's work and they were
her . . . *(Checking himself)* Come to think of it, when
you get right down to it, I was probably the one . .
in a way . . . who had . . . But shucks, call it collaboration, if you like.

ULF *(snorting)*

Collaboration! Collaboration between marriage partners? Know what? I become terribly thirsty when I
hear things like that.

ÅKE *(with forced laughter)*

No illusions about marriage, eh?

ULF

My idea of what can be called collaboration between
the sexes ought to end when the man puts his pants
back on in the morning.

ÅKE *(coldly)*

You don't say? You don't say? *(Sadly)* It suddenly
struck me how proud she was of this collaboration of
ours. She was always fond of that word. Ah, but sometimes . . .? Sometimes she exalted in the word, raising it up in pride, in triumph . . . as if it were the pin-
nacle of life. The word: *we* . . .? *(In quiet wonder)* I
don't know. Was I a conscious member, a conspirator
in a tiny little joint effort — without realizing it?
Without understanding it? Unable to see it? *(Quietly)*
I don't know . . .

ULF *(quickly)*

And you, old chap, you kept yourself in the wings, of
course. Anonymous. Much too modest. *(Trembling)*
You're quite a man, Åke Vendel, and the injustice that's
been done to you is going to be set to rights again by
me!

ÅKE *(unhappy)*

Forget it, Ulf. Let's drain our cups of joy.

ULF *(putting on his coat)*

Yes, let's. You and I have quite a lot to talk about

this evening. You're not going to sit up here and rot away in this attic any longer.

ÅKE (*with his coat on*)

It's been a bit hard, perhaps. A bit hard . . . every now and then.

ULF

It's a crime . . . that a man like you . . .! (*Earnestly*) What I mean to say is: we're not just going to straighten out your economy, my friend, but your old position as well. Your influence. Your power, dammit.

ÅKE (*smiling, palely*)

Yes. . . Here, late at night, I feel a strange spring flooding my heart: the filthy undercurrent that has been frozen all winter is now breaking up. It's gaining strength. Force. Yes, power. It'll soon merge with my brother's sewage. Together we'll do all that's in our power to make the world no better than it is. This is our vow. Amen.

ULF (*staring in dumb amazement at first, then in deep admiration*)

What a poet . . .!

Both move upstage. They turn in the doorway towards Erik.

ULF

Just take a look at The Big Bad Wolf. Does he think he's going to have Little Red Riding Hood all to himself?

ÅKE (*to Erik*)

Ulf and I'll have a smoke in the car. Then we'll blow the horn. (*Pointing at him*) Then you'll come on down. (*In sad mockery*) We need a trusty soul to fetch our soda water tonight. (*Exeunt Ulf and Åke*)

ERIK *(standing up, paces a little. He listens at the bedroom door, then knocks carefully)*

Helle . . . .? You can open up now.

HELLE *(in a dressing gown)*

Have they gone?

ERIK

Yes, they've gone.

HELLE

Over to — Gram's?

ERIK

They're sitting down in the car waiting — for me. Are you coming?

HELLE

Do you think I look as if I want to go to a party?

ERIK

No. No, you don't look as if you want to go to a party. But I don't like your being up here alone. It's too beastly.

HELLE

I don't know . . . But, in a way, it's right. Because that's the way things are. That's the way it's been the entire time. Only I never realized it.

ERIK

No, Helle . . .!

HELLE

Oh, yes, Erik. It was nothing but a dream, an illusion, a misconception . . . . these four years! He and I together, on equal terms. I was terribly naive.

ERIK

Can't things be straightened out, Helle? Between Åke and you?

HELLE

Are they sitting down there?

ERIK

They were going to smoke a cigarette in the car.

HELLE *(sits down and smiles palely)*

.... While you dished out comfort and explanations.

ERIK

What do you want me to do?

HELLE

Go on to the party, little Erik. Go and be of use to your two friends.

ERIK

Christ. You should have seen them.

HELLE

Bosom buddies?

ERIK *(furious)*

Hah, pals ...! They almost melted into one another, that's how interested they were in one another.

HELLE

I knew it. Deep down inside me ... I believe that that was what frightened me so — that I ran away from you this evening. Because I knew it: if you don't get Åke on your side at once, completely .... well, one day he's going to turn against you. Become a man you've never known. A stranger — who hates you more than you thought possible.

ERIK *(pacing, restlessly)*

Åke was jealous. Completely confused. He meant everything he said and nothing.

HELLE

He meant something when he threw his keys at me. He meant only one thing.

ERIK *(as before)*

Åke. Åke. Whenever we two are alone, we do nothing but talk about him. *(Stops)* You're a human being. I'm a human being.

HELLE *(after a short pause, says cautiously)*

Perhaps he's owned me too long? Perhaps he's owned me so long that I've gone to pieces. My will, I mean. My ability to be free.

ERIK *(with feeling)*

No, never! Not like that.

HELLE *(tense)*

No?

ERIK

He's never owned you. You've never buckled under to another's will. Not for a moment. Not to the extent of self-annihilation.

HELLE *(as before)*

... No?

ERIK *(bitter)*

Why do you say things like that?

HELLE

Because ... *(Is silent, then says cautiously)* I do so want to help you.

Sound of car horn

ERIK *(bothered)*

Yes, I know. I know that I've let myself be used — misused — by other people. I do things for other people

when they want me to. Is that a weakness? It's nothing
but a weakness, isn't it?

HELLE

I think it's wonderful that there are people who ...
(hesitant) do things for others.

ERIK *(tense)*
But ...?

HELLE *(thoughtfully)*
But why do you have to ... just because another person
asks you to?

ERIK *(stops, says curtly)*
What are you going to do?

HELLE
You mean: what am I going to do now? — tonight?

ERIK
I mean: generally speaking. What are you going to do?

HELLE *(in a flat voice)*
Oh ... live ...? Work?

Sound of a car horn

ERIK *(paces, more and more upset)*
Oh! ... Those two down there. *(Pointing towards the
street)* They're sitting down there ... *(Pointing at himself)* — But they're sitting in here, deep down in here,
as well. They're expecting me. *(Desperately)* But I always come when people expect me to. I have to. I hate
it. That's precisely what I hate. To know that I, deep
down *(trembling)* ought to do something, well, something completely different! I only hear a pounding
somewhere inside me, inside me *(pauses, listens, then
says in a monotone)* with my father's voice: Are you

13 — Modern Nordic Plays: Norway

coming, Erik? Are you coming, Erik? Are you coming,
Erik?

Sound of car horn

ERIK *(to Helle, in panic)*
    Choose me.

HELLE *(quietly)*
    The bitter hour of decision... *(Tenderly)* My dear
    Erik.

ERIK
    Choose! Do you think the choice is mine? Whether I
    shall go down to those two disgusting creatures down
    there?

HELLE *(tense, in a whisper)*
    Or...?

ERIK *(in a low voice, desperate and bitter)*
    Choose me.

HELLE *(tired)*
    You mean: choose for me, Helle, because I, Erik, am
    unable to choose you. Oh, no, my friend. *(Quoting)*
    'Whenever you're bothered by a choice, it's because;
    deep down, you've already rejected both possibilities
    the choice offers you.'

ERIK
    Helle ...

HELLE
    Goodbye, Erik.

ERIK
    Helle ... !

HELLE
    Goodbye, Erik ... *(Exit Erik)* My only ... my last
    friend.

HELLE *(stands still for a moment, then mechanically begins to tidy things up, with stiff, slow movements)*
Well, there's nothing left . . . I've said goodbye to everybody and have to go — go the rest of the way alone. *(Stops, looks down and whispers)* Don't touch those keys. Let them stay where they are. They're not your keys, Helle. Let them stay where they are . . . because you know what he meant when he threw them at you: death, Helle, death! Oh . . . what a dreadful thing to wish for another person. *(Near the table, downstage)* No, it's not dangerous to walk in the woods alone. The path is never as long as you think. One day you'll reach your goal. And then . . . ? *(Turns off the reading lamp. Moonlight floods through the panes. Whispers)* And night falls. *(Towards the bedroom door)* Then no more tears. Then the injustice you've done to others and others to you — shall sleep. It shall sleep . . . sleep . . . sleep.

Erik enters quietly. During the following, he stands half-hidden by dark shadows . . . in the door in the background.

ERIK
I forgot something.

HELLE
What is it? Who's there? Are you here again?

ERIK
I've come back. *(Smiles)* I forgot to return your keys.

HELLE
Just put them there on the table.

ERIK
I've come back to you, Helle.

HELLE

Did the others drive off and leave you?

ERIK

They drove off when they realized that I meant what I said. They smiled as they drove off. One of them looking like sin, the other like death. *(Laughs quietly)* He forgot his keys. But I didn't. I didn't forget yours.

HELLE

You can put them on the table.

ERIK

Do you want me, Helle?

HELLE

The moonlight was so bright that I put out the light. I was so tired.

ERIK

Do you want me, Helle?

HELLE *(in a thin little voice)*

It's so hard to hear what you're saying . . .?

ERIK

Do you want me?

HELLE *(is silent, presses her hands to her eyes, and says in deep pain and relief)*

Yes . . .!

Erik walks into the moonlight, towards Helle, who lets her hands fall, standing immobile, but expectant, as the curtain falls.

The Bleaching Yard

By Tarjei Vesaas

Translated from the Norwegian
by James Wesley Brown

All rights, including professional, amateur, motion picture, recitation, lecturing, public reading, radio broadcasting, television, reproduction by recording or any electronic or mechanical means, and the rights of translation into foreign languages are strictly reserved. Permission for any of these rights must be obtained from Halldis Moren Vesaas, 3890 Ytre Vinje, Norway.

Tarjei Vesaas

Tarjei Vesaas (1897-1970) is regarded by most people as Norway's greatest author in the period after the Second World War. He grew up in Vinje, in Telemark, and his New Norwegian language reflects the dialect of his native district. Vesaas has written plays, radio dramas, and lyric poetry. Nevertheless, he has achieved highest acclaim as a writer of short stories (his collection *Vindane (The Winds)* was awarded the 1952 Venice Triennale Prize), and as a novelist. His early works are realistic descriptions of people and their problems in a rural community — among these is *Det store spelet (The Great Cycle)* (1934). Vesaas' later writing becomes more symbolic. *Huset i mørkret (House in Darkness)* (1945) treats the German occupation of Norway as a suggestive allegory, and in his next novel, *Bleikeplassen (The Bleaching Yard)* (1946), the action and symbolism are interwoven into a whole.

The Bleaching Yard was first written as a play in 1939. In 1953 Vesaas dramatized the material once again. During the same year, it was performed by The Norwegian Theatre in Oslo. It is undoubtedly the most successful dramatic work from the author's hand, even though several of his radio dramas also rank high.

The play is about loneliness. In his corrosive, spiritual isolation, Tander, the owner of the laundry, is struggling against the unknown depths, the dangerous forces in his own heart — here is an abyss of evil, an urge to kill. Contrasting with this spiritual darkness is the white laundry at the bleaching yard — a frequent symbol in Vesaas' writing, a picture of cleanliness, of the purging of the soul. Old Krister feels drawn to the white cloth, he wants to die in a clean shirt.

And the play ends with Tander conquering the darkness in which he has been living. As is often the case with Vesaas, this redemption is due to the assistance of someone else — here it is Elise, who has been wanting to wrench him out of his isolation in a drastic manner.

The ending is tragic in that Tander dies. But Vesaas emphasizes, both symbolically and in so many words, that the tragedy contains a catharsis. After Tander's death, the others remain and feel that something just and proper has happened: only by his death was Tander able to 'reach people the way he wanted to', and help them out of the darkness.

Characters

JOHAN TANDER

ELISE TANDER

VERA

ANNA

MARTE

JAN VANG

STEIN

AMUND

KRISTER

ACT ONE

A summer evening. The bleaching yard. The tall side of a house rests upon a stone wall. A double door is in the wall. It is closed now. 'Tander's Laundry' is written on the wall. Lines of wash are strung across the yard to dry. There is a lamp out in the yard, but it is not turned on now. Johan Tander restlessly walks around out in the yard, thinking. A shadow is seen behind the curtain to a window on the second floor. . . Elise is watching him.

TANDER *(stops suddenly, looks straight ahead, says loudly and threateningly)*
Jan Vang! *(Begins to walk back and forth again)* It'll soon be all over! Jan Vang. *(Repeats as he walks restlessly)* It'll soon be all over. *(Walks. Stops suddenly and says in a new, frightened, helpless voice)* Give me light!

KRISTER *(an old, decrepit man appears, seemingly drawn by something. He starts and stands still when he sees Tander. Tander does not notice him. Krister calls softly)*
Johan Tander.

Tander jumps, then quickly walks over and turns on the light which illuminates the linen. Elise is seen for a second in the light as she stands in the window. She disappears behind the curtains.

TANDER
Who's there?

KRISTER *(frightened)*
   Johan Tander.

TANDER
   Oh, it's you, Krister.

KRISTER
   Yeah.

TANDER
   What are you doing here?

KRISTER
   I haven't done anything.

TANDER
   You had better go on home. It's late. You're a pretty
   sorry sight.

KRISTER
   Oh? I wanted to look at all the shirts. As I walked over
   here, this strong longing rose up in me. I don't think that
   I'm going to live much longer, that's why.

TANDER
   Nonsense.

KRISTER *(starts when he sees Tander's face)*
   Do you also have that feeling?

TANDER
   What are you talking about?

KRISTER *(helplessly)*
   It struck me when I looked into your face.

TANDER
   Go on home now, Krister.

KRISTER
   Oh, yeah ... home ... There's nobody *there* ... *(Looks*

at Tander) I can't figure it out, but your face is so dark ... I can't tell you how dark. When you're as alone as I am, you know that something's going to happen soon.

TANDER
Why did you call out my name a while ago?

KRISTER
I don't know ... It's hard to say.

TANDER *(sharply)*
Well, go now ...

KRISTER
That's just what I'm going to do.

Tander, hearing someone approaching, disappears in a flash behind a clothesline with tablecloths and sheets ...

KRISTER *(in a little cry)*
Tander, what's the matter?

TANDER
Shut up. And leave. Go on home.

KRISTER
My, my ... *(Exit)*

Jan and Vera enter. They embrace.

VERA
One more ...

JAN
But it's getting late, Vera.

VERA
And tomorrow's another day. Is that what you mean?

JAN
I don't suppose you want me to go around thinking about *that,* do you?

VERA

We don't think about that very *often* now. Let's sit down for a while, Jan. It's so nice and quiet here.

They sit down. Jan pulls Vera up against him.

JAN

This is the way you want things to be, don't you? You usually end up having your own way. Is there anything the matter, Vera?

VERA

I am happy.

JAN

This evening as well?

VERA

This evening and every evening, Jan. You know, we're going to be happy for a long time. A long time.

JAN

Let's hope so.

VERA

It's not a question of hope . . . I'm sure of it. Jan, just suppose I had never met you! That could so easily have been the case. *(After a little pause)* Jan . . .

JAN

What now?

VERA

Oh, nothing I guess. But you seem to be thinking about something all the time. Something else. Something you *don't* like.

JAN

Hm. Yeah. Shall we go in now? *(They remain seated just the same)* I'm going out into Old Man Olsen's woods

to mark some new trees for cutting. I'm going to have
Amund and Stein with me.

VERA

Is that what's bothering you?

JAN

No, far from it.

VERA

Is it Anna?

JAN

Don't be silly.

VERA *(frightened)*
What is it then?

JAN *(lets slip)*
I'm thinking about Johan Tander, and the fact that he's
headed straight for hell . . .

VERA *(starts)*
Ugh. Be quiet. Why do you have to say such unpleasant things?

JAN *(continuing)*
I think it's going to happen soon, too.

VERA

Why can't you let Tander just be the way he wants to
be?

JAN

Don't you see how he is?

VERA

No. I don't pay him much attention. He's always busy inside with his tubs. I think it's awful of you to say that
he's going to go to hell.

JAN

At any rate, that's what strikes me . . . whenever I meet
him in the hallway or on the stairs. I don't know why,
but he's up to something evil. Lately, chills run up and
down my spine whenever I meet him. Now you know.

VERA (*staring at Jan*)

I don't understand all this.

JAN

There's something bothering Tander, and he's walking
around planning something. And it all concerns me.

VERA

You?

JAN

Yes.

VERA

But what in the world for?

JAN

I'm standing in the way . . . to you. Now you know.
(*Vera laughs*) Don't laugh!

VERA

I can't help it, when you come up with such things as
this.

JAN

Haven't you noticed the way his eyes follow you, Vera?
I have.

VERA (*carefree*)

Bosh.

JAN (*shaken*)

Oh?

VERA

Yes, there's no need for you to be jealous.

JAN

I'm not jealous. Not at all. But I'm in his way, and he's up to something. He'll soon be stretched out there.

VERA *(suddenly frightened, hoping that she has not heard clearly)*

Stretched out there? Who? You?

JAN

No, him. I think I'll manage to take care of myself. But Tander will soon be lying right there.

VERA *(frightened)*

What are you going to do, then?

JAN

Nothing.

VERA *(sad)*

You've got to go away for a while, and wait and see. After all, with you living here in the same house and all that. Me too. Don't you think it best that . . .

JAN

No, I'm not going to run away from him. I like my job here as forester for Old Man Olsen. He's not going to chase me out of the house. He's the one who's going to have to leave. If I were Old Man Olsen, I'd clean my house of my tenant Mr. Tander.

VERA

Now, now, don't get yourself all worked up, Jan. You're just making mountains out of molehills.

JAN

I'm absolutely sure that he's up to something evil.

VERA

Well, let's not worry about that now. Jan!

JAN

Hm?

VERA

Nothing . . . just this. (*Kisses him*)

JAN

I'll follow you up to your room.

VERA

Not tonight. It's so late. Some other time. After all, we're not Old Man Olsen, you know, who can stay in bed as long as he likes in the morning.

JAN

Yes, thank God we're not Old Man Olsen. He's had his fun. Now we're going to have ours.

VERA

Yes . . . now we're going to have ours.

They exit. Tander emerges, straightens up. One of his feet has fallen asleep. When he brings life back into it, he puts his heel down slowly in a crushing manner — as if he had something underneath it. He thinks.

TANDER (*mumbles in a low voice*)

So I'm going to hell, am I? (*Starts suddenly, frightened*) It's a long way to hell for somebody who doesn't want to go there! (*Stands completely still*)

KRISTER (*creeps back in again*)

Are you still here, Tander? (*Tander does not answer*) I didn't think that I'd find anybody here now. (*Tander is still silent*) Why don't you speak? But, then, I didn't come here to talk to you. I came to look at the linen.

TANDER *(without moving)*
The linen?

KRISTER *(walks past him towards the back of the stage)*
Strange thing — linen. A lot of things can be said about linen.

Stein and Amund enter

STEIN
There's nobody here, Amund. We'll have to wait for our ladies' man.

AMUND
He'll be here soon. It's going to be a real scorcher today, believe you me. *(Looks up at the house above the wall)*

STEIN
What are you looking at? Vera's room? Jan has probably just left her room. *(Sits down)* I think I'm going to take over his job as forester for Old Man Olsen. Jan has enough to do chasing girls. What's so special about him that he's got to have both job and girls? What have we got? We're just his errand boys. Hell, we've studied forestry too.

AMUND
Unfortunately, good jobs and women go together in this here world.

STEIN
Yeah, Amund, there's nothing to be done about it now. You were just too slow.

AMUND
Yes, I know.

STEIN
You can probably get Anna, the one who does the ironing. She's free now that Jan has chosen Vera.

AMUND

  It's easy for you to talk.

JAN *(entering)*

  Hi, fellas.

STEIN *(to Amund)*

  My, my, just look at the way he looks. Red-eyed and ugly.
  Sleep poorly, Don Juan?

AMUND

  It's not hard to see. Or maybe you got up too early this
  morning?

JAN

  There's no need for us to rush out into the woods. The
  job won't take long with the three of us working.

STEIN

  It's a good thing that Old Man Olsen doesn't know how
  little he gets in return for what he pays you. There
  ought to be a clause in your contract that requires you to
  stay in at night. I just said to Amund that I can take
  your job so that you can devote all your time to your
  girl.

AMUND

  I'd rather have the girls than the job.

JAN

  Aw, shut up. Do you two think you're being funny?

STEIN

  We'd better ask Tander to keep a better eye on that
  pretty book-keeper of his.

JAN *(angrily grabs Stein by the collar)*

  Shut up, will you? I don't want to hear anything about
  Tander.

STEIN

Jesus, you can't even open your mouth today.

AMUND

What has Tander done to you?

JAN

He's going to stab me in my back soon, that's what. I'm sure of it.

AMUND

Well, I never! What are you getting at?

STEIN

In the back, too.

AMUND

This is just something you must have dreamed up.

STEIN

In the room of the lovely book-keeper, Vera . . .

JAN

I told you to stop all this foolishness . . .

AMUND

So you think Tander's out to get you?

JAN

Yeah, I have chills all over when I see him.

AMUND

But, Christ, what for?

STEIN

Is it because of the girl?

Amund pooh-poohs this.

JAN

Stein's hit it right on the head.

AMUND

You mean that Tander's got his eyes on Vera?

JAN

He's walking around, at any rate, with me and a lot of evil on his mind . . . I'm not the only one who's frightened.

AMUND

Who else? Vera?

JAN

No, Elise Tander.

STEIN

Mrs. Tander? Has she said anything?

JAN

I can tell by the way she looks that she's frightened of something.

STEIN

You're just imagining things. I've seen her every day.

AMUND

Really, Jan, you are exaggerating things, you know. You just can't stand to have anybody else look at Vera.

JAN

Neither you nor Stein knows what this is all about. I feel as if I'm surrounded by something, something deadly and invisible, and it's getting closer and closer.

STEIN

Shh!

ELISE *(enters, falters)*

Good morning.

AMUND

Good morning, Mrs. Tander. I guess you're ready to light the fires down in the laundry.

ELISE

Yes. (*Quickly to Jan*) Jan Vang, there's something I want to ask you.

JAN (*turns towards Elise*)

Yes, what is it?

ELISE

Can't you go in and talk to my husband for a while?

JAN

Tander?

ELISE

When he comes down. He's been out for a while, but I think he's up in the house now.

JAN

We're on our way out into the woods to mark out a new parcel for felling, ma'am.

ELISE

I see. But if you could just go in before you went out into the woods . . .

JAN

I don't have anything to talk to him about.

ELISE

Perhaps *he*'s got something he wants to say to you.

JAN

Has he said so?

ELISE

No, no. But you never know. I think there's something or other that you two ought to talk about.

JAN

    Concerning what?

ELISE

    I don't know ...

JAN

    Can't you even tell me what it is?

ELISE

    Would you please do this for me?

JAN

    I can't. I don't think we're very good friends. I've noticed that there's something wrong.

ELISE

    Please?

JAN *(losing his self-control)*

    As far as I'm concerned, he can go to ... *(Stops)* I'm sorry, Mrs. Tander, but you've asked me to do something that I just can't do.

ELISE

    It would have done him a lot of good.

JAN

    In what way?

ELISE

    There's something hurting him.

JAN

    Well, I haven't hurt him. I think the best thing for me to do is just leave him alone. I've noticed the way he's been acting around here lately.

ELISE

    What have you noticed?

JAN
I don't know. That's the problem.

ELISE
I'm afraid something is going to happen, Jan Vang. We two understand one another, don't we? Do you think I would approach you like this if I weren't sure?

JAN
I don't want to have anything to do with all this. I haven't done anything. I just told these guys here that I had better keep out of his way . . . as long as something seems to be bothering him.

ELISE
I understand . . . But if . . .

JAN (*interrupting her*)
I'm sorry, but would you please stop all this?

ELISE (*looks at him*)
You just want me to leave?

JAN
Sure, why not?

ELISE
Well, if you can't do it . . . (*Leaves*)

JAN
Whew! (*Signals to Amund and Stein, who return*)

AMUND
What did she want?

JAN
She wanted me to go in and talk to Tander! Can you figure that out?

STEIN
Well, I never . . . What were you supposed to talk to him about?

JAN
  She didn't say. But *I'm* not going in there.

AMUND *(as Vera enters)*
  I'm beginning to get scared too. *(Sees Vera)* Morning,
  Vera.

VERA
  Good morning. I thought that you all would be out in
  the woods by now.

AMUND
  Jan doesn't seem to be able to pull himself together today.

VERA
  Oh?

AMUND *(looks at Vera and says in a new tone of voice,
  as if he had completely other things on his mind)*
  Vera.

VERA
  What's your problem.

AMUND
  Just let me look at you. It could just as easily have been
  me and you instead of Jan, don't you think?

STEIN
  Perhaps we can work up a little drama here as well.

VERA
  Who's been talking about drama?

AMUND *(pointing to Jan)*
  He has. No, I have no intention of starting any sort of
  drama.

STEIN

Jan, at any rate, thinks that he's going to take part in one.

JAN

Come on, let's leave.

AMUND

Start marching, Stein. We'd better get out of here so that he can hug his gal. That's what he's been waiting for the whole time.

STEIN

Yeah. Don't take too long, will you, Jan? We're not going to do all your work for you, you know. *(Stein and Amund leave)*

JAN

Have you ever had to? *(Sees Vera following Amund with her eyes)* Looking at Amund, are you? You can be sure that he meant what he said to you.

VERA

I'm quite aware of that.

JAN *(grabs hold of her)*

Let me look at you. It's no wonder that everybody wants you! *(Kisses her)*

VERA

There, now, Jan.

JAN

But they're not going to get you. Because I want you all to myself.

VERA

Is this what's bothering you, Jan?

JAN

What do you mean?

VERA

You're not your usual self today. Haven't you slept?

JAN

I've had too much on my mind. But I can't let you hold me up any longer. I've got to join Stein and Amund.

VERA

Oh, they're waiting for you over there in the shade. Are you going to be gone all day?

JAN

No. We'll be gone until early this afternoon. *(Suddenly)* And he's going to be after you again.

VERA

Don't get yourself all worked up, Jan. Do you want me to quit my job in his laundry? Jan, here I am . . .

JAN *(sees Anna, frees himself)*

Shh. Let me go now. Anna's coming. I'll be up to see you this evening.

VERA

Okay. Be seeing you. *(Jan leaves)* Jan. *(Jan stops)* Don't do anything, do you hear? *(Exit Jan)*

ANNA *(entering from the other side)*

Good morning. What are you standing out here for?

VERA *(not really at ease)*

Good morning, Anna.

ANNA

Aren't you going to go inside?

VERA

Of course I'm going in. *(Walks toward the cellar door)*

ANNA

Well, was he nice and sweet today?

VERA

Why would you say a thing like that, Anna?

ANNA

I guess I've got a right to say something. After all, you took Jan away from me . . .

VERA

That's not true.

ANNA

Oh, I don't know. He was mine, at any rate, and now he's yours.

VERA

Anna, I . . .

ANNA *(interrupting her)*
Shh. Elise's coming.

ELISE *(entering)*
Have either of you seen Johan?

ANNA

No, I haven't seen him.

VERA

Nor have I.

ELISE *(entering the cellar door)*
Well, we'd better light the fire.

VERA

Did you hear how scared she was?

ANNA

Scared? No. She was just her usual self.

VERA

She seemed to be trembling, if you ask me.

ANNA

Okay, what is it then? You look like you know something.

VERA

I don't know anything. But you can tell that there's something wrong between them.

ANNA

Oh, everybody's seen that. But I don't know which of them is to blame. Tander's all right in many ways but . . .

VERA

Sure, Elise seems to love him.

ANNA

I don't know. He seems to be so lonely. Both of them seem to be lonely.

VERA

Well, there's obviously something bothering Elise today.

They are about to leave, but Anna stops suddenly as if she sees something.

ANNA

What in the world! Come over here and see what's written on the wall!

They stand in dismay, reading the writing on the wall.

VERA

'Nobody has ever cared for Johan Tander.'

ANNA

That's the most awful thing I've ever seen. Who could have done that?

VERA *(frightened)*
I don't know.

ANNA
Ugh, here he comes. *(They hurry off)* We don't want to meet him now.

They disappear down into the cellar. Tander has entered without having seen them. He notices the writing on the wooden wall across from the laundry. He stands there as if nailed to the spot. Marte enters. She looks at Tander in surprise. He turns stiffly toward her.

MARTE *(startled)*
Christ, what's wrong, Tander?

TANDER *(stiffly)*
Oh, it's you, Marte.

MARTE
I won't tell you what I thought I saw.

TANDER
Tell me. Was it ugly?

MARTE
Yes, it was the ugliest thing I have ever seen.

TANDER
You don't say?

MARTE
But it turned out to be you, that's all. Good morning. I know I'm rather late, but I'm not as spry as I used to be in the morning.

TANDER
Don't worry about it, Marte.

MARTE
No, I guess I'm about the best person you've got down in

the laundry when it's a question of tackling dirt . . .
(*Looks at him*) Has anything happened, Tander? You
look like a gloomy murderer.

TANDER

Have you ever seen one?

MARTE

No, but I imagine that he would look just the way you
just did, no matter what you say. Aren't you going to go
inside?

TANDER (*suddenly*)

Marte?

MARTE

What do you want?

TANDER

Have you ever heard that anybody cared for me?

MARTE

What's all this? Is there something bothering you?

TANDER

That was not an answer to my question.

MARTE

I don't intend to give you an answer either. We've got to
go inside and empty the bags of dirty laundry. I have
worked in this laundry for too long to pay any attention
to your moods, good or bad.

TANDER (*looks stiffly at her, then repeats*)

Marte, have you ever heard that anybody cared for me?

MARTE

I don't know.

TANDER

Are you sure!

MARTE

No, I've never given the matter much thought. But, God,
Tander, what do you want to bother me with this for?
Why don't you just keep quiet?

TANDER

A man can't always do what he wants to do.

MARTE

What's all this about, Tander?

TANDER

Walk over there and look at what's written on the wall
on the other side of the road.

MARTE

What . . .

TANDER

Go ahead. Use those old eyes of yours, and you'll find
out something about Johan Tander. Go on, I said.

MARTE

What's there . . . *(Walks over and reads the writing)*
'Nobody has ever cared for Johan Tander.' Really, how
. . . who could have . . . I think that this was a terrible
thing to do.

TANDER

Maybe yes, maybe no . . . The question is: Is what is written there true?

MARTE

Listen here, Tander . . .

TANDER

You're not answering my question.

MARTE

I think that this was a terrible thing to do.

TANDER *(not listening to her)*
Do you think that Elise cares for me?

MARTE
There's no need your worrying about this, Tander. Somebody just wants to hurt you, that's all. *(Makes up her
mind)* I'm going to go over and wipe it off.

TANDER *(loudly)*
No, let it stay there.

MARTE
But . . .

TANDER
Just let it stay there now that it's there.

At this moment, Krister enters.

KRISTER
Good morning.

MARTE *(brusque)*
Good morning, Krister.

TANDER *(in a hard voice)*
There's no point in your coming here.

KRISTER
This is the place I belong, first and foremost. Don't you
think so?

MARTE
Is the end drawing near again? *(Krister doesn't answer)*
How many times have you come by here thinking that
your days were at en end?

KRISTER
They are now. I felt it last night.

MARTE

You don't say. I would prefer to lie in my own bed then. I'm sorry, Krister, but I can't take all this about your end drawing near very solemnly. Go on home now. *(Looking at Tander)* And you, Tander, get on inside. We've got to get you working at your tubs. Don't stand here. It's better that you talk this over with Elise. *(Tander stands, thinking, doesn't answer)* Oh, well . . . I'm going in now. *(Marte goes down into the laundry in the cellar, shaking her head)*

KRISTER *(to Tander)*

It looks like we'll all wind up here. *(Tander says nothing, has turned toward the writing on the wall)* It looks like we'll all wind up here, I said. There are a lot of things that are troublesome.

TANDER *(energetically)*

Anything in particular?

KRISTER

I thought that I had better go out and see whether anybody cared for me.

TANDER *(stunned)*

What was that you said?

KRISTER

Whether I mean anything to anybody, been anything, understand? You get a lot of thoughts like that when your end is drawing near.

TANDER

Maybe you're right.

KRISTER

Do you think I can take one of the white shirts from off the lines here?

TANDER

No, you can't. This is all washing that people have delivered here.

KRISTER

Oh, I see. But I can go and lie down in the grass over there, can't I? It's so nice and warm in the sun, and I'm freezing.

TANDER

We don't usually use our bleaching yard to let people lie around in, but . . .

KRISTER

You look like you are afraid of me, Tander.

TANDER

I can't figure out why you keep coming here, time and time again.

KRISTER

Are you trying to chase me away again?

TANDER (*short*)

No, go on.

KRISTER

I came to ask about something.

TANDER

Oh, can't you do that later? (*Leaves him, walks over toward the house, notices that there are people reading the writing on the wall*)

KRISTER

I came to . . .

Stops, notices that Tander has left him. He walks slowly and calmly over to a rise and lies down so far away that he can't hear what follows. Elise comes out. She stands

*for a moment looking at Tander. She is carrying an emp-
ty basket. She walks over to the clotheslines and starts to
take down some laundry.*

TANDER *(becoming aware of her presence, looks at her for
a while and then says)*
Elise.

ELISE
Oh, so this is where you are.

TANDER
Come here, Elise.

ELISE
Haven't got time. I've got to take this in to Anna.

TANDER
Well, take the time. Come here. *(Tander looks at the
writing and doesn't see the strange face she has when she
enters into battle)*

ELISE
What do you want, Johan?

TANDER
Look at what's written on the wall over there.

ELISE *(looks at the writing)*
Hmm. That was a silly thing for somebody to do.

TANDER
Silly thing to do?

ELISE
Yes, what else am I supposed to say?

TANDER
You talk as if there's nothing at all wrong with my being made fun of on a public wall, to be laughed at by

everybody who passes by. This is not just somebody's little prank.

ELISE *(controlled and calm)*
I didn't mean to imply that it was a trivial thing. Not at all.

TANDER
Well, who do you think it is then . . . who would attack me like this?

ELISE *(looking steadily at him)*
This is probably something that had to happen, don't you think?

TANDER
What do you mean?

ELISE
It must have been written by somebody who thinks that this is the way things are.

TANDER
Maybe you know who has done it?

ELISE
What would make you ask me a thing like that?

TANDER
You blushed when you saw it. Why did you blush?

ELISE
If I blushed, it was because of you.

TANDER
What's the matter with you, Elise?

ELISE
What about you, then?

TANDER *(pointing at the writing)*
This is not true!

ELISE

Well, you'd better see whether anybody goes over and wipes it off, Johan.

TANDER

You have cared for me! *(Elise remains silent. Looks down)* Won't you answer me, Elise? *(Elise looks at him)* What are you doing!

ELISE

I'm standing here looking at you.

TANDER

But . . .! *(Continues)* Are things that bad between you and me? Oh well, I guess I knew it, come to think of it. . . .I have loved you, Elise.

ELISE

I haven't seen much evidence of that lately.

TANDER

Well, what do you think I have seen and felt from you for a long time now? Ever since our child died, and we found out that we couldn't have another, you have been . . .

ELISE *(interrupting)*

Don't bring that up . . .

TANDER

Are you sure I shouldn't? None of that was my fault.

ELISE *(has for a moment dropped her role, but now pulls herself together again and becomes cold and remote)*

You know you turn everything upside down.

TANDER *(starts)*

In what way?

ELISE

I'm not the one to be cross-examined. You're the one who has problems today, Johan. You had better hurry up and think things over.

TANDER

Have you been . . .

He stops because Vera and Anna come out carrying a basket of wet wash and start hanging it up. They are lightly clad because of the warm weather and the heat of the cellar.

ANNA

Ah, there's a little air up here, at any rate. It's impossible to stay down in that cellar in weather like this. Standing over a hot iron . . .

ELISE *(more sharply than she realizes)*

Well, you've just about taken off all your clothes.

VERA

Yes, we have. And thank God that they are made in such a way that you *can* take them off.

TANDER *(to the girls, referring to the laundry)*

We should have done that. We have just been standing here talking.

ANNA

Oh, Marte chased us out with it. I don't mind. At least you can breathe out here.

TANDER *(involuntarily)*

Do you think that you can breathe here?

MARTE *(appears in the doorway)*

Am I supposed to stay all alone with these dirty tubs all day, Elise?

ELISE

No, I'm coming. *(Remains standing where she is)*

MARTE *(to Tander)*

And what about you, standing there looking at the girls, do you think you can come in?

ELISE

Pay him no mind. Nobody cares about him. *(Marte disappears into the cellar. Elise suddenly points at Tander, as if attacking him)* There stands Johan Tander, the man nobody cares for.

TANDER *(stands as if nailed to the spot)*

Why, Elise . . .

ELISE

He stands there as if he were lame. You have surely noticed Johan today, haven't you, girls?

TANDER

Elise?

ELISE

It just shows that nobody wants to have anything to do with him.

ANNA *(exclaims)*

What's gotten into you?

VERA *(to Anna)*

Are you through? Marte is motioning to us.

ANNA

Yeah, I'm through. *(Suddenly)* Who's that lying over there like a corpse?

TANDER *(starts)*

There's nobody there.

ELISE (*who has also started, quickly looks over at Krister*)

It's just Krister lying here sunning himself. (*Forced*) How are you feeling, Krister?

KRISTER (*turns his head a little, then lies down again*)

It'll soon be here.

ELISE

He really gave me a start.

ANNA

Yeah, lying there just as if he were dead. All of a sudden I thought that now . . . ugh.

Anna and Vera go back down into the cellar, looking at Elise in an embarrassed and frightened way.

TANDER (*to Elise*)

Aren't you going to go, too?

ELISE

Do you feel hurt, Johan?

TANDER

Elise, why did you act like that? Explain yourself.

ELISE

No, you're the one who had better think things over, and in a hurry too.

TANDER (*frightened*)

Why?

ELISE

Isn't time running out on you? You had better think matters over before it's too late. You know better than anybody else what's wrong. (*Turns away and walks over to her basket*)

TANDER

Wait! Don't go, Elise. I've got to talk with you some more about this.

ELISE *(taking down some laundry)*

I don't have time. Large bags of laundry have arrived.

TANDER

But I have to . . .

ELISE

No, you're all alone now with your problems.

TANDER

You have made me be alone with them, you mean.

ELISE

Yes, you'll see whether anybody comes along to help you.

TANDER

This can't be true, Elise. This is not you. Elise, don't you think that at least our child cared for me?

ELISE

I don't think that a little dead child is going to be of much help to you today, Johan.

TANDER *(staring at her)*

What is all this!

ELISE *(turns toward him, firmly)*

Let me ask you, then, what do you think about when you walk around here? *(Tander hardens, doesn't answer)* There's something bothering you, Johan. *(Tander remains silent)* You walk and walk.

TANDER

I'll walk whenever I feel like it.

ELISE *(continues)*

> You don't even have any peace at night. You're restless. You just walk and walk.

TANDER *(with difficulty)*

> Don't get mixed up in all this.

ELISE

> Well, look over there, Johan. Look at the people standing there reading all about you.

TANDER

> Will you leave me now?

ELISE *(urgently)*

> What are you planning on doing? *(Tander stares at her)* You'll see today, Johan, whether anybody will wipe it out. You'll be looking for a long time.

TANDER

> Elise, tell me . . .

ELISE

> You are hurt, Johan. Think it all over. *(She moves toward the door)*

TANDER *(calling after her)*

> But what about your own shame, then?

ELISE

> What kind of shame?

TANDER *(pointing)*

> Over there. It's to your shame as well. It's just as great a shame for you as it is for me.

ELISE

> Yes, I know. *(She leaves)*

TANDER *(stands for a long time, completely lamed. Suddenly*

*he is aware of Krister's presence. He walks over to him.
Stops again. Finally he calls out in a low voice)*
Krister.

KRISTER *(stirs)*
Do you finally see something?

VERA *(comes out through the cellar door, quickly, but as if
against her will. She walks over to Tander, who turns
away from Krister when he notices her)*
Well, here I am.

TANDER *(sees how beautiful she is in her slight airy clothing)*
You have come, have you?

VERA
Yeah, what do you want?

TANDER
It was strange to see you come up out of the cellar there.
It was a beautiful sight. You're wonderful to look at,
Vera. *(Vera remains silent. They look at one another.
Tander comes closer)* Vera . . .

VERA
What do you want?

TANDER
Let me look at you.

VERA
No.

TANDER
Vera . . .

VERA
I asked you what you want with me. Elise told me to
hurry on out here.

TANDER *(struck)*
  Did Elise . . .

VERA
  She said that you had to talk to me before it was too
  late.

TANDER
  Did Elise . . .?

VERA
  But it seems that I can just as well go back, right?

TANDER
  You'd like to go back, wouldn't you?

VERA *(feels sorry for him. She knows about the writing on
  the wall, but has to say all the same)*
  Yes. *(Tander looks at her, flinching beneath the blow)*
  What's the matter?

TANDER
  I have never touched you with so much as a finger,
  Vera.

VERA
  No, you haven't. But I have felt your presence all the
  same. That has been enough.

TANDER *(flinches, then says)*
  You like it, don't you?

VERA
  Any woman who tells the truth would have to admit
  that she likes it. *(Suddenly frightened)* What are you
  about to do now?

TANDER
  You have no idea what it is I see in you, do you, Vera?

(Vera looks away from him. He says bitterly) And here you are, taking a close look at me in my moment of mockery and humiliation, right? That's what Elise wanted to achieve by sending you out here to me.

VERA

Do you think so?

TANDER

Yes. That's what it was. I'm sure you have seen what's written on the wall over there.

VERA

Yes.

TANDER

What was the first thing that entered your mind when you saw it, may I ask?

VERA

I don't remember.

TANDER *(pointing at the writing)*

Well, you had better read it again, then. And read it correctly. Or would you like me to help you read it in the way it's supposed to be read? *(His voice becomes biting)* Why didn't he just go on and write it out so there would be no misunderstanding? Let me help you. *(He points)* Do you see what's written there? Johan Tander, and he's headed straight for hell, that's what's written there. *(Vera, confused, recognizes the words from the previous evening)* Yes, isn't that where he's headed, this Johan Tander? *(Vera, frightened, remains silent)* How do you think it feels?

VERA *(frightened)*

You've got to let me go. I don't know what all this is about. But I do know that you were listening to us last night.

TANDER
I had to. I had no choice other than to hear it.

VERA
Are you sure about that?

TANDER
Now that it's written on the wall over there, Vera, do you think that anybody will do the slightest thing to prevent me from going where I'm headed?

VERA *(not knowing what to say)*
I don't know. I don't know everybody.

TANDER
Vera, could you go over and wipe it out?

VERA *(calmly)*
No.

TANDER *(collapses)*
No, I guess not. *(Wildly)* But there must be somebody who can interfere.

VERA
Interfere?

TANDER
Yes, before it's too late. *(Continuing)* Vera ... wait.

VERA *(she rushes into the cellar)*
No. *(Tander stands without moving)*

KRISTER *(rises up, looks at him. Calls in a low voice)*
Johan Tander.

Curtain

ACT TWO

Inside the laundry in the cellar. Various laundry machines, buckets and wash-tubs. Rather old-fashioned equipment. A stair leads up into the house. A door to the right opens on a room used for ironing and packing. A door leads from this room to the outside. The double door that leads to the bleaching yard is wide open, revealing a white wash hanging on lines in the bright sunshine.
Marte and Elise are working. It is very hot. Steam and sweat. Vera and Anna are in the ironing room. Anna is ironing. Vera is busy with some packages at a counter. All are dressed as before. Nothing is being said. A man fetches a package at the counter and leaves.

MARTE

It was written with chalk on the wall right across from the laundry. Nobody has ever cared for Johan Tander, it said. In plain daylight. Letters that could be seen a long way away. I've never seen anything so awful. Somebody must have written it early this morning.

VERA

I wonder who would do a thing like that. It's not right.

ELISE

This is none of your business, Vera, so keep out of it.

VERA

Tander thinks that it was Jan. But he would never do a thing like that.

ELISE

Keep out of it, do you hear me? After all, I'm the one

who has to bear the greatest part of the shame involved in such a public announcement.

MARTE

It was an awful thing to do, no matter who did it.

ELISE

What do you think, Marte?

MARTE

I think he's been an all right guy. But his main problem is that he's unhappy.

VERA

Jan didn't do it.

ELISE

I've asked you to stay out of this, Vera.

ANNA

Where is Tander now?

MARTE

He's upstairs standing by the window looking at it. In plain view. He didn't even notice that I saw him. He just stood there staring out.

ELISE

Is he standing by the window looking at it?

MARTE

He stands there looking at people walk up and read it. Nobody has wiped it out.

ELISE

Nobody's going to, either.

MARTE

I really feel like going over and taking it off the wall. It looks so damned unpleasant. And, if you ask me, the person who did it must have done it for a reason. To write things like that about somebody on a wall! Not that I care very much for him, but we do work together.

VERA

Well, it wasn't Jan.

ELISE

Keep out of this, Vera.

VERA

Why did you trick me into going out to see him. You could have spared me your little prank.

ELISE

I can't be bothered about what people think today . . .

ANNA

Vera is cross today because she went to bed so late.

VERA

Why do you always have to be picking on me, Anna?

ANNA

I think the problem is that I simply can't forget things as quickly as I should. (*Marte closes the door*)

ELISE

Ugh, that door.

MARTE

What do you mean?

ELISE

Oh, nothing. (*Groans*)

MARTE

What's wrong? (*She sees that Elise wants to say something*) Is it the writing on the wall over there?

ELISE

I've got to talk to you. I can't keep this all to myself.

MARTE

Oh?

ELISE

No, you had better share this with me. I'm too lonely.

MARTE

I'd better light the fire under these tubs, that's what I'd better do. Tander's not going to be here for some time today. Elise, I'm not in any mind to get involved in all this funny business. You ought to understand that.

ELISE

Marte, I can't stand it. I had no idea what I was bringing on myself.

MARTE

You're going to have to talk more clearly than that.

ELISE

That about Johan out there . . .

MARTE

Well, I can't tell you whether it's the truth or not. You know best yourself. I just think that it was a dirty thing for somebody to do.

ELISE

But do you think that it ought to stay there? . . . It *shall* stay there.

MARTE

Did you say that it *shall* stay there?

ELISE

Yes, it shall stay there. Because I'm the one who wrote it, Marte.

MARTE

You!

ELISE

Yes, I did it.

MARTE

Well, of all things . . .

ELISE

Yes, it must be hard for you to believe. God, I don't know what I have done. But I have had a feeling that we were going to fall off a cliff someplace soon if I didn't do something.

MARTE

What's this all about?

ELISE

Haven't you noticed anything strange about Johan lately, Marte?

MARTE

No, I can't say that I have.

ELISE

He's planning a crime.

MARTE

What are you saying?

ELISE

Or something like that. He walks around the place all night. He can't sleep any longer.

MARTE

You must be imagining things. Don't worry.

ELISE

Imagining things, you say. I'm at my wit's end today, and am doing one stupid thing after another, but I'm not imagining things. He does nothing but walk around. Last night he was out in the yard most of the time. Will you help me, Marte? All I know is that he is up to something and that we have got to stop him.

MARTE

Does it have anything to do with Jan Vang?

ELISE

You know about that?

MARTE

We're not so blind here in the laundry that we don't see a thing or two. But what did you expect to achieve by writing on the wall?

ELISE

The idea just popped into my head. I wanted to frighten him away from thinking about Vera . . . to put a stop to the whole thing. That's why I wrote it.

MARTE

And now you're just going to let it stay there, are you?

ELISE

Yes, it can just as well stay there, now that it's up. And he's sitting up there in his chair like a petrified man. But I had to do something.

MARTE

And do you think you made matters any better by sending Vera out to see him? Did you want her to see him standing there lamed?

ELISE

He should have looked at her at that moment. Don't think that Vera cares for him. It was probably a stupid thing for me to do as well, but the idea just struck me.

MARTE

Well, well, don't worry about it.

ELISE
You've got to try to help . . . I can hardly stand on my
feet. I have exposed him to mockery and shame.

MARTE
Yes, you have. And yourself as well.

ELISE
I know.

MARTE *(warmly)*
I think you had better go over and wipe that sentence
off the wall, Elise.

ELISE
Me?

MARTE
Yes, you and nobody else.

ELISE
No, it can just as well stay there now.

ANNA *(enters)*
Excuse me for interrupting you two and your secrets.

ELISE
What's the matter?

ANNA
Nothing. I just have to have some more things to iron,
that's all.

ELISE
I'll get you something right away. *(Grabs a basket)*

MARTE
Now that you're here, Anna, grab a hold of this here.
The boss isn't here at the moment.

ANNA

Ugh, these old-fashioned things of Johan Tander. Why can't he get us some more modern and handy equipment.

MARTE

I've complained about that until I'm blue in the face.

ELISE *(as she goes out)*

It would cost too much, Anna. He can't afford it.

ANNA

Well, this is a pretty sad laundry, if you ask me.

MARTE *(with a stiff sound in her voice)*

Maybe, yet we still manage to wash things here as clean as snow . . . I wouldn't object, however, to his coming down now.

ANNA

He's spoiled. Perhaps he thinks that we like him.

MARTE

There, there, there's no need your being cross, Anna.

ANNA

I'm scared today, Marte.

MARTE

Nonsense.

ANNA

Where is he?

MARTE

Don't worry, he'll pop up.

ANNA

It was a dirty thing for somebody to do to him. Who do you think it was? And Elise, who . . .

MARTE

It's none of your business. Just keep out of it.

ANNA *(angry. Sees Vera in the other room)*
Look at Vera yawning.

MARTE
Do you think there's going to be a wedding soon?

VERA
Not that I know.

ANNA
Oh, you know all right.

VERA
Well, it's none of your business what we're going to do.
You can just leave me alone.

ANNA
My, my!

MARTE
It appears that Anna seems to think that *she* ought to
be the girl.

ANNA
Don't start that up again. *(Works)* Why in the world
would anybody want to work in a laundry? All the dirt
to be found near and far winds up in our tubs to soak.
They send it all to us. *(Elise enters)*

MARTE
But when we return it, it's as white as snow. It's not the
worst job you can find. And you've got an easy job,
haven't you, standing there ironing, you young, lovely
thing you.

ANNA
Oh, shut up.

MARTE
But that's the way it's supposed to be. There ought always
to be young, lovely girls in Johan Tander's laundry.

ELISE

What was that, Marte?

MARTE

All I'm saying is that they are useful. I wasn't thinking that it would be a good thing for Johan Tander.

ELISE *(to Anna, who is about to leave)*

Don't go, Anna. You mustn't all leave me alone.

MARTE

There's nothing we can do to help you.

ELISE

Come on in here, you too, Vera.

VERA *(unwilling)*

What's the matter now?

MARTE

You're wrought up, Elise. Why don't you calm down some?

ELISE

Hasn't it dawned on you yet what I'm involved in?

MARTE

Sure, sure, sure. Is the stuff in this basket dry enough to iron?

ELISE *(rebuffed)*

Yes, it's dry enough.

MARTE

Well, why don't you carry it over to the table over there and stop worrying about all this.

ELISE

You're right.

MARTE

I'm going to look for the man in the house who can never come when he's needed.

ELISE *(piling clean laundry up in front of Anna)*

See here, Anna. Do you notice the way it smells when it's brought in off the line after bleaching in the sun? *(Loudly)* Do you want me to bury you in it, Vera?

ANNA *(yells, frightened)*

Marte.

MARTE

Elise, don't carry on so.

ELISE

I'm not going to pay you any mind. Here you are, surrounded by dirt and have no idea that somebody's life is in danger today. Smell this aroma, I said. It's as if there never was any evil in the world ... That's the way it smells. Here, sniff, Vera.

MARTE

Look, don't say things like that.

ELISE *(buries her face in the pile of clean laundry)*

As if there was never any evil here. Can you all tell me what I have done?

ANNA

Watch out, it's falling on the floor.

MARTE

Don't lie like that.

ELISE

Don't touch me. I give up. Che sarà, sarà *(Tander comes down the steps)*

MARTE

Elise, he's coming. *(Elise stands up, starts working)*

TANDER

So. What has brought all you women together? It was rather a lovely sight, seeing you among the black tubs.

MARTE

You've finally come, have you? You didn't come any too soon to take over your work. I don't like doing work for two.

TANDER

I was held up.

MARTE

Yes, I can believe that!

TANDER *(noticing that Anna is watching him)*

What are you looking at, Anna?

ANNA

I can't see that there's anything here to look at. I'm ironing.

TANDER *(begins to crank wash through a wringer)*

Well then, keep on ironing. Come here and help me, Marte.

MARTE

I've got enough to do over here. Things rather have a habit of piling up for people who shirk their work.

TANDER *(working)*

You don't say.

VERA *(enters with bags of laundry)*

Some more bags of laundry have come, Marte.

TANDER

Empty the bags, Marte. We've got no time to waste.

MARTE

My, my, aren't we all keyed up!

TANDER

We've got to finish this stuff. In a hurry. Today. Not all days are the same.

MARTE *(rummaging in the sacks)*

My, my, all the stuff people send to the laundry. My word, look at that . . . Yes, the things people send here.

TANDER

Come on, come on. Get started. That's none of our business.

MARTE

Poor people. And it all winds up here in the laundry.

TANDER

Shove it down, I said. I'm tired of hearing all this every time you empty those sacks, Marte.

MARTE *(without listening to him)*

My, my, all the stuff people send to a laundry.

ELISE

My Lord, what's this? *(Moves some dirty laundry)*

ANNA

What is it?

ELISE

Look at this. Doesn't it look like it's been dragged through blood?

ANNA

Look out, you're falling.

MARTE

You're sick. It's the heat and . . .

ELISE

I don't understand . . . but it immediately struck me that it had been dragged through blood.

MARTE

It's the heat and all the hard work you've been doing.

TANDER

Let's get to work. Go on up to bed, Elise, and let the rest of us work.

ELISE

Yes, look here, Johan.

TANDER

Go on up.

MARTE *(to Tander)*

And how do you feel, Tander? Looks like you're having a hard fight with something inside you.

TANDER

Anything else?

MARTE

You'll just have to fight the good fight, Tander.

ELISE

Oh, hush, Marte.

TANDER

Do I have any account to settle with you?

MARTE

No, you've treated me all right all the years I have known you.

TANDER

You're going to have to explain yourself.

MARTE *(looking at him)*

Yes, as you like, Tander.

KRISTER *(entering)*
Hello, again.

ELISE
Hello, Krister.

MARTE *(walking over)*
Are you out for a walk again?

KRISTER
Yes, there's something I've got to do.

MARTE
Oh, I see. *(Pulls out a stool)* Why don't you sit down first. I don't want to have you falling into my tubs here.

KRISTER *(remains standing)*
My time's running out.

MARTE
Don't be silly.

KRISTER
If anybody should know, it ought to be me. Both of us are finished.

MARTE
Krister, I don't want to have any more of this kind of talk. It's not that I really pay it any mind, but . . .

KRISTER
I didn't mean you. I meant him. Him over there.

ELISE *(softly)*
Krister, won't you please be quiet.

KRISTER
But there's something I've got to do.

ELISE
What is it, Krister?

KRISTER

I have a great wish to have a good shirt to die in. One of those that smell so nice. *(Decisively to Elise)* Can you get me one like that?

ELISE

Me? Sure, what?

KRISTER

Can I have a shirt? It mustn't cost anything.

ELISE

Oh, that's what you ...

KRISTER

You've got so many hanging on the lines outside, so I thought ...

ELISE

Those shirts don't belong to me, Krister. Why don't we talk about the question of a shirt some other time?

KRISTER *(frightened)*

That's the way it is wherever I go.

ELISE

What's the matter now?

KRISTER

I don't have anything else to talk to you about, at any rate.

ELISE

Krister ...

KRISTER *(walks over to Marte)*

Do you have a shirt?

MARTE

I don't have a husband, so I don't have any shirts either.

KRISTER

Yes, maybe, but . . .

MARTE

Well, I'll see if I can find a shirt for you. Perhaps tomorrow.

KRISTER

Tomorrow will be too late for me and for you as well. That's the problem. If a person cares for you, he gives you a shirt the moment you ask for it.

MARTE *(looking at Tander)*
Cares for . . .

KRISTER

You've got to find out in the end whether anybody does. I don't understand a thing. Things turn out so differently from what I had hoped. *(Krister turns toward Tander who is looking at the floor and not working)*

TANDER *(starts when Krister moves)*
What do you want?

KRISTER

A person can have a lot of troubles.

TANDER

How right you are.

KRISTER

Things are particularly troublesome for us today. *(About to leave)*

TANDER

Wait, Krister, maybe . . .

KRISTER *(cutting him off. Trudges over to Anna)*
You didn't have any.

MARTE

Please . . .

KRISTER *(next to Anna)*

Who is this?

ANNA

Anna.

KRISTER *(looks at her as she works)*

That's a nice shirt.

ANNA

Yes, linen is very nice.

KRISTER

That's really a nice one.

ANNA

Listen, Krister, if you want . . .

KRISTER *(shy and frightened)*

I've got to go. Things to do . . . *(He starts to hurry out as quickly as he can)*

TANDER

I'll get you a shirt, do you hear. Tomorrow, when I . . .

KRISTER *(trudges out)*

It'll be too late. I can't stay here any longer with you all.

MARTE

Ugh, it was a good thing that he finally left.

VERA

It looked like he was telling the truth this time.

TANDER

About what? Oh, never mind.

VERA

About everything. That he's not going to live until to-morrow and everything.

MARTE

It's not fair, but Krister gives you a bad conscience whenever you meet him. He just stands there, self-righteous
and holy.

ELISE *(leaving)*

He's probably going to lie down outside now. We can't
have him lying out there like that. It's obvious that he's
sick.

MARTE

He's used to lying in the grass everywhere.

ELISE *(leaving)*

I'll see how he's doing.

MARTE *(to Tander)*

Elise has left!

TANDER

So what?

MARTE

You're all by yourself when she leaves you, you know.
You're not a very pretty sight to look at this afternoon.
You look like they're going to come for you soon.

TANDER

Come for me?

AMUND *(enters)*

Blessèd be your work.

MARTE

There's not very much here that is worth blessing. Well,
you're back from the woods, are you?

AMUND

Yeah, we finished early. *(To Vera)* Hasn't Jan been by
here?

VERA
No.

AMUND *(giving Vera a package)*
Well, take this.

VERA *(writes a receipt)*
Okay.

AMUND
How are you?

VERA
Fine. Is Jan coming here?

AMUND
I don't think he'll be down. But you're going to join us this evening, aren't you? Are you tired?

VERA
Are you?

AMUND *(looking at her)*
It should always be so warm here that you need so little clothing. *(Turns toward the others)* I was given quite a scare out in the bleaching yard. I just about put my foot right in Krister's face out there.

TANDER
Is Krister dead?

AMUND
Dead? No.

MARTE
We've been thinking a lot about such things today, you see.

AMUND
He does look pretty bad. Elise is with him now. Well,

I'd better get on home. See you this evening, Vera. You and Anna. *(Leaves)*

MARTE

Dinner break. Thank God.

ANNA

I'll take care of the shop, Marte. I just have to run out and get a bottle of milk.

VERA

Won't you come up to my room today, either? *(Anna shakes her head)* We used to have such a nice time up there.

ANNA

There's a lot of things that were nicer before.

VERA *(defiant)*

I have no regrets. I think I've deserved the joy I have been given.

ANNA

Deserved. Why do you say that?

VERA *(walks toward the stairs)*

I just have.

ANNA *(walks toward the back door)*

Deserved.

VERA *(as she passes by Tander)*

We are not afraid of you. *(Goes up the stairs)*

MARTE

You're going to get a beating.

TANDER

Shut up, will you.

MARTE

What are you conjuring up in all the corners here today?

TANDER

I want you to leave me alone.

MARTE

Aren't you the man of the day? Your name's written right across a wall like some sort of public matter. If you were any sort of man, you'd go and wipe it off yourself, Tander.

TANDER (*flares up*)

No, it can just stay there. The guy who wrote it is going to be punished for it. He's never going to be able to do anything like that again.

MARTE

Ugh, don't look like that, Johan. I almost expect somebody to come right up out of the wash boiler and grab you.

TANDER

Be careful what you say. I'm going to kick you out if you don't leave me alone.

MARTE

Well, go right ahead and do it. I think that something ought to be said, so I'm going to tell you just what's on my mind. (*Tander doesn't answer*) You've got troubles this evening, Johan.

TANDER (*in a different tone of voice*)

Yes, I have.

MARTE

Let me give you some advice . . . and I want you to listen to me.

TANDER

No, you may go.

MARTE

What are you going to do when I leave, huh?

TANDER

Nothing that's any of your business, I've said. Leave.

MARTE

Don't do anything you'll come to regret, Johan.

TANDER

They have forced me to this.

MARTE

No, that's just something you say to put the blame on others. I don't want to hear another word about that. *(Tander is silent)* Is it all over with you.

TANDER *(startled)*

What do you mean?

MARTE

Is that the way it's going to end?

TANDER

Leave me.

MARTE

I repeat: Don't forget Elise. She's on your side.

TANDER

There's nobody on my side.

MARTE *(looking at him)*

Well, I've said what I had to say. I'll just stand here for a moment and look at you before you leave us ...

Tander can't stand any more of this, raises his arm as if to strike. Elise has entered.

ELISE

Johan. *(Tander looks stiffly at Elise, then leaves. Elise says beseechingly)* Johan, Johan.

MARTE

He won't listen to you, poor outcast that he is.

ELISE

But he might do something foolish . . . in the state he's in now.

MARTE

That's just the chance you're going to have to take, you know.

ELISE

I'm so terribly frightened. The ugly way the two of them carried on!

MARTE

I usually don't stick my nose into other people's affairs, but things are different this afternoon.

ELISE

I just hope he doesn't do anything wrong.

MARTE

Yes, I'm sure you know what you have taken on today.

ELISE

I'm just as lonely as he is, Marte. It seems you just talk about him.

MARTE

Are you lonely too? (*In a slightly bitter tone of voice*) Well, I'm not, if we have to talk about such things.

ELISE (*lowers her head*)

You?

MARTE (*laughs*)

But there's no need to make a big thing out of it.

ELISE

Come upstairs with me today, Marte.

MARTE

Are you afraid now?

ELISE

I feel so strange.

MARTE

Come on, then.

ELISE (*as they go up the stairs*)

Thanks. I couldn't do anything for Krister. He insists on lying out there. He would just start yelling if you tried to make him move.

The stage is empty for a while. Then Jan Vang enters and looks around the cellar. He jumps when he hears somebody coming.

JAN

Oh, it's you, Anna.

ANNA

Yes, it's just me. She's gone up to eat dinner.

JAN

Already?

ANNA

Well, what's the matter with you today? Upset stomach?

JAN

You gave me quite a shock entering as quickly as you did. I thought it was . . .

ANNA

Tander?

JAN

He's after me, Anna. Oh, you know what's going on, so there's no need for me to explain.

ANNA

Are you so sure about that? He's unhappy. You know what's written on the wall over there. Did you write it?

JAN *(sharply)*

No, I wouldn't think of doing anything like that.

ANNA

What would you do if you found out that nobody cared for you?

JAN

Oh, many people have found that out, but they manage to live with the fact.

ANNA

Tander can't take it. You can tell it by just looking at him.

JAN

Are you going to defend Tander?

ANNA

He hasn't done anything to you yet. He's simply become an outcast. *(In another tone of voice)* And here you are, alive and kicking, Jan.

JAN

Only by accident, I believe.

ANNA

Well, so long, Jan.

JAN

What's the matter?

ANNA

Oh, I don't know. It's something I can't seem to forget.

JAN

Are you thinking of always being in my way, Anna?

ANNA
I don't know.

JAN
There's an aroma of freshly-ironed cloth about you, Anna.

ANNA
Ha, you've always said that.

JAN
You are lovely, Anna.

ANNA
Jan.

JAN *(becomes uneasy, wants to leave)*
Well, be seeing you. I've got to get hold of a bottle.

ANNA *(darkly)*
What kind of a bottle?

JAN
I've asked Amund and Stein to sit with me this evening, and we need a bottle.

ANNA
So you need a bottle to lift your spirits, do you?

JAN
We've got to do something when we get together.

ANNA
Isn't Vera going to be with you?

JAN
She'll probably come down and join us.

ANNA
Yes, I guess she will. She'll come down and join you. How convenient. God, Jan.

JAN
Maybe you would also like to come?

ANNA

No, thank you. I wasn't invited either. I can't take all this as easily as you can, Jan. It was just us once, you and I.

JAN

I can't help it that that's all over now. We hadn't promised each other anything, you know.

ANNA

I felt that we had.

JAN

I don't think that I have anything to be sorry for, Anna. We just happened to be together. Quick, thoughtless.

ANNA

There's something completely different I've got to say to you.

JAN *(retreating)*

Don't. I don't want to hear it.

ANNA

It's got to be said whether you want to hear it or not. You've got to know that I have never loved you more than I do now.

JAN

Is that ... Is that what's been on your mind?

ANNA *(standing there like a gift)*

I had to say it.

JAN

Like some sort of accusation against me.

ANNA

Why no, Jan.

JAN
Do you think that I like hearing such things.

ANNA *(at a loss)*
I thought it would make you happy.

Jan remains silent. Krister enters from the bleaching yard.

KRISTER *(from a distance, poorly)*
Excuse me . . .

JAN
Like I said, I've got to go. *(About to leave)*

KRISTER
Excuse me. Wait a moment. There's something . . .

JAN *(stopping)*
Be quick about it, then.

KRISTER *(approaches them)*
Who's this? My sight is so poor. Do I know you?

ANNA *(in a tired voice)*
It's Anna. You talked with me earlier today.

KRISTER
Yes, you're the one who irons the linen. Why did you
say it like that? Have I done anything to you?

ANNA
No, Krister. It's just that I gave a gift to somebody
this evening and it was turned into a thing of shame.

KRISTER *(turns to Jan)*
Who are you?

JAN
Oh, just somebody who dropped in.

KRISTER
Why won't you tell me your name?

JAN

For Anna's sake.

KRISTER

You wouldn't happen to have a shirt for me, would you?
I've got to get one today.

JAN

A shirt? I don't know if I do. I'll look.

KRISTER

So you don't have one either . . .

JAN

I didn't say that. I'll look when I get home . . .

KRISTER *(interrupting him)*

I won't ask you again.

JAN

It was just that I didn't . . .

KRISTER *(interrupting)*

It's too late, do you hear? . . . But what would it have
cost you to lose a shirt? You're going to lose more than
that.

JAN *(startled)*

What did you say?

KRISTER

You're going to lose everything someday, you too.

JAN *(out of sorts)*

Oh, that . . . Well, so long, Anna. *(Leaves)*

KRISTER

There he goes. They're all so strange. I won't be able to
ask anybody else.

ANNA
    You were too abrupt, Krister. He didn't have time to
    think.

KRISTER *(bent over)*
    There shouldn't be any need for you all to think. That's
    the whole point.

ANNA *(carefully)*
    Was it that important?

KRISTER
    A man's got to find out whether there's anybody who
    cares for him at all. There's nothing else a man searches
    for.

ANNA
    Are you doing that, too? Tander's also doing that.

KRISTER
    Why did you mention Tander?

ANNA
    I don't know. Because I was looking at you, I guess.

KRISTER
    He's going to die today, I think. I have seen it on him.

ANNA
    Don't keep on talking such nonsense, Krister. Look out
    there, you're about to fall over. *(Supports him)*

KRISTER
    I'm going out into the yard. There's nobody else for me
    to ask. *(Becomes aware of something)* How nice you
    smell. Freshly washed and new. A lot of things could
    be said about you.

ANNA
    Well, say some, Krister.

KRISTER

Can't. No, don't let go of me.

ANNA

I'm not going to let go of you.

KRISTER

No, I'm sure you won't. I thought for a moment, however, that you were going to. Do you think you could come out into the yard with me and sit by me this evening?

ANNA

Sure, I'll be glad to.

KRISTER

No matter what happens?

ANNA

I'll stay by you, Krister.

KRISTER *(wondering)*

My, how things can change. I thought I was going to have to be all by myself. The moment you held me up, however, I changed my mind. Shall we go?

ANNA

I've got to stay here until we're through for the day. Then I'll walk you home and sit up with you.

KRISTER *(quarrelsome and cross)*

Home? I'm not going home. I'm staying out in the yard.

ANNA

You're not planning on lying out under the open sky all night, are you? You know you're not well.

KRISTER *(in revolt)*

I guess I can be where I want to be. You don't understand anything about this. You have just lived for a few

years ... *(Suddenly frightened of what he has just said)*
You're not going to leave me because I said that, are you?
*(Anna shakes her head. Folds up a shirt she has just
ironed)* That's good. What was your name again?

KRISTER

Anna.

KRISTER

Yes, Anna, that's what it was. I won't be at peace until
I'm out in the bleaching yard. *(Suddenly blurts out)* But
nobody had a shirt for me. *(Looks at the shirt Anna has
ironed)* I have to have that one.

ANNA

Oh, no you don't, Krister. We can't. It belongs to somebody.

KRISTER

He's also going to pass on some day. If he's a just man,
he'll understand. *(He carefully takes the folded, white
shirt out of Anna's hands)*

ANNA *(can't bring herself to take the shirt back. She just
stands there)*
Was that the end ...

KRISTER

You don't understand how it feels. You haven't walked
around and asked and asked. We have.

ANNA

We? What do you mean by 'we'?

KRISTER

Just we. Will you help me to put it on? I'm so stiff. I
can't raise my arms.

ANNA

Not now, not here, Krister. Folk can still come in. I'll

help you with it this evening. *(Is aware of something about Krister)* What's bothering you?

KRISTER

It's not an easy thing being alone.

ANNA *(startled by his behaviour)*

Whom are you expecting?

KRISTER *(hides himself up against the wall)*

It's not an easy thing being alone.

Tander enters, dark and reserved. Anna starts, frightened, and moves toward Tander. Tander is unaware that Krister is in the room.

ANNA

What have you done, Tander?

TANDER *(stiff and distant)*

It's not an easy thing being alone, Anna. You don't know that yet. But you will . . .

ANNA *(stiffly)*

Have you done anything yet?

TANDER

It'll soon be night, Anna. What a child you are. It's dark here.

ANNA *(points to the sunlight in the door)*

No, it's still mid-day here. What have you done?

TANDER

You can go, Anna.

ANNA *(frightened)*

Go? What do you mean. It's the dinner break.

TANDER *(wild)*

Yes, you can go. Get out. This is no place for you. We're talking about things you're too young to understand.

ANNA

You probably thought that Vera was here? But you're
not going to have her.

TANDER *(as before)*

Don't speak of her. I've told you not to speak of her.
Things have gone farther now ... We're beside dark
streams ... where judgement takes place. He who has
sinned shall fall.

ANNA *(frightened)*

No.

TANDER

Justice can then prevail.

ANNA

I think you're out of your mind. Have you followed
Jan's tracks like a dog?

TANDER *(dangerous)*

It's night, Anna. You can go.

*Anna is now so frightened that she moves toward the
door. She has forgotten Krister.*

ANNA

Don't you touch Jan!

TANDER

Go, Anna. *(Anna runs out. Tander suddenly says to
himself)* The time will soon be ripe. *(He suddenly becomes aware of Krister, who is trying to sneak out.
Krister presses the shirt close up against his chest. Tander
stares at Krister)* Did I have to meet you now? *(Notices
the shirt. Looks at it, then at Krister)*

KRISTER *(pressing the shirt against him)*

Somebody cares for me.

18 — Modern Nordic Plays: Norway

TANDER

Have you found yourself a shirt?

KRISTER *(shy)*

Yes, I'm going to put it on now.

TANDER

What have you done now?

KRISTER

What I had to. Anna is going to help me put it on, now.

TANDER *(in a different tone of voice)*

Has Anna helped you?

KRISTER

Somebody cares for me.

TANDER *(blurts out)*

That's not true.

KRISTER *(starts to leave)*

I'll meet you out in the yard this evening.

TANDER *(as if struck)*

I hadn't thought so. *(Krister tries to trudge out. Tander says suddenly)* Don't go, Krister. I've got to talk to you. Now, right away.

KRISTER

I don't have time, now.

TANDER *(grabs a hold of him)*

But I have to . . .

KRISTER *(blurts out)*

It's too late. When I didn't get it when I first asked, well . . .

TANDER *(pushing him down on the stool)*

Sit down . . .

KRISTER
I'm afraid of you.

TANDER
Why?

KRISTER
You are just like you were when I saw you out in the
yard yesterday evening. You seem to be completely
black.

TANDER *(beseechingly)*
I need help, Krister. *(Krister nods. Tander says
bitterly)* Yes, no matter how bad off you are, you always
find out things like that. *(Angry)* Nobody's wiped it off,
you see. It's going to stay there for ever. *(Krister
doesn't answer. Tander comes to the point)* Can you
help me, Krister? I feel inside me that you can.

KRISTER *(shakes his head)*
I can't. I haven't time.

TANDER *(angry)*
You have to.

KRISTER
I've got other things to think about now.

TANDER
Will you try to keep me from taking a man's life?

KRISTER *(confused)*
I'm the one who is supposed to die. *(Suddenly,
frightened)* Is somebody going to be destroyed?

TANDER *(nods, trembling)*
I'm going to do it. *(Krister still acts confused)* Will
you stay with me?

KRISTER

That's no question to ask me. I'm going to die myself.
I don't have time to stay with you. (*Attempts to rise,
but Tander holds him down*)

TANDER

Don't leave. You look at me in fear, but I'm the one
who is so frightened that I tremble.

KRISTER (*with strange authority*)

Let me go.

TANDER (*seized by fear*)

What's this? Am I to receive no sort of help?

KRISTER (*confused*)

Help?

TANDER

Yes, you have to stay with me wherever I go.

KRISTER (*standing up*)

It's too late. You'll have to manage by yourself.

TANDER (*afraid*)

Don't leave me alone.

KRISTER

You'll just have to ask somebody else, Tander. Just as
I have had to do.

TANDER (*wild*)

No, I've asked the two people who could have helped
me and have been refused. I'm not going to ask anybody
else. All I want now is to have this *other thing* happen.

KRISTER

You'll have to get out of my way. I'm going out.

TANDER (*bitingly*)

Well, get out, then. (*Krister toddles off*) Because there's no point in your staying *here.* (*Krister exits out into the bleaching yard. Tander is left alone. His whole body trembles*) Your hour has come, Jan Vang. (*Repeats as if calling*) Jan Vang, I'm ready for you.

Someone is suddenly heard on the stairs. Tander slides underneath the stairs, pressing himself up against the wall. Jan slowly descends the stairs, as if drawn by something. He walks a short way out onto the floor. He suddenly becomes aware of something. He quickly turns and stares at Tander. He stands as if nailed to the spot, stunned by the unpleasant sight.

JAN (*in a low voice*)
What's up, Tander? Why are you standing there as if you were nailed to the wall? What's this behaviour supposed to mean? (*Tander remains silent*) Do you want to say or do anything to me? Is it dangerous here? Answer me, man! (*Tander remains silent. Jan bursts out*) What have I done to you, Tander? Why won't you leave me alone?

TANDER (*in a low voice*)
You have caused me to have a great day today, Jan Vang. You know that as well as I.

JAN
I didn't have anything to do with that writing on the wall, if that's what you're thinking about.

TANDER
The darkness has gathered closely about you, Jan Vang.

JAN (*startled*)
The darkness? You're sick! Do you hear me?

TANDER
If you're so innocent, why are you trembling?

JAN

It's no wonder I'm trembling with you threatening me like that. I would very much like to get out of this unpleasant cellar. But I realize that we've got to have a showdown, Tander. There's no point in postponing it.

TANDER *(with difficulty)*

Did you say showdown? Well, if this is the last time we're going to talk with one another, what do you have to say?

JAN

What do you mean?

TANDER

You're not going to be able to say anything soon.

JAN *(low-voiced)*

What did you say?

TANDER *(with difficulty)*

Don't you understand, Jan Vang? Don't you understand how all this is going to end?

JAN *(whispers)*

You're mad.

TANDER

You have to be gotten rid of. That's the way I see it.

JAN

But what have I done to you, man?

TANDER

You have ruined Vera for me. She was just supposed to be here. Among the linen. Always. No one was supposed to touch her with so much as a finger. But then Jan Vang came along and messed up everything. Perhaps you understand me a little bit better now. You've got to be gotten rid of.

JAN *(moved)*
> All I understand is that all this has got to end. It'll have to be *one* of us. Maybe you don't expect me to fight back.

TANDER
> You won't have a chance to.

JAN
> I've got a chance right now. *(Is about to attack Tander)*

TANDER *(calls out)*
> Stay where you are. The time has not yet come.

JAN *(is stopped by the power of Tander's words, but says in a threatening voice)*
> Tander.

TANDER *(breathless, as if after a big jump)*
> Stay there. The time has not come yet. But we'll soon meet again.

JAN
> Tander.

TANDER
> I've given you a warning, Jan Vang. It's best that you know so you can prepare yourself somewhat for what's going to happen.

JAN
> Well, this ... *(At this point Vera enters. She stands in the sunlight inside the door)*

VERA
> Are you here, Jan?

JAN *(stares at Tander for a moment ... then runs quickly up to Vera. He takes her in his arms, kisses and caresses her)*
> Here I am, Vera.

VERA *(weakly, enjoying his embrace)*
>   Oh, Jan. You. Not here. Somebody might come.

JAN
>   Aren't we all by ourselves, Vera? Vera?

VERA
>   Jan, dear Jan . . . not here . . . you mustn't.

JAN *(keeping it up)*
>   I'll keep on as long as I like. As much as I like. And
>   that's what you want me to do, too.

*Tander stands stiffly. Vera has no idea that he is there.
Suddenly Elise and Marte are heard descending the stairs.*

VERA *(tearing herself away)*
>   They're coming. Go now.

JAN *(as he leaves)*
>   See you this evening.

*Exit. Vera walks out onto the floor. Suddenly she sees
Tander and stands still. Tander just looks at her. She walks
a few steps across the floor. Marte and Elise have come
down. Vera runs into the room where the ironing is done.*

TANDER *(excitedly turning toward Marte and Elise)*
>   Oh, so you've finally come back, have you? I was afraid
>   we weren't going to get started.

ELISE *(nervously)*
>   What's been going on here?

MARTE
>   God help me, I thought I saw something black, but it
>   was nothing but Tander.

ELISE *(to Tander)*
>   Where's Anna? *(Tander doesn't answer, but walks over
>   to the mangle)* Vera, do you know where Anna is?

VERA *(uneasy)*
Have no idea. I haven't seen her. Do you want her for
something? Is anything wrong?

ELISE *(calling)*
Anna!

MARTE
Just listen to the sound that's inside people today.

ANNA *(in the doorway)*
Here I am. I haven't been far away. *(Walks over to
where she works)*

ELISE
You usually sit in here, that's all.

ANNA *(prepares to start ironing)*
Yes, I usually sit in here all by myself.

TANDER *(yelling at them)*
Let's get to work now. *(He darts here and there. He
bends over a tub and the sound of rushing water is
heard)* Let's get to work!

VERA *(entering with some bags of laundry)*
Yes.

ELISE *(bent over a tub, straightens up and looks at Vera)*
Yes?

TANDER *(by the mangle)*
There are some more bags of laundry, Marte. Empty
them!

MARTE *(in the process of doing so)*
Yes, you don't have to yell and tell me what to do. I
know what has to be done.

TANDER

The place is full of laundry bags! We'll probably have to work overtime today.

MARTE *(emptying the bags)*

There's no more here today than usual. My, my, some of the stuff people send to a laundry.

TANDER *(turning the mangle)*

We'll have to work all night.

MARTE

No, thank you. I don't want to hear anything like that.

ELISE

Johan? What's the matter?

TANDER

Will you all stay with me and work all night?

MARTE

I've already said no thanks.

TANDER *(trembles)*

I'm asking you all to stay with me and work all night!

MARTE

Why don't you just keep quiet. You're not well. If we work all night, we won't be able to work tomorrow. What will we have gained by it, then?

ELISE

He was just kidding.

TANDER *(in a hard tone of voice)*

I didn't ask you to, either. I told you to empty those bags. *(Everybody busily at work)* I hope you are aware that I'm not asking any more.

MARTE *(emptying bags of laundry)*

Just look at this . . . I can't remember things being worse!

TANDER *(laughing in a way)*
Ha, the laundry is really working now! *(Something sud-denly strikes him. He calls quickly)* Hey, Anna!

ANNA *(stops ironing)*
Yes, what is it?

TANDER
Can you hear me?

ANNA
Hear you?

TANDER
Where is he now?

ANNA *(at once, interested)*
Out in the yard. In the grass.

TANDER
What were his last words? *(They are all startled)*

ELSIE
Whom are they talking about?

MARTE
Oh, Krister.

ANNA
He's not dead *(To everyone)* Nobody's dead.

Curtain

ACT THREE

Outside in the bleaching yard. Twilight. The doors are shut. The lights have been turned on. Krister is lying in the grass. Anna is with him.

KRISTER

Are they working now?

ANNA

Oh, no. We're through for the day. We were through a long time ago. He wanted us to keep at it all evening, but . . .

KRISTER

There was a lot of yelling for a while.

ANNA

Yeah, that was before we were through. He wanted us to keep on. He's been crazy all day.

KRISTER

It was a good thing that it eventually stopped. I would like to have it quiet here now.

ANNA

Are you feeling bad, Krister?

KRISTER

I'm very tired and weak. *(They sit without talking for a while)* Where is he now?

ANNA

Who?

KRISTER

He who's going to die. He was flying all around the place.

ANNA

Let's not talk any more about people dying. We've got to
see that you get into the house. It's late and it'll be getting damp.

KRISTER

I'm not moving. I'm not going home any more.

ANNA

You can't lie here on the ground all night, Krister. You're
sick, don't forget.

KRISTER

I'm not moving. What do I need a house for when everything inside of me is all used up?

ANNA

But it seems so strange to me.

KRISTER

Are you chilly?

ANNA

No, I'm wearing a warm coat.

*Faint sounds of voices from inside the house are heard...
from Vera's room. The voices of Jan, Amund and Stein.
They have been drinking.*

JAN

Open the door, Vera, it's me.

STEIN

And me and Amund. We've decided that we're going to
have to stand watch for you.

JAN

Aren't you in there, Vera?

AMUND

No, she's not there, Jan. But where on earth can she be?

JAN

    I don't like this. We'll have to look some place else.

STEIN

    Yeah, we are supposed to be her guards, aren't we? Sure we are. Her guards. (*The voices die away*)

ANNA

    Shh. Don't pay all that any mind, Krister.

KRISTER (*frightened*)

    Do you hear anything? It sounded to me like there's something strange going on tonight.

ANNA

    It's nothing, Krister. Just take it easy.

KRISTER (*after a short pause*)

    Isn't it wonderful, Anna.

ANNA

    What?

KRISTER

    I'm speaking of all this hanging on the clotheslines here. The air is filled with it. Don't you smell it?

ANNA

    No, I guess I work too much with it every day.

KRISTER

    Aw, that's too bad. (*He says after a pause*) I think you are like linen.

ANNA

    What did you say?

KRISTER

    Like linen. I don't know any other way of putting it. There is so much I've just known the smell of, you know.

(Anna strokes him on his forehead) You'd probably like to go to bed now, Anna.

ANNA

Don't worry about me.

KRISTER

No, you're right. It doesn't matter whether you stand watch one night, does it? You have so many other nights to sleep in.

ANNA

Do you feel any worse now?

KRISTER

I don't know. It's as if I didn't have any feeling at all. *(After a pause)* Anna, this new shirt is bothering me.

ANNA

Just don't you worry about it. Just think about the fact that it's clean. Isn't that what you wanted?

KRISTER

It's upsetting me. I shouldn't have put it on. *(Suddenly, loudly)* Take it off!

ANNA *(sorry that this is bothering Krister)*

Just don't worry about it, do you hear? I'll fix it all up for you. There'll be no trouble. None at all. Just calm down and take it easy.

KRISTER *(relieved)*

Well, if I don't have to worry then . . . .

ANNA

Try to sleep for a while, Krister. *(After a while)* Krister! *(Krister doesn't answer. He has dozed off for a while. Anna thinks aloud)* Like linen. *(Bitterly)* Poor old man, you haven't had that ruined for you, then. That's nice. *(The boys' voices are heard down in the cellar)*

JAN

No, there's nobody here, either. I don't like the looks of this, I say ... What with him prowling around the place ...

AMUND

Don't get upset, Jan. Something has probably delayed her. Let's look out in the yard.

STEIN

Yes, let's get out of this black hell of Tander's ... It's so unpleasant here.

AMUND

Shut up. You're going to wake up the whole house.

Jan has now come out into the yard. He sees Anna and walks over toward her.

JAN

Vera! *(Discovers who it is)* Aw, so it's ...

ANNA

Yes, it's just me again, Jan.

STEIN *(who has followed him, along with Amund)*

Good, good, you've found her ...

AMUND

Hush up ... don't you see that it's .... Excuse us, Anna.

ANNA

What's going on? You all ought to be ashamed of yourselves for making so much noise ...

KRISTER

It's supposed to be quiet here now.

STEIN

Is that old Krister lying there? Well, he doesn't frighten us, at any rate.

JAN

Frighten? We're not afraid of anything.

AMUND

Don't get all excited now, Jan . . .

JAN *(interrupting)*

Are you in this as well or are you not?

AMUND

You know that I am. What's the matter with Krister, Anna?

ANNA

He's feeling poorly. You all had better go now. We don't want to have any noise here. I see that you're drunk, all of you.

STEIN

We drank ourselves into courage, as the saying goes.

ANNA *(mockingly, to Jan)*

So you've had a big party? But what about Vera? Where's she?

JAN

She didn't come. Has she been here?

ANNA

No.

AMUND

We're looking for her.

STEIN

We are going to protect her. We have formed a troop of faithful guards that are going to protect her from Tander. Protect Jan, too.

19 — Modern Nordic Plays: Norway

ANNA
  Oh, so you need protection now, Jan.

JAN
  Don't think so. We'll see when I meet up with him.

KRISTER
  No!

JAN *(to the others)*
  There's no need of our staying out here. Come on.

They turn to leave, but stop suddenly. Elise has come out without their knowing it.

ELISE
  May I speak with you, Jan Vang?

JAN
  What? Again? No, this time I want to talk to Tander personally.

ELISE
  But there is something that you don't know ...

JAN
  All I know is that I don't want this hanging over my head any longer. I can't take it any longer, do you understand?

ELISE
  I understand. But I don't know what I can do ...

JAN *(interrupting)*
  There's one thing you can do, Mrs. Tander. You can keep your husband away from Vera. *(He leaves. Stein follows)*

ANNA
  Jan!

AMUND

Excuse us, Mrs. Tander, but Jan's afraid now, and when
... (*Elise just stands there, stiffly. Amund follows the
others in*)

ANNA (*looking at Elise*)

Don't stand like that, Elise. He didn't mean what he
said. He's drunk and frightened of Tander.

ELISE (*stiffly*)

I saw him!

ANNA

What did you say? Whom did you see? Tander?

ELISE

Yes, I saw him, Anna. He stood there, alone, wiping the
writing off the wall. (*Bursts out*) Oh, God, what have
I done? I can't stop it any longer. I can't stop it. Can
you tell me what I have done, Anna?

ANNA

What's the meaning of all this, Elise?

ELISE

Don't you understand, Anna? I was the one who wrote
on the wall over there!

ANNA

You?

ELISE

Yes, me. Anna, I didn't know what I was doing. But I
wrote it.

ANNA (*alarmed*)

But I don't understand. What in the world were you
thinking about?

ELISE

I thought I had to think of something. In one way or

another I had to turn his thoughts from Vera. *(Bursts out)* I wish I had never done it!

ANNA
But why did you let it stay on the wall, then?

ELISE
I thought I had to ... It was too late. But tonight I realized that I had to wipe it off myself, and so I went over there ... and that's when I saw him.

ANNA
Tander?

ELISE *(nods)*
Yes. I had almost reached the wall. But then I saw that there was somebody already there, and I stopped. I could glimpse something moving in the darkness. At that moment the glare from a flashlight streaked across the wall, and I recognized who it was. It was Johan. He was rubbing out what was written there. A lonely man standing in the darkness wiping it out. I wanted to go over to him ... but my legs refused to carry me there. I just stood there in the darkness ... and then stumbled back home.

ANNA
But what about Tander?

ELISE
He's still out there in the darkness ... alone.

ANNA
I don't understand a bit of all this ... I have just lived for a few years, as Krister said. *(Elise just stands there)* But how did he become the way he is now?

ELISE
I don't know, Anna. All I know is that I am to blame

for a large part of it. He's so lonely. It might have been our child that died. Something ended then. I think it's mostly because he has probably had a longing inside him that I have been unable to define.

ANNA *(thoughtfully)*
I understand him better now.

ELISE
I've got to find him ... I've got to tell him that it was me. You'll have to go with me, Anna. I'm so scared. The way he's acting now ... We've got to stop him ... Something terrible can happen at any moment now.

ANNA
I can't. Krister's lying over there and I have promised ...

ELISE
What's this about Krister?

ANNA
I've promised to stay here with him.

ELISE *(uneasy)*
I've got to stop Johan before he does something wrong! I've got to get a hold of Marte ... *She'll* help me.

KRISTER *(calls)*
Anna.

ANNA *(walks over to him)*
Yes, here I am, Krister.

KRISTER
I'm still in the yard with all the linen, aren't I?

ANNA
Yes, you are.

KRISTER
Yes, linen.

ANNA

Calm down now.

KRISTER *(weakly)*

It's this shirt.

ANNA *(gently)*

Well, what's wrong with your shirt, Krister?

KRISTER

It wasn't given to me. I took it from you.

ANNA

No, you didn't, Krister. I gave it to you. Calm down now.

KRISTER *(fearfully)*

Come. Tander. Are you here? *(Tander has entered. He stands there, dark, with pent-up feelings)*

ANNA *(rises, frightened)*

What are you doing here, Tander! Go away. Please, go.

TANDER

It's dark now, Anna.

KRISTER

Come here, Tander.

TANDER *(to Anna)*

You're right. There's no point in my staying here. *(Walks toward the house)*

KRISTER

No.

ANNA *(tempted to stop him)*

Don't go in there, Tander. Please, go away from here. Elise is looking for you. She . . .

TANDER

Anna, child, you don't understand anything of this. I'm

just an instrument. Everything has been put into my hands.

ANNA

Listen, Tander, it wasn't Jan who wrote that on the wall.

TANDER

I won't listen to you, Anna. You don't understand this here, I've told you.

ANNA

No, listen. It wasn't Jan who wrote it. It was your wife, Elise.

KRISTER

Tander . . .

TANDER *(stands looking stiffly at Anna)*
You're lying! Why should she? . . . You're lying.

ANNA *(stutters)*
She t-t-told me so just now, Tander.

TANDER *(grabs a hold of her)*
You're lying!

KRISTER

There's somebody who cares for me.

TANDER *(Stares at Anna for a long time. He fights with the lightning that has struck him. It is obvious that he is won over and believes)*
Elise? Was it Elise, Anna?

ANNA *(nods)*
Yes.

TANDER

Elise? But why? . . . Elise. But then . . . *(Suddenly)* I've got to talk to her, immediately . . .

ANNA *(happy, points)*
She went that way . . . She was going over to Marte's.

TANDER *(leaving)*
Elise! Was it Elise?

KRISTER
You mustn't go, Tander.

ANNA
Hush, Krister.

KRISTER
Who are you?

ANNA
Anna, from the laundry.

KRISTER
Yes, of course.

ANNA
I'm not going to leave you, Krister. *(Vera enters)*

ANNA
Vera, where are you coming from?

VERA
Nowhere.

ANNA
Are you looking for your splendid guards?

VERA
Have you seen Jan?

ANNA
Yes, you have such fine guards that . . .

VERA
Maybe you would also be out of your mind if you were

Jan now. It has been proven that he was the one who wrote that on the wall.

ANNA

Proven? By whom?

VERA

By Tander. He'll kill Jan if he gets the chance. I had better stay here so I won't run into him.

ANNA

Do you mean Jan is so scared that he's gone and gotten himself drunk?

VERA

I'm talking about Tander. And you know very well (*quickly*) that Jan is not drunk.

ANNA

He had at any rate drunk up a little courage.

VERA

The whole house seems to be bewitched. (*She is about to leave, when she suddenly sees Tander, who has come in*)

TANDER

Good evening, Vera.

VERA (*frightened*)

What do you want?

TANDER

Can I tell you something, Vera.

VERA

About what?

TANDER

About myself and what has happened to me.

VERA

What does that mean?

TANDER

Just that I want to tell you about something that has happened to me. Will you listen to me?

VERA

I don't know. You're acting so strange.

TANDER

You know that I have been so mad at Jan that I have just about choked. I won't try to describe what it was all like. You can probably guess.

VERA

Was? Have things changed, then?

TANDER *(calmly)*

I'm free of it all.

VERA

Free?

TANDER

Yes, I haven't been abandoned . . . I am being cared for.

VERA

Cared for? *(Pause)*

TANDER

And nothing more is going to happen now between Jan and me.

VERA

Have you spoken to him recently, then?

TANDER

No, but I have found out who wrote that on the wall . . . and at that moment, everything changed. All at once I could think of Jan Vang in a different way.

VERA *(slowly)*

How strange . . .

TANDER

Elise wrote it. Can you imagine?

VERA

Was it Elise?

TANDER

She didn't do it because she wanted to hurt me, Vera. She has hurt herself in the worst way possible for my sake . . . because she was the only one who knew that what was written there wasn't true. She did it because she cared for me.

VERA

Cared for you?

TANDER *(nods, happy)*

And that has changed everything for me.

VERA

How strange . . . Did Elise tell you herself?

TANDER

No, she told it to Anna. And now I've got to find her. She is supposed to have gone over to Marte's, but there was nobody home. I also think that I can look at you in a different way now.

VERA

How strange . . . *(Suddenly)* Do you think that this is going to last?

TANDER

Yes. *(Looks at Vera)* Are you happy? *(Vera is overwhelmed. Tander says softly)* I just asked you if you were happy?

VERA *(barely nodding)*
  Yes.

KRISTER *(in fear)*
  Tander! *(Jan, Amund and Stein have come out of the laundry)*

JAN
  My, oh, my . . . Why it's *Tander.*

STEIN
  And together with Vera. Look at him . . .

JAN *(immediately excited)*
  What's up? You haven't managed to kill me yet.

KRISTER
  Tander.

TANDER *(stares at them)*
  I had hoped that this wouldn't happen . . .

ANNA *(has jumped to her feet)*
  Jan, get out of here!

VERA
  Jan, listen to me!

JAN
  I don't have to listen to anything . . . after all, there he is, standing right next to you.

VERA
  But he's not thinking of doing you any harm, Jan.

JAN
  I have felt him after me long enough for me to know that he intends doing something to me.

TANDER
  Listen here, Jan Vang!

JAN

No, sir! We're not going to listen to anything. We have seen enough.

STEIN *(hard)*

You're right. We formed a troop, didn't we?

VERA

What does all this mean, Amund?

JAN *(grabs a hold of Tander)*

Well, Tander. I don't like to have anybody threaten my life.

AMUND *(to Vera)*

We've promised each other to stick together and protect you, Vera. And whom do we run into but Tander there.

VERA

Yes, but he hasn't done anything ... other than take a load off my heart.

JAN

Come on, Amund. We're all going to take part in this.

VERA

Let him go, Jan. Something has happened. He's changed

TANDER

Yes, it's all over now, Jan Vang.

JAN

And you fell right into his trap, didn't you, Vera?

TANDER *(frightened)*

What do you mean?

JAN

Shut up. Words are of no use now.

TANDER *(frightened)*

  Is this the way things stand? I didn't know . . . I thought
  I was free now.

KRISTER

  He mustn't . . . he and I . . .

ANNA

  Hush, Krister . . .

KRISTER *(staggers to his feet)*

  You don't know what it feels like. *(To Tander)* I had
  to *take* that shirt. Do you hear me?

ANNA

  We're not going to leave you, Krister.

KRISTER *(falls down to the ground)*

  He and I, we . . .

TANDER

  I've got to go over to Krister.

JAN

  Oh, no, you don't. Stand still. We're not going to listen
  to that foolishness.

STEIN

  No, the troop is going to go into action.

JAN

  We're going to give him a good ducking.

STEIN

  A ducking . . . that's a good idea. Let's wash him, boys . . .
  down in the cellar in his own tub.

JAN

  Wash him, yes. In searing lye.

STEIN
Then we'll set him out to bleach . . . so that he'll be real nice.

VERA
Jan, you mustn't.

JAN *(interrupting)*
Shut up, Vera!

TANDER *(to Vera)*
Thanks, Vera.

JAN
Shut up! Don't interfere with this, Vera!

TANDER *(weakly)*
Let me go.

JAN
Oh, no, sir. We have come for Tander at last. Come for you, do you hear that?

STEIN
Look at the way he's shaking. The moment you said that we had come for him, he started to tremble.

AMUND *(who has long stood stiff, becomes more and more involved)*
Yes, look at how he's trembling.

VERA
You have to listen to me, at any rate, Amund.

AMUND *(stiffly shakes his head)*
Not this time, Vera. *(He walks stiffly over and grabs Tander by the arm. Jan makes room for him)*

VERA *(frightened)*
How horrible you all are! You mustn't do this! He's

innocent! *(Seizes hold of Jan)* Jan, you mustn't do anything that you'll . . .

JAN *(shaking Vera off)*
Don't interfere with this! *(Turns toward Tander and
says in a low voice)* Okay, Tander . . . your tub is waiting.

TANDER
But I've got to find Elise. Elise, who . . .

JAN
No more noise out of you now that you've been captured.

KRISTER
What's going to happen?

TANDER *(firmly)*
I'm going in.

KRISTER
Do you see me?

TANDER
Yes.

KRISTER
Help me. *(He collapses again)*

ANNA *(trembling)*
Don't you all see that he's a . . . a dying man.

VERA
Stop all this, Jan.

TANDER *(strangely excited)*
I'm going, Vera.

VERA *(at a loss)*
You're going?

TANDER *(in a firm voice)*
   Yes, I've got to do it.

The boys, struck by something they don't understand, have let go of Tander.

VERA
   Run away from them, Tander.

TANDER *(tottering)*
   I must.

VERA
   I can see that you're hardly able to stand on your feet, Tander. Run away from them.

TANDER *(trembling from tension and effort)*
   I must, Vera. I must.

VERA
   Why?

TANDER
   It's the only way for us to end the whole thing, Vera. *(Turns toward Jan)* Shall we go?

Jan no longer dares to speak. He stands completely still. Tander starts to move toward the cellar door. The three boys immediately follow him, but do not touch him. They just follow him, helpless, frightened by what they have begun.

ANNA *(bursts out)*
   I can't stand this. You mustn't.

TANDER *(stops)*
   But I haven't seen Elise.

AMUND *(in a stiff monotone)*
   Move on, Tander. *(Tander nods, walks on. They dis-*

appear into the cellar. Anna and Vera have come in to-gether)

VERA *(in fear)*
They seem to be transformed.

ANNA
He won't be able to take it. I could tell from the way he looked. What's that? *(Jan's voice is heard from the cellar)*

JAN
Okay, Tander, we've reached your tub.

VERA
Oh, God. *(Anna and Vera seem to be drawn by something towards backstage, where they can look down into the cellar)*

STEIN
Let me turn on the water.

ANNA
Look at the way he's standing ... *(The loud sound of running water is heard)*

STEIN *(wildly)*
We are the one's controlling the streams today.

VERA *(calling, wildly)*
Leave them, Tander.

JAN *(from the cellar)*
We're ready, Tander.
Nothing is heard for a while but the sound of running water.

VERA *(startled by something she sees, whispers in fear)*
No, no.

ANNA *(similarly)*
My God.

JAN *(from the cellar, yells in fear)*
Tander . . . Tander, listen to me. *(Stein and Amund also yell)* Tander.

AMUND
Grab him, Stein. We'd better carry him out into the fresh air.

STEIN
He fell?

VERA *(trembling)*
No, no, not this. *(Stein and Amund come out carrying Tander. Jan follows)*

AMUND
Give him some fresh air.

STEIN *(confused)*
He just fell, didn't he? *(They lay Tander down)*

ANNA
Has he fainted?

AMUND *(confused)*
I don't know. We didn't do anything to him. He just . . .

JAN *(to Vera who has joined him)*
He simply walked over to the tub and then suddenly collapsed.

ANNA *(who has bent over Tander)*
Can't you all see?

JAN *(frightened)*
See what?

ANNA
Tander's dead.

VERA

Oh, no, not that!

JAN

Don't say such things, Anna.

AMUND

Yeah, don't scare us like that.

JAN

He has just fainted. We've got to get the doctor.

STEIN *(running out)*

Yeah, I'll go and call.

JAN

He can't be dead.

AMUND

I simply don't understand what I have done. We didn't touch him. He just stepped forward.

JAN

Yes, we can't be blamed for what happened, Amund.

AMUND *(trembling)*

Oh, I don't know. I think we can be blamed. We had something to do with it.

ANNA *(over by Krister)*

Krister's dead too.

VERA

What? Krister?

ANNA *(with guilt feelings)*

And nobody even noticed it.

JAN *(pained)*

That was just something that had to happen, poor Krister.

ANNA *(in wonder)*
All at once Krister's gone too.

JAN
He too? Who else? Tander's not dead. He can't be dead.

VERA
Tander's dead. You've got to admit it, too. *(Elise and Marte enter)*

ELISE
Where is he? Stein said that . . .

JAN
Here, Elise. He . . . I . . .

ELISE *(bends down over Tander)*
Johan . . .?

JAN
He can't hear. Stein has run for the doctor, but . . .

MARTE *(looking at Jan and Amund)*
What have you all done?

JAN *(trembling)*
He was free, not bound or held. But when he was about to climb up into the tub, he collapsed.

ELISE
What was he going to do up in there?

JAN *(desperate)*
He wanted to do it, Mrs. Tander. We had decided that we had to wash him . . . but he was the one who was all for it in the end.

AMUND
Yes, that's what happened, Mrs. Tander.

MARTE

Did you all threaten him? You seem to have something on your consciences.

JAN

Yes ... but not in the end. He was so strange.

ANNA

He told Vera that it was something that he had to do.

ELISE

Oh, my God, what have I done?

VERA

He knew that you did what you did because you cared for him, he said. And that as a result, everything had changed. Because somebody cared for him, he said.

ELISE

Cared for him ...

VERA

He was freed from what had been bothering him, he said. Because somebody cared for him ...

ELISE

But ... he then went through this?

JAN

What can I say? I made him go in there.

ELISE

We've got to help each other, Jan Vang.

JAN

Help each other?

ELISE

Yes, I think so.

JAN

But I wouldn't listen to him.

VERA *(comforting him)*
He was the one who finally insisted on it, Jan.

ELISE
Yes, that's what happened. *(To Vera)* Did he *say* that he was sure I did it because I cared for him?

VERA
Yes.

ELISE
There was no one here who was in greater need of being cared for than Tander. *(They stand motionless, turned toward Tander)*

ELISE
It's as though I have changed.

ANNA *(over by Krister)*
Krister is dead too.

MARTE
Krister, too?

ANNA *(bitterly)*
And nobody even noticed it.

MARTE *(walks over to Krister)*
But I see that he finally got a white shirt to put on.

ANNA
He had to take it. It caused him nothing but uneasiness.

ELISE
Poor thing. He had to sneak away in the end.

ANNA
Sneak away?

ELISE
But that isn't what Johan did, at any rate. He walked right up and faced his fate. He got what he wanted.

MARTE

But that finished him.

ELISE

Yes ... (*Stands for a while, and finally says, in wonder*) And yet, it's as if ... (*Something seems to become clearer for her*) He has helped me at the same time.

MARTE

Has he helped you?

ELISE

Yes, I think that I have come out of the darkness. (*They look at her in wonder*)

VERA

He could act so strange. I realize now that I was fond of him.

ANNA

He never found out that we were.

MARTE

He was unable to reach the people he wanted to reach. Every now and then he was nothing but a helpless child.

ELISE

You have to say that he reached somebody when he helped me out of the darkness ... Yes, I think that I have come out of the darkness.

Curtain

The Lord and His Servants

A Play in Three Acts

By Axel Kielland

Translated from the Norwegian
by Viola K. Stabell

All rights, including professional, amateur, motion picture, recitation, lecturing, public reading, radio broadcasting, television, reproduction by recording or any electronic or mechanical means, and the rights of translation into foreign languages are strictly reserved. Permission for any of these rights must be obtained from Agni Krein Kielland, Ivar Aasens vei 37, Oslo 3, Norway.

Axel Kielland

Axel Kielland (1907-63) was a journalist — even when he was writing dramas. His newpaper experience, not least as a courtroom reporter, characterizes his plays, in which courtroom scenes play a central role.

In 1952, Professor Dick Helander was appointed Bishop of Strängnäs in Sweden. The following year, he was indicted for having sent anonymous letters to the electors in which he maligned his competitors for the position. Helander was found guilty and suspended from his bishopric in 1954. Since then, there has been considerable controversy about the case. Many people maintained that Helander had been convicted on unsound circumstantial evidence, and that the trial had not been satisfactory. The case was not reopened until 1964. Helander was again found guilty, but this sentence was rescinded. Instead, Helander was fined a comparatively small sum.

While the discussion was at its peak, Axel Kielland made use of this material in a play, *Herren og hans tjenere*. (*The Lord and His Servants*) (1955), in which he launched his theory about the question of guilt in the celebrated case. At the same time, he introduced a new theme that was attracting considerable attention in Norway: the debate about the existence of hell. This debate split the Norwegian clergy into two camps: the puritanical, low-church circles — which attached considerable importance to external punishment, and believed that the doctrine of infernal torment was a necessary part of Christian dogma and belief — and the more liberal, high-church circles, which interpreted the conception of hell symbolically, and did not wish to scare the believers with threats of hell.

In *The Lord and His Servants,* the newly appointed Bishop is called Helmer, not Helander. He is portrayed as representative of the latter category of clergymen, while the opponent and competitor he has maligned in anonymous letters is a typical advocate of the belief in hell.

The play is a good example of the utilization of topical material in dramatic form. When it was performed, it excited considerable interest. It is one of the plays that has had the most performances in Norway after the war.

At the end of the play, Axel Kielland tries to elevate the action to a higher level. Helmer's fate is presented as a kind of wandering to Golgotha. The author endows him with traits that remind one of Christ. In addition, it seems as if Helmer allows himself to be innocently convicted, 1) in order to save Miss Monsen's peace of mind, 2) because he regards himself as morally guilty: he has thought and said the things that Miss Monsen has written in the anonymous letter. This is a solution that is debatable on both the artistic and religious levels. But Kielland's main purpose was undoubtedly to start a discussion.

Characters

BISHOP SIGURD HELMER

MARGRETHE HELMER *his wife*

AGNES *his daughter*

LEIF *his son*

DR. ARVID TORNKVIST

MISS MONSEN

PROSECUTING ATTORNEY

COUNSEL FOR THE DEFENSE

JUDGE

POLICE CHIEF

JENS GREN *shop-owner*

GUNNAR BERG *building superintendent*

BJERKE *police detective* .

Maid, newspaper reporters, photographers, two police-men, a court clerk, two assistant judges, a court stenographer.

The action of the play takes place in our day, in a northern European country where the Church is a state institution.

ACT I.
The Bishop's Residence in Elveness.

ACT II. SCENE 1.
The Bishop's office in the church building.
SCENE 2.
The coutroom.

ACT III.
The Bishop's Residence.

ACT ONE

It is noon on Sunday in the bishop's drawing room. In the background are wide sliding doors which open onto the dining room, where a long table can be seen, festively decorated for many guests. A maid walks back and forth in the dining room with Agnes, the bishop's daughter, making last-minute changes in the arrangements. Now and then they go out through a door into the kitchen and return bearing platters, flower decorations, etc.

At stage left, Mrs. Helmer, the bishop's wife, sits with her embroidery on a sofa beside a sewing-table near a window. She is a strikingly beautiful woman between 45 and 50. Her son, Leif, stands in the open sliding doorway with his back to her and his hands at his sides. He turns and looks at his mother with a slightly defiant glance.

LEIF

Well, the family's austerity has come to an end. He's got himself a bone.

MRS. HELMER

It's usually referred to as a 'call'.

Pause. Leif wanders about a bit, stops and smiles.

LEIF

I don't believe I've ever seen you embroider before, mother.

MRS. HELMER

It's not what you might call my favorite occupation.

LEIF *(bitterly and scornfully)*
  But the congregation expects you to, is that it?

MRS. HELMER
  Oh — they expect so much — and usually in vain. But
  today for some reason, my hands needed something to
  hold on to.

LEIF
  What is it?

MRS. HELMER
  Some sort of teacloth. I started on it in 1928 when I
  was carrying you.

*Leif laughs, goes to her, sits on the arm of the sofa and
gives her a hug.*

MRS. HELMER *(winking at him)*
  We're going to have roast veal — the fatted calf. In
  honor of the prodigal son.

LEIF *(immediately less cheerful, stands and walks away
from the sofa)*
  There's someone else who ought to feel more prodigal
  than I.

MRS. HELMER
  I know you think that.

LEIF
  You think it yourself.

MRS. HELMER
  No, that's where you're wrong, and it's really quite unjust of you. Toward me, I mean. You can think what
  you like about him. He has the strength to bear it. But
  you ought to know me, Leif. Do you believe I would
  have lived all these years with a—sham?

LEIF

I've never been able to understand it.

MRS. HELMER

You won't understand it until you find the one who means everything to you. You can be sure that I see all that other people see. You can be sure that I see his faults. But it's easy for me to forgive those faults because I know that he's a *man*. I know that there's a heart beating inside him . . . That's what you call happiness, my son. I sincerely hope that you may experience it some day.

LEIF *(laughs, in a good humor once again)*

You're the one who ought to have been the bishop! Funny to think that with only a little change in the law you could have been!

MRS. HELMER

No, Leif. Never.

LEIF

All the same, you are a Doctor of Theology. The first woman in the country ever to receive that degree.

MRS. HELMER

Yes, but I'm a renegade. A defrocked minister.

LEIF

Defrocked?

MRS. HELMER

I saw to it myself. I peeled off my mantle and collar.

LEIF

I always thought that was something that just happened naturally. Because you married — him — and were busy with a home and children . . .

MRS. HELMER

That's what everybody thought, and it was for the best.

LEIF

I think that's really very funny. Are you sitting there, you, a Doctor of Theology, you, Margrethe Helmer, the bishop's wife, telling me that you broke with the church and the only true faith?

MRS. HELMER

In a manner of speaking. I had too much intelligence. And it soon dawned on me that God had not given it to me in order for me to believe in things that could scarcely be true.

LEIF

That sounds rather simple.

MRS. HELMER *(reminisces, smiles)*

It was much more complicated than that, of course. In my youth, in my milieu, the word 'free thinker' was considered something monstrous. It came as something of a shock when it eventually dawned on me that I was a free thinker. And so — well, I had to laugh, for I realized that that hideous term of abuse was the most beautiful in the language. Free thinker! One who thinks 'free'! Can you imagine a more splendid title!

LEIF

And so you broke away. I'm proud of you, mother!

MRS. HELMER

You mustn't be, because I didn't *break* away. I simply went on thinking freely in quiet. And . . . who knows whether I might have corrupted my intelligence, just as so many others have done. If the law had allowed a woman to rise to the bishop's seat then . . . perhaps I might have fallen for the temptation . . . yet . . . no!

LEIF

Well?

MRS. HELMER (*thinks a moment*)

Well . . . you see, I had something which was more dangerous than intelligence . . .

LEIF

And that was . . .?

MRS. HELMER

Taste, my son. A certain sense of what one can and cannot do . . . in the Lord's name.

LEIF

I think I see what you mean. (*Walks about. A bitter thought has again struck him. He turns suddenly*) Then perhaps you didn't despair completely when I kicked over the traces and went to sea?

MRS. HELMER

Not at all, I was delighted. Finally a little fresh sea spray in these two incarnate clerical families. I climbed the mountainside in solitude and sang. (*Whispers, with a smile*) Can you guess what I sang?

LEIF (*near her, eagerly*)

No . . ?

MRS. HELMER (*sings softly. He joins her on the second line, and they forget themselves and sing gaily*)

'Better and better day by day,
Better and better day by day.
Enjoy yourself, don't care.
Though others think you ought to sorrow.'

AGNES (*alarmed, comes to the sliding door. She is a radiantly beautiful, but all too serious, young girl of 24. Severely dressed*)

Mother! What are you two doing?

MRS. HELMER *(unabashed)*
We're singing. Or rather trying to.

LEIF *(with a touch of bitterness)*
We're so happy, you see, because he's become a bishop.

Agnes looks at them for a second, turns abruptly, and closes the doors after her with a bang.

LEIF
Well!

MRS. HELMER
She's not particularly happy. *(Resignedly)* There, the thread has come out again!

LEIF
Well, we'll just put it back in again.

MRS. HELMER *(putting her embroidery aside)*
No ... I'm tired of trying to creep through this eternal needle's eye.

LEIF *(nodding toward the door)*
What's bothering her?

MRS. HELMER
Savonarola.

LEIF
Savona ... what the dickens ... ?

MRS. HELMER
I keep forgetting that it's been five years since you were last at home ... It's a question of a man!

LEIF *(whistling lengthily)*
A man! At last!

MRS. HELMER
And when I say a man, that's exactly what I mean. I

call him Savonarola. Or Ibsen's Brand. It comes to about the same.

LEIF *(laughs)*
Well, her name *is* Agnes!

MRS. HELMER
We couldn't foresee everything when we christened her.

LEIF *(shaking his head)*
Another preacher in the family.

MRS. HELMER
A preacher . . . Yes. And a thundering preacher at that. I can't stand him, but I can well see that he has dangerous power over many people.

LEIF
And she loves him?

MRS. HELMER
That's like calling a typhoon a light breeze.

LEIF
And he . . . ?

MRS. HELMER
Savonarola?

LEIF
No, him . . . does he know?

MRS. HELMER *(smiling)*
Try to say 'father.' It can be done with a little practice. And he really is your father. That I can assure you. *(In a different tone)* Do you hate him?

LEIF *(slightly shocked, thinks a moment)*
No . . . no, I don't hate him . . .

MRS. HELMER
Are you ashamed of him?

LEIF

I don't know.

MRS. HELMER

Because he has become a bishop?

LEIF *(almost a little hysterical)*

I don't know, mother. I honestly don't know. There are some things which ... which I've always pushed away from me ... didn't want to think about ...

MRS. HELMER

Try to think about them. *(Pause)* You asked if your father knew about Agnes and Dr. Tornkvist ... that's his name. No, your father, during the last half year, has thought of nothing but his fight for the ordination. It's just like when America elects a president ... just as tense and just as ...

LEIF

Dirty?

MRS. HELMER

Just as brutal.

LEIF

But now it's over. *(At this moment the church bells nearby ring loudly as a sign that the service is over)*

MRS. HELMER *(as if she cannot believe it)*

Well, it's over now. Now he's Bishop of Elveness!

Pause. Leif goes to the window, looks out, the bells continue to ring steadily.

LEIF

There he comes out of the church ... *(Impressed against his will)* How proudly he carries himself ... right through the common herd ... alone. *(Turns)* He must feel lonely today, mother. None of us in church ...

MRS. HELMER *(firmly)*
I'm a renegade.

LEIF
And I'm a heathen. But what about Agnes?

MRS. HELMER *(softly, weakly)*
You'd better ask her.

LEIF *(at the window again)*
Alone . . . only little Miss Monsen in his wake, as always.

MRS. HELMER
She's a faithful soul.

LEIF *(quickly away from the window)*
Here he comes.

Mrs. Helmer rises. Together they stand and look toward the door. In spite of all they have just said to each other, there is something deferential in the way they stand, as if they await a great man. The doors are thrown open and Bishop Sigurd Helmer enters in canonical robes. He is tall, erect, and handsome, in his early 50's, a clever man. He bears himself as a prince of the church. At the sight of his wife, he smiles, broadly, warmly, and openly. And her expression changes . . . one understands that she loves him. They stand thus for a moment, looking at each other with this mutual smile . . . then she breaks the mood by snatching up a cigarette box from the table and holding it out toward him.

MRS. HELMER
A cigarette, Sigurd? I can imagine that it was exhausting. *(Miss Monsen has slipped in quite unnoticed behind the bishop. She is an insignificant, colorless woman, about 35. At Mrs. Helmer's remark she bursts out)*

MISS MONSEN
> It was great! It was wonderful!

The bishop says nothing. Shakes his head and smiles. During the following, his wife lights his cigarette, he inhales deeply and happily.

MRS· HELMER *(to Miss Monsen)*
> You say that as if you had seen the heavens open.

MISS MONSEN
> I saw the dawn of a new day. A new day for the church.

MRS. HELMER
> For mankind too?

MISS MONSEN
> Yes!

MRS. HELMER
> Let's hope so . . . Won't you sit down?

HELMER
> We have only a few minutes. The guests have already begun to arrive and I must change. Is everything ready? . . . Hello there, Leif.

LEIF *(embarrassed)*
> Hello . . . and congratulations.

HELMER *(with a broad smile)*
> Does that come from the heart?

LEIF *(looks down)*
> I . . . I don't know.

HELMER
> All right, my boy. Thanks all the same.

AGNES *(coming in quickly through the sliding doors which she closes behind her)*

They've started to come. You must get yourselves ready.

HELMER *(arms outstretched toward her)*
Good day, my little friend.

AGNES *(looks down)*
Good day, father. *(Looks up, right at him, coldly)* You must hurry.

HELMER *(looks at her, his smile fades, his arms fall . . . a pause)*
Well, well, all right, we'll go.

He takes his wife with him, his arm around her shoulders. Leif follows, and finally Miss Monsen. Agnes remains standing alone after the others leave. She looks after them, her face stiff with bitterness, almost hate. Arvid Tornkvist comes into sight behind her through the door. He is a tall, impressive man, an important theological scholar, about 40. There is something dark and fanatical about him. At the moment he is full of a violent inner excitement and anger.

AGNES *(after a moment, turns and sees him)*
You? Have you come?

TORNKVIST
Yes.

AGNES
To join them in there?

TORNKVIST
No.

AGNES
That would have been too much!

TORNKVIST
He didn't think so . . . He invited me.

AGNES
  And so you have come?

TORNKVIST
  To speak to him.

AGNES *(tense)*
  About us?

TORNKVIST
  No.

AGNES
  Shall . . . shall I take your hat and coat?

TORNKVIST
  No.

AGNES
  You're so strange, Arvid. It's almost as if you can't
  bear to speak to me.

TORNKVIST *(standing by the sewing table, emphasizing each
  word with a blow of his fist on the table, not in a violent manner, but with a strange, inexorable rhythm)*
  I have come to speak to Bishop Helmer! Fetch him!

AGNES
  They are just going to sit down at the table.

TORNKVIST
  Fetch him!

AGNES
  But, Arvid, isn't it best to . . . ?

TORNKVIST
  What I have to say to Bishop Helmer cannot wait. Fetch
  him!

AGNES
  Yes . . . yes . . . *(She goes to the sliding doors, parts*

them slightly, we hear the voices of the guests. She looks back for a second at Tornkvist, who stands motionless with his black hat in his hand, then she goes into the dining room. A moment later the sliding doors are opened wider so that we see more of the party. The bishop hurries in with a broad smile, shuts the doors behind him and walks toward Tornkvist with outstretched hand. He is wearing a dark suit.)

HELMER
I'm pleased that you wanted to come, Tornkvist!

TORNKVIST *(ignoring the outstretched hand)*
Had you expected it?

HELMER *(smiling with slight embarrassment)*
No, not really, to be perfectly frank. But you give me great pleasure. Peace between us is my highest wish.

TORNKVIST
He who has won the bishop's crozier can afford to bury the hatchet?

HELMER *(laughs)*
Yes, exactly. *(Seriously.)* I well understand that you think the bishop's crozier would suit your hand better, and I do not presume to judge to what extent the best man won . . . but, in any case, the struggle is now at an end.

TORNKVIST
That I do not believe.

HELMER *(laughs a little)*
Nor do I, not really! We two will never agree . . . But take off your coat. Let's go in and dine.

TORNKVIST
I have come to talk to you.

HELMER

Yes, and I look forward to that . . . but later . . . over coffee, perhaps?

TORNKVIST

We will speak here and now!

HELMER *(pulled up by Tornkvist's tone, at last understands that there is war in the air)*

I don't think I quite understand you, Dr. Tornkvist. I cannot let my guests wait . . . Bishop Steen . . . the district governor. . .

TORNKVIST

That you will have to do!

HELMER *(taken aback, takes a step toward him. They look each other in the eyes. They are both strong men)*

That . . . I . . . will . . . have . . . to . . . do! If it weren't so absurd, I'd think that you were threatening me.

TORNKVIST

I may come to that.

HELMER *(the prince of the church speaks)*

Dr. Tornkvist, I know that there are forces behind you. I know that you speak for a large part of the people, for a powerful . . . and in my opinion . . . an unpleasant faction of the church. I know that you are a highly respected scholar. But you are also a pastor. Don't forget that. You stand before your bishop. Take care how you threaten him.

During the last five or six lines, Agnes has come in and shut the doors behind her. She stands, dark clad, against the white doors and listens pale and tense. Neither of the men has noticed that she is there.

TORNKVIST

You sit in my bishop's chair, Helmer.

HELMER *(he is furious, but laughs)*

You go too far, Tornkvist. You have lost the battle we two have fought. It is the law of life and the law of God that one shall accept his defeat like a man. You didn't lose because you would make a poorer bishop. No, you and your cohorts lost because a hell lies between your Christianity and mine; because, at last, God be praised, mankind is rising up, throwing off the yoke of dogma and seeing a greater, more beautiful God; casting off the fear of everlasting hell with which you and yours have held them down for a thousand years!

TORNKVIST

You preach your godlessness to me, Helmer . . . in your rash anger, more audaciously than you dare to preach it from the bishop's pulpit. And you can go on preaching as long as you have breath. Preach to that slack humanity which arrogantly dares to select and reject from God's Holy Word. Those who comfort themselves with leniency and mercy . . . but cast aside, as worn-out dogma, that warning written in blood in the heavens, that warning of punishment for evil-doing!

HELMER *(throws out his hands in a gesture of resignation)*

Here we go again, Tornkvist . . . and I really haven't the time . . . *(Glances toward the door, sees Agnes)* What are you doing in here?

AGNES

I'm listening.

HELMER

You'd better go in there.

AGNES
  I prefer to stay here.

HELMER
  Go in there.

TORNKVIST
  Let her listen. It will do her good. What I have to say
  may have significance for her.

AGNES *(strongly)*
  What you say means everything to me.

HELMER *(genuinely curious)*
  What's this, my child? What do you mean by that?

AGNES
  Arvid and I love each other, father.

HELMER *(amazed)*
  You want to marry?

AGNES
  Yes.

TORNKVIST
  That's possible . . . I don't know. If she's able to make
  a choice. It's difficult, perhaps an impossible choice.
  *(Neither Agnes nor the bishop understands the meaning
  of his words. Helmer misunderstands positively)*

HELMER *(with a sudden hearty laugh)*
  Oh, Tornkvist, Tornkvist! I'll never understand you. So
  that was what *had* to be said . . . here and now, while
  the roast veal gets cold!

TORNKVIST
  You don't understand . . .

HELMER *(continuing)*
  And as always you start your negotiations by con-

demning me to your everlasting hell! Yes, you are magnificent, and that's just what I like about you. Never in
agreement, always in conflict. We are enemies in many
things, but you are a real man!

TORNKVIST *(bitterly)*
Listen to me, Helmer . . .

HELMER *(interrupting)*
Indeed, this is all so unnecessary, my friend. You
must understand that I'm delighted. Delighted and flat-
tered . . . and happy on my child's behalf. She couldn't
find a better man. Margrethe will be enraptured.

TORNKVIST *(about to explode)*
You understand nothing. . . .

HELMER
Of course I understand. It's you who do not understand
a simple human truth. . . that I'm proud to have you as
my son-in-law, even though I despise you as a theologian.
That I heartily stretch out my hand to you as a straightforward man, even though I shall fight against your
beliefs with all the means at my command. Come now,
both of you . . . *(Hurries toward the dining room)*

TORNKVIST *(bangs his fist on the table)*
I came here to discuss neither marriage nor theology . . .
but the penal code.

HELMER *(at the sliding doors, turns)*
What . . .?

TORNKVIST
I have said that you sit in my bishop's chair and I say
it again! Yes, you have truly fought against me with all
possible means . . . with the basest, vilest means.

HELMER (*more shocked than angry*)
 In God's name, what are you saying, man?

TORNKVIST (*with an icy, unpleasant calm*)
 That you have stolen your holy office, that you have
 disgraced that office, that you shall, in shame and ignominy, be cast out of it.

HELMER
 You must be mad!

TORNKVIST
 Like a creeping mole you have dug the earth from under
 me . . . confident that no one could find your trail. And
 you have won. But now comes the reckoning, Helmer.

HELMER (*surprisingly calm*)
 I ought to ask you to leave. But that would solve nothing, Tornkvist. What is all this? What strange hallu-
 cinations are you suffering from? I have no idea what
 you're referring to.

TORNKVIST (*contemptuously*)
 Oh, no? You have no idea?

HELMER (*on the verge of becoming angry, controls himself*)
 There is so little purpose in quarrelling and it little becomes men of the church. I beg you, quite quietly and
 calmly: Explain what you mean by all this? (*Tornkvist
 takes a letter from his pocket, unfolds it, and lays it
 on the table. Helmer takes the letter and reads it, show-
 ing no reaction on his face*) I have heard, naturally,
 that such letters exist . . . there are probably dozens
 which blacken me too.

TORNKVIST
 No, strangely enough, there are none against you.

HELMER

No? Well, that's gratifying to hear. *(Gives the letter back)*

TORNKVIST

What would you say about a man of the church who spreads that sort of anonymous letter? *(Drops the letter on the table where it lies)*

HELMER

I would call him a vile rascal, Tornkvist, and you should know me well enough to be aware of that. The church, unfortunately, is not infallible. We both well know that there is hatred, intrigue, and malice. This isn't the first time that such cankers have burst forth in one or another parish council. Some hysterical eccentric dips his pen and spreads venom.

TORNKVIST

That letter was not written by any hysterical eccentric, Helmer. It was written by a crafty and calculating man, a man with insight and knowledge; one who knew exactly where to strike.

HELMER *(takes a cigarette with great calm and lights it)*
Am I to understand that you, in one way or another, make me responsible for these letters?

TORNKVIST

Yes.

HELMER

That I can simply have written them myself?

TORNKVIST

Yes.

HELMER *(exhales, stretches his chest, controlling his anger, speaks calmly)*

I agree with you that we must talk this out ... here and now. I cannot, unfortunately, offer you the bishop's seat, but will you take another?

TORNKVIST

I will stand.

HELMER *(puts his cigarette aside, walks to the dining room doors. Agnes, who has been standing motionless before the doors, steps aside and during the following, she remains in the darkened background, listening. Helmer opens the doors, and speaks, facing the dining room)*
Dear friends, forgive me for having so unpardonably kept you waiting. And forgive me that I must stay away from my own celebration for a short time longer. I take it as a good sign for my work here in the bishopric that duty has already called me. A man in spiritual need has sought me out, and he has first claim on my time and energy. I ask my colleague, Bishop Steen, to be host in my stead for the time being. I bid you sit down and partake of what we have to offer. And I wish you all as heartily welcome as I myself have been welcomed here today. *(Voices and the reaction of the guests are heard.)* And I must ask my secretary, Miss Monsen, to come and help me for a moment. *(Miss Monsen comes in after a second, uncomprehending, sees Dr. Tornkvist, and an anxious expression crosses her face. Helmer shuts the doors, draws the portieres across them so that the noise from the dining room is no longer heard, turns and walks quietly to the table where he sits while indicating a chair for Miss Monsen at the other end of the same table)* Take your notebook, Miss Monsen. *(Sees that she has nothing with which to write)* You'll find pencil and paper there. *(Indicating the desk. She goes and gets what she needs, while he continues)* Dr. Tornkvist

has certain things to say to me of which I wish to have an accurate record. You are presumably aware, Dr. Tornkvist, that your words to me are of such a character that they cannot be considered as a personal altercation between us two?

TORNKVIST

I am entirely aware of that. *(Miss Monsen takes her seat)*

HELMER

Then perhaps you will be so kind as to formulate your contention.

TORNKVIST *(fluently and easily)*

I accuse Sigurd Helmer, at present Bishop of Elveness, of having obtained his position by underhanded means, illegally, and in a manner unworthy of a servant of the church; by means which should make him unwarranted to hold that office. I accuse him further of having, in writing, spread mendacious rumors and charges aimed at disparaging me, Dr. Arvid Tornkvist, in the public's esteem . . . Do I speak too quickly?

MISS MONSEN

Not at all.

TORNKVIST

He has done this by composing an anonymous letter appealing to everyone to withhold his vote from me in the election of the Bishop of Elveness. He has written this letter on his typewriter, mimeographed it, and sent it out to at least thirty-six persons, primarily ministers, members of the parish council, and others who had influence in the election of the Bishop of Elveness. Thank you.

HELMER

Did you get all of that, Miss Monsen?

MISS MONSEN

Yes.

HELMER *(lights a cigarette)*

And you really believe this about me?

TORNKVIST

Yes. *(To Miss Monsen)* If you will type that out, I'll
be glad to sign it.

MISS MONSEN

I have no typewriter here.

TORNKVIST

You can send it to me in the morning.

HELMER

I had no idea that your defeat in this election had hit
you so hard, Tornkvist. I am greatly distressed over
this. In many ways, you are a fanatic; that can be a
strength, but not always. For all your quick intelligence,
you do not always think clearly. Is there really nothing
that tells you that all this is absurd?

TORNKVIST

No.

HELMER

And you stick to this grotesque accusation? Perhaps
even publicly.

TORNKVIST

Of course, publicly. This is not something I confide to
you for your own pleasure.

HELMER

Well, in that case, I cannot help you very much. But

have you thought of the sad, unpredictable consequences for our church when I'm forced to call you to account?

TORNKVIST

Yes, I have. But in the long run it will benefit the church to be rid of an unworthy servant.

HELMER *(rises, takes a few steps)*

I ought to be angry. I'm usually not a patient man. But I find this only tragic. Good Heavens, Tornkvist, there are certainly chasms between our points of view, but we have always fought on a straightforward basis. *This* is surely not worthy of you. *This* you must not do!

TORNKVIST

You bid me keep silent?

HELMER

Yes, I certainly do. It will profit no one to start a church dispute over this slanderous nonsense.

TORNKVIST

It's not nonsense. It's the wicked truth.

HELMER

Listen here! You are right when you say that all this is more than a discussion on theology. You are right when you say that this is a question for the penal code. You obviously have no great respect for your bishop, and that is, as far as I'm concerned, quite immaterial. But you should have respect for the law. You should know that you cannot make such accusations without proving them.

TORNKVIST

I intend to prove them.

HELMER

You intend . . . what? How?

TORNKVIST

I'll tell you how. In spite of all your slyness and cal-
culation, you have forgotten that nowadays a typewriter
has peculiar characteristics as clear as handwriting.

HELMER (*crushes out his cigarette with an indignant gesture*)

That's enough! Now I must ask you to go! And if you
really mean what you say, then you ought to go to the
police!

TORNKVIST

I've already done that. (*Bows formally and goes toward
door*)

AGNES

Wait for me, Arvid! (*Tornkvist stops, turns, waits in
the open door. She walks toward him*)

HELMER (*quietly*)

Are you going with him?

AGNES (*without looking at him*)

Yes.

HELMER

After all that he has said to me?

AGNES

Yes. (*Walks quickly past Tornkvist. He follows her, and
shuts the door*)

*Helmer sits motionless, with no outward sign of emotion.
He slowly takes a cigarette, puts it in his mouth, strikes
a match, and sits with it burning in his hand in deep*

thought.

MISS MONSEN

I beg your pardon, Bishop . . .

HELMER

Yes? *(Drops the match in the ashtray, turns slowly toward her)* Yes?

MISS MONSEN

May I . . . may I go now?

HELMER *(with a weak smile)*

Do you believe him too, Miss Monsen?

MISS MONSEN *(with violent emotion)*

No! How can you . . . how can you . . .? I? I know that you could never do such a thing! *(Sobbing)* Oh, this is horrible, horrible! I must tell you that . . .

HELMER

Another time, Miss Monsen! Go home now. Calm yourself. Don't think any more about this.

MISS MONSEN

But if he really . . .

HELMER

No, no, my dear. *(Laughs bitterly)* We must try to understand him. We must remember that for many years he has felt himself called to this office. Is it any wonder that his world crumbles before his eyes today . . . when he sees his worst enemy put in his place? I myself would have felt it as a burning wound, as an intolerable defeat if he had won . . . I could hardly have borne it.

MISS MONSEN

I know that!

HELMER *(smiles warmly)*

Yes, you know that better than anyone else. Often you have had to comfort me, strengthen me when things looked black. And how incredibly black they looked at times. You, you know that! *(Rises, walks back and forth)* But you also know that it was something more than the bishop's title I fought for. I had to defeat him. Had to! It was and is the whole purpose of my life! Because he, pious and sincere though he is, nevertheless bears something evil within himself. Because he is the symbol of reaction, of the rockbound orthodox claims to power, power at any price. Power over minds. Power over words and meanings. Power over life and knowledge. Power through fear . . . My God is no bogeyman. My congregation shall not be a flock of cowards. I will be a freeborn bishop, midst freeborn people who do not drop their gaze in terror because of some mystical retribution in the great hereafter!

MISS MONSEN *(carried away)*
Yes! Yes!

HELMER *(hearing this emits a little laugh)*
Here I go sermonizing again! Well, well, go home now. All this has been upsetting, but now it's over.

MISS MONSEN
But think if . . .

HELMER
My dear, he is an intelligent man. Tomorrow he will see quite clearly how meaningless it all is. Just go on home now.

MISS MONSEN
But . . .

HELMER *(decisively)*
I would like to be alone now. We'll meet at the office tomorrow as usual.

MISS MONSEN
Very well . . . *(She walks hesitantly toward the door. He watches her with a smile)*

HELMER

Don't worry. Everything will work out all right.

She goes out with a bowed head. Helmer stands a moment, seems to shake off some thought, walks to the window, opens it. He stands there looking out. It has begun to grow dark. After a short pause, Mrs. Helmer comes in hurriedly from the dining room, looks about and sees him.

MRS. HELMER

Has he gone, Sigurd?

HELMER *(turns and smiles)*

Yes, he has gone.

MRS. HELMER

What did he want?

HELMER

He has gone mad. Completely mad.

MRS. HELMER

And Agnes?

HELMER

She too. She left with him.

MRS. HELMER

I sat in there and had such a   strange feeling that you needed me, Sigurd . . .

HELMER

And I do . . . But ought we not join our guests?

MRS. HELMER

Will it help you to tell me about it?

HELMER

Yes, of course. It's only so utterly stupid. *(Walks over*

to the table, picks up the anonymous letter and hands it to her) Read this.

MRS. HELMER *(reads gravely)*
Does he blame you for this?

HELMER
He maintains that I have written it with my own hand!

MRS. HELMER
Have you?

HELMER
Have I? Do you ask me if I have written that filthy letter and sent it out in order to destroy Tornkvist? You *know* I have not!

MRS. HELMER *(looks directly at him and nods)*
Yes, I know it now . . . and I'm glad.

HELMER
That you could even ask at all! As if anyone could believe a thing like that about *me.*

MRS. HELMER
Many will believe it, Sigurd.

HELMER
What are you saying?

MRS. HELMER
Many will believe it. Didn't Agnes believe it?

HELMER *(seems to be shocked by this thought. Stops suddenly)*
Yes, without hesitation. My own daughter believed it without the slightest hesitation.

MRS. HELMER
That doesn't surprise me very much, Sigurd. If I knew only the clergyman in you, I might have believed it my-

self. But I also know the man you are, the man I love. I know that there is still something in you which is pure metal, something upright and honest which your dangerous career has not yet been able to destroy.

HELMER

Do you call a life in God's service a dangerous career?

MRS. HELMER

Yes, I do. From a lifetime of experience, I do. The older I become, the more I revere God and despise his servants.

HELMER

Do you despise me too?

MRS. HELMER

I love you. You are my whole life. And one must take life as it comes.

HELMER

What you say is shocking. It is out and out blasphemy.

MRS. HELMER

But it's true, Sigurd. My father was a clergyman, as was yours. The first sound I can remember is the ringing of church bells; the second, my father's voice intoning the service. It seemed to me to ring beautifully then; in a certain way, it still does. But now I hear, first and foremost, a hollow ringing. I have learned to abhor the ecclesiastical profession; religion has become a handicraft; piety a trade.

HELMER

No! No, and again, no! To me it's a life work; for me, the only conceivable life work.

MRS. HELMER

How easy it was to believe that long ago when we first

began; long ago, when you toiled around the clock as a seamen's pastor, in dirt and poverty. How easy it was to love you then! It became harder when you, like all the others, began to climb; when you began looking about for greener pastures, when you set your sights on the bishopric, when every fellow-pastor who dared to compete with you for the position became an enemy . . .

HELMER

No, listen here . . .

MRS. HELMER

An enemy, I say! Whom you heedlessly made small and ridiculous with your sharp tongue and your dangerous intelligence.

HELMER

So this is what you have thought about me all these years!

MRS. HELMER

Yes. It's good to be able to say it for once. And it had to be said sometime or other. For you have pushed yourself so far out on the edge of the precipice that a thing like this . . . *(points to the letter)* is not inconceivable. This is why the world will so easily believe it. This is why your own children will doubt you. Because to them you are a climber, a man with the morals of a Jesuit: that the end justifies the means.

HELMER *(coldly)*

And I say no! No one will believe it. People know me! An upright man of the church, severe in dispute, but honest. They will search in vain in this letter for my way of thinking.

MRS. HELMER

That's where you're wrong, Sigurd. In this letter, they'll

find your way of thinking. It's a clever letter; it strikes as you and only you can strike.

HELMER

Give it to me. (*He seizes the letter and reads as she continues to speak*)

MRS. HELMER

Many of your opinions about Tornkvist are in that letter . . . much of what you have said about him in intimate circles. Everything in the letter has an ugly and twisted form, a malice, a scornful spite which is not like you. But the thoughts, you *have* thought them.

HELMER (*putting the letter quietly on the table*)

It's appalling to hear you say all this. Because it's so untrue, so bitterly unjust. I'm not a climber. It is written that no man shall bury his talents in the earth. I have seen the path before me as God staked it out! I have fought and struggled because God's church needs my abilities, because I am destined to be one of its leaders. In a time of fear and uncertainty, I stand where God has placed me, in order to give the light of faith and mercy to frightened souls.

MRS. HELMER

Take care that you don't concern yourself so completely with the souls of others that you lose your own.

HELMER

Margrethe! Are you turning your back on me? Is everything falling to pieces between us? Is all that seems so great to me, only small and paltry to you?

MRS. HELMER

No, Sigurd. I'm not turning my back. Never! Whatever happens, you have me. Whatever you say or do, for me, you are the only one. Whatever you do, you are my beloved, for whom I shall fight to my last breath.

HELMER

You speak as if I were in danger.

MRS. HELMER

You *are* in danger.

HELMER

Nonsense. Tornkvist was completely off-balance today. When he's had time to think about it he will send me an apology. *(Pauses)* Hadn't we better join our guests?

MRS. HELMER

Yes, I think we must.

HELMER

So we'll forget about all this! *(With forced gaiety)* I've already completely forgotten about Tornkvist. And Agnes will surely come home this evening. We'll burn this letter . . . and cancel out the well-meant little sermon delivered by the bishop's wife.

MRS. HELMER

Yes, we'll do that. *(They walk toward the dining room)*

MAID *(enters)*

Excuse me, Bishop Helmer.

HELMER

Yes, what is it?

MAID

There's a gentleman here asking to speak to the bishop. He's from the police.

Curtain

ACT TWO

Scene 1

*In the bishop's office, the next morning. It is an old room,
in an old church, with thick walls and gothic-arched doors.
The modern equipment, ugly desks, etc. . . . seem out of
place. The bishop's inner office is in the foreground; the
outer office can be seen back stage through a large wide
door. Miss Monsen sits in the outer office. In the bishop's
room there is a large old-fashioned fireplace in the right
wall. As the curtain rises, Bishop Helmer is sitting at his
desk reading the morning newspaper. He is dressed in an
ordinary dark suit. We hear the sound of Miss Monsen's
typewriter.*

HELMER

Oh, Miss Monsen. *(The machine stops. She comes to the
door)*

MISS MONSEN

Yes?

HELMER

Do you have the letter to the Ministry of Ecclesiastical
Affairs ready?

MISS MONSEN

Yes, Bishop. Would you like to sign it now?

HELMER

I'd better. They're waiting for it. I think you ought to
run down to the post office and send it off at once.

MISS MONSEN

Very well. *(Goes out. The bishop picks up his newspaper, stretches, hums. He seems untroubled. Miss Monsen enters with the letter, which he signs)*

HELMER *(smiles at her)*
Well, Miss Monsen, did you get any sleep last night?

MISS MONSEN
No.

HELMER *(chuckling)*
I rather thought not. You know, every now and then I'm quite alarmed by your fidelity. Indeed, you take my small worries much more to heart than I do myself.

MISS MONSEN
But it was so unpleasant. He was so . . . so relentless.

HELMER *(laughs)*
Tornkvist is relentless both by profession and by nature. We're used to him. But I admit that I wouldn't have believed he could make himself so completely ridiculous.

MISS MONSEN
Has he . . .?

HELMER
Can you believe that he has sicked the police on me?

MISS MONSEN *(terror-stricken)*
The police!

HELMER
Yes, indeed. A very pleasant officer paid me a visit. Now, now, take it easy; it was only a formality. He understood at once that the whole matter was pure nonsense. Believe me, my friend, we'll hear no more of this business. And I've decided to consider the matter closed. We can all lose our heads at times. One must look at such things with forbearance. I would like to forget the whole affair too. It's nothing one should talk about.

MISS MONSEN

No, naturally . . .

HELMER

Now run along to the post office. The letter should get off on the eleven o'clock train.

MISS MONSEN

Very well. (*She exits. We see her through the door putting on her hat and coat. Suddenly she turns, startled. Someone we cannot see has come into the outer office. She goes toward him out of our sight*)

VOICE (*outside*)

Good morning, miss. I'd like to have a word with the bishop. (*A second later, Miss Monsen comes to the door. She is pale as death and supports herself a moment on the door frame, then enters the bishop's office, shutting the door behind her*)

HELMER

Yes?

MISS MONSEN

It's . . . it's the Chief of Police.

HELMER

The Chief of Police? He wants to speak to me?

MISS MONSEN

Yes.

HELMER (*shakes off a moment's uneasiness, smiles*)

Well, indeed. Show him in, then. (*Laughs*) And take it easy. You look as if you'd seen a ghost. (*Miss Monsen leans against the door, is silent, looks frightened*) And don't forget the letter. (*She goes out, leaving the door open. The Chief of Police and a police detective, Bjerke, enter. The Chief is an elderly, jovial cynic; Bjerke, a*

*thin, melancholy, taciturn man who looks on everything
and everyone with extreme suspicion. The Chief walks
toward the bishop with a large, hearty smile and an
outstretched hand. Helmer rises)*

POLICE CHIEF

Good morning, Bishop. And welcome to our little community. We have met briefly, if you remember, but you
are hardly an old acquaintance of the police as yet,
eh? Do you play bridge?

HELMER

Very badly.

POLICE CHIEF

Same here. We must get together ... Well, now ...
excuse us for disturbing you. This is Detective Bjerke.
An able man. Suspicious as the dev ... Well, hm ... er ..

HELMER

Won't you sit down?

POLICE CHIEF

Thank you. *(Sits)* Ugh ... it's cold in this old vault!

HELMER

Cigarette?

POLICE CHIEF

No, thank you ... It's about those letters, naturally.

HELMER

But ... I explained everything to the police yesterday.

POLICE CHIEF

Yes, yes, that's true. As far as that goes. Have it here.
*(Takes a report from his pocket; puts his glasses on his
nose with a quick gesture, reads, mumbling)* Yes, here it
is ... 'when questioned about the said document, the

above-named declared ...' (*Mumbles further, stops, snaps off his glasses, smiles broadly*) in short, nothing but chitter-chatter and twiddle-twaddle 'ad infinitum,' eh, Bishop?

HELMER

I beg your pardon?

POLICE CHIEF

You state emphatically that the whole business is tommy-rot and rubbish which the police should consider themselves too smart to take seriously?

HELMER

Yes, exactly.

POLICE CHIEF

Well, Bishop, that's putting it on the line. But we can't call it much of an explanation.

HELMER

How can I explain something with which I haven't the slightest connection?

POLICE CHIEF

Well, that's easy for you to say. Yes, *you* can say that. But I'm expected to find an explanation.

HELMER

Well, then ... so you must try, of course. Yet I fail to see what purpose it will serve. A stupid, anonymous letter without any significance ...

POLICE CHIEF

Without significance? No, I disagree with you there, Bishop. I don't think you should belittle this matter.

HELMER

Very well, make the matter as big or as little as you like. It's completely irrelevant to me.

POLICE CHIEF

I don't doubt that for a second. But ... *somebody* wrote that letter. And mimeographed it. And paid postage to send it out into the world.

HELMER

It looks that way, yes.

POLICE CHIEF

And that somebody had a motive. Are we in agreement thus far?

HELMER

What motive?

POLICE CHIEF

Isn't that as clear as daylight? The motive was to ruin Dr. Tornkvist's chances and get *you* ordained as Bishop of Elveness.

HELMER *(stiffly)*

There's an implied suspicion in what you say. Police Chief.

POLICE CHIEF

Not at all ... it's a fact.

HELMER

A suspicion, I say. And I say as well that I am above such absurd suspicions.

POLICE CHIEF

Well, above and above. I know nothing more about you than that you are a bishop. And, frankly speaking, that's not enough in itself. My hobby is history, you see. History's full of enterprising bishops.

HELMER

I don't like your tone, sir!

POLICE CHIEF

Then I beg your pardon. I spoke quite generally, you understand . . . How many typewriters have you?

HELMER

Typewriters?

POLICE CHIEF

Exactly. You have been formally accused of having written anonymous letters on one of your typewriters. That's why Bjerke is here to take a look at them.

HELMER

So you're starting a regular investigation on this absurd basis.

POLICE CHIEF

Have I any other choice? I'm a public official. I can as little shelve cases as you can refuse to officiate.

HELMER

And you don't take into consideration the painful scandal such an investigation can mean for the whole church?

POLICE CHIEF

Why, yes, Bishop. And, to tell you the truth, I'm enjoying this a bit. So little happens in my district. I must say that this case interests me, and its ecclesiastical aspect adds a spicy touch to the whole business.

HELMER *(has been walking back and forth during the last remarks, now stops and speaks coldly)*

Well, the typewriters are in the outer office. Go ahead.

POLICE CHIEF

Thank you. Well, Bjerke, get started. *(Bjerke hesitates, wants to say something. The Chief of Police understands)* Oh, yes, that's right. We've sent a couple of the letters we've been able to get hold of to the police laboratory. It may be possible to get some fingerprints from them. Have you any objections to Bjerke's taking yours?

HELMER

My fingerprints?

POLICE CHIEF

It doesn't hurt. Just takes a second.

HELMER

Like a common criminal!

POLICE CHIEF

Far from it. Merely a routine matter. But you can refuse, of course.

HELMER

I have no reason whatsoever for refusing.

POLICE CHIEF

No, I thought not. All right, Bjerke.

Bjerke has placed a white sheet of paper and an inked pad on the desk. Helmer goes to the desk. Bjerke takes his hand and makes routine fingerprints.

BJERKE

Thank you. (*Puts his equipment in his briefcase, goes into the outer office and during the following conversation we hear him taking samples of the typewriter scripts*)

HELMER (*wiping his fingers on his handkerchief, angrily*)
I feel degraded and dirtied.

POLICE CHIEF (*dryly*)
It comes off with warm water.

HELMER *(formally)*

Is there anything more you wish to ask me?

POLICE CHIEF

There is, unfortunately. It's my duty. You may think I perform my duty in a rather unpleasant manner and I have to agree with you there . . . You have a mimeograph machine out there, I see.

HELMER

A mimeo . . . Yes, and what of that?

POLICE CHIEF *(as if thinking aloud)*

Nothing. The letters were mimeographed, but there are plenty of those machines about.

HELMER

I assume so.

POLICE CHIEF *(as if thinking aloud)*

Yes, I am perhaps unpleasant. . . . It's because I'm so democratic, Bishop. I don't like being awakened in the middle of the night by the Minister of Justice with orders to investigate this case *personally* just because it concerns such a fine gentleman! As if Bjerke wasn't good enough!

HELMER *(dismayed)*

The Minister of Justice?

POLICE CHIEF

None other. This is a serious matter, you see. *(Bjerke has come in again.)* Well, Bjerke?

BJERKE

It's none of those. But we knew that already.

HELMER

Well, are you satisfied now?

POLICE CHIEF

Not entirely. (*Mentions somewhat off-handedly*) As
you probably know, the police have samples of practi-
cally all makes of typewriters in use. We can therefore
see at once that the anonymous letter was not written
on an ordinary office machine like those out there . . .
Have you a portable typewriter?

HELMER (*has become pale and uneasy. Looks about*)

A portable?

POLICE CHIEF

Listen, now, Bishop. That's an easy question to answer.
Either you have one or you don't. A portable typewriter!

HELMER

As a matter of fact, I do have such a typewriter.

POLICE CHIEF

Good! Let's have a look at it.

HELMER

Certainly. (*Goes to a cupboard, opens it, stands still,
surprised*) It's not here!

POLICE CHIEF

Well, then it's somewhere else. Shall Bjerke help you
look?

HELMER (*nervously*)

No . . . no, thank you . . . Where in the world can it be?
(*Searches, opens cupboards, drawers, etc.*)

POLICE CHIEF (*pleasantly*)

There's no hurry. We have plenty of time. (*Rises, shakes
off the cold, rubs his hands*) You keep it ice-cold in
here. I think I'll put on my coat. (*Walks into the outer
office, comes back at once putting on his coat. Sits*

again. Bjerke stands motionless, following all the bish-op's movements with his eyes)

HELMER *(speaking as he searches)*
It's a very small machine, you see . . . Very practical for travelling . . . flat as a little box . . . very light-weight.

BJERKE
A Romeo, perhaps? Green. Light metal. German make?

HELMER *(nervous, but nevertheless **unaware of its full significance**)*
Yes . . . as a matter of fact it *is* a Romeo.

POLICE CHIEF
It would be nice if you could find it.

HELMER *(slightly desperate)*
Miss Monsen! Miss Monsen . . . No, I forgot, she's gone to the post office.

POLICE CHIEF
When did you have it last?

HELMER *(thinks)*
I . . . I really can't remember . . . There has been so much lately . . . moving . . . the ordination . . . my trips here and there . .

POLICE CHIEF
I can understand that. Perhaps you left it behind some-where on one of your trips?

HELMER
That's possible, of course . . .

POLICE CHIEF
Lost it, perhaps?

HELMER
No, no no! I can't have lost it!

POLICE CHIEF

Or somebody might have stolen it?

HELMER

Who could that have been?

POLICE CHIEF

Don't ask me. *(Yawns slightly. Rises)* It's not here, in any case. We can all see that. Will you please ring us as soon as you have located it?

HELMER

Yes, of course.

POLICE CHIEF

Then I guess we'd better be going. You undoubtedly have things to do.

HELMER

Surely you believe me when I tell you that I . . .

POLICE CHIEF

What I believe is of precious little importance, Bishop.

HELMER *(stiffens)*

Yes . . . naturally. I'm sure that I'll find the portable in the course of the day.

POLICE CHIEF

I'm sure you will. Goodbye, then. And thank you. *(Walks toward the door and signals to Bjerke to precede him. Turns toward Helmer when Bjerke has left)* I advise you to talk to a lawyer, Bishop. A good lawyer! *(Exit. Helmer stands a moment, looking after him, quite at a loss. Then he slowly walks to his desk and sits, staring into space. Lights a cigarette. More bewildered than frightened . . . one has the impression that he shakes his head and murmurs. 'The Minister of Justice!')*

Curtain

Scene 2

*The courtroom. In the back, large windows high up
on the paneled wall. On the left, slanting in toward stage
back, is the judges' bench on a raised platform. The judge
and his two assistant judges sit in black robes on high-
backed chairs behind the bench. The court stenographer
sits a little lower, near stage back. In the middle of the
stage, facing the judges' bench, is the witness box, an open
bar. Near the back is the Prosecuting Attorney's desk.
Toward the right are the defendant and his Counsel. Far
forward in the foreground, preferably halfway down in
the orchestra pit, is the press table, where five or six reporters, a couple of photographers with cameras, etc. can
be seen. On the right of stage back are chairs where Leif
and Mrs. Helmer sit...
As the curtain rises, two policemen force shut large doors
and lock them. Loud shouting of people is heard outside.
The two policemen take their places on either side of the
doors. Everyone is in his place except the judges. Bishop
Helmer is talking in a low voice with his lawyer, Lind.
The Prosecuting Attorney sits erect, looking into space. The
uniformed court clerk comes in through the door behind
the judges' bench, quickly puts some documents at the
judges' places, straightens up and announces.*

CLERK
   Will the court please rise. (*All stand. Sit quickly again
   after the judges have taken their places*)

JUDGE

The Court is in session. The criminal case against Bishop Helmer continues. *(Looks threateningly toward the public)* The court will not tolerate demonstrations such as those which occurred yesterday. I will not give further warning. At the slightest indication of contempt for the dignity of the court, I shall clear the room. This case has stirred up the whole country, yes, many other countries as well. I cannot, and will not, exclude the nearly one hundred reporters for national and international newspapers who are here in the courtroom. What they write is their business. Here in this court, however, nothing but clear, dispassionate facts will be tolerated. I insist that this be understood. And I further insist that the parties *(with a severe glance at the Prosecuting Attorney)* take my words to heart!

PROSECUTING ATTORNEY

Am I to interpret that as a criticism from the honorable judge of my conduct of the case?

JUDGE

The Prosecuting Attorney heard the words of the court. Next witness!

DEFENSE COUNSEL

Honorable judges! I request that this case be dismissed by the court, that the proceedings be discontinued without delay, and that the accusation against Bishop Helmer be withdrawn.

JUDGE

Such a request at this point in the trial is quite unusual. Defense Counsel has the floor in order to give his reasons for making such a request.

DEFENSE COUNSEL

Nothing is easier, Your Honor. And yet . . . I find it
bitterly difficult. Standing here, as I am now doing, with
thirty years at the bar behind me, I should have thought
that the court itself would have stopped this revolting
comedy without any need of argument from me . . . A
line must be drawn somewhere!! I am pleading a bishop's case although I myself am more or less on non-be-
liever. Nothing is sacred to me but justice! I have taken
this case because I know that an injustice has been committed here, a cruel injustice, against an upright and
honorable man in whom there is not a trace of guilt or
fraud. And I rise in protest because now the limit has
been reached. What is going on here in this courtroom
. . . in this highly cultivated community . . . is that the
court itself, justice itself, is allowing itself to be used
by the vile interests of the powers of darkness. Is allowing itself to be used in a planned action to destroy an
innocent man. During the past two days, the court has
heard the Prosecuting Attorney's line of argument. Can
anyone fail to see that he has not produced a shred of
evidence? Can anyone fail to see that there isn't even
an intention to prove anything? The powers which lie
behind this monstrous attack against Bishop Helmer do
not expect the impossible, do not expect to have him
condemned. But they do hope to so sully him, so discredit
him, that, in the end, when he leaves this courtroom
an acquitted man, he will, nevertheless, be a ruined
man. And they expect to achieve this with the very help
of the court. If that happens, then my faith . . . and the
faith of many . . . in justice will collapse in ruins. And
therefore I say . . . stop this performance. Now! At

once! Before it's too late. Before the dignity of the court has received a mortal blow!

PROSECUTING ATTORNEY

Your Honor, I protest, for the sake of form, against these pleadings ... aimed at the gallery and the press.

JUDGE

I have a profound respect for the high ideals of the Counsel for the Defense and the principles he maintains have the full support of this court. It must never be said that a court of justice allows itself to be used in the interest of one party or another. That shall not be said of this court. Proceed, Counsel for the Prosecution!

PROSECUTING ATTORNEY

I do not intend to engage in any sort of polemics. I submit an absolute and emphatic protest against a dismissal of this case. I have made a charge against Bishop Helmer on behalf of the Ministry of Justice. When I now demand that the proceedings continue, I am speaking for the highest legal authority of the land. Thank you.

JUDGE

I then ask the Prosecuting Attorney: Does the prosecution expect further evidence to provide concrete proof of the accused's guilt.

PROSECUTING ATTORNEY *(emphatically)*
Yes!

JUDGE *(after a short parley with the assistant judges)*
The proceedings will continue. Next witness ... *(Defense Counsel is silent but manifests obvious indignation and agitation)*

PROSECUTING ATTORNEY

I continue the examination of Dr. Arvid Tornkvist.

CLERK *(at the door in the right background)*

Dr. Tornkvist! *(Tornkvist enters quickly and goes over to the witness box. He does not glance at the bishop nor does Bishop Helmer change his expression at the sight of him)*

PROSECUTING ATTORNEY

Dr. Tornkvist, yesterday you went so far as to state your absolute conviction that Bishop Helmer must be the author of this anonymous letter. We must go into further detail. On what do you base your conviction? *(He counts the following arguments on his fingers)*

TORNKVIST

Helmer is my most implacable opponent. The attack on me served his and only his interests. Besides, there are matters referred to in the letter which he, and only he, knew about.

PROSECUTING ATTORNEY

Three good arguments. Continue!

TORNKVIST

The conflict behind this recent episcopal election was undeniably sharper than those outside the church can realize. Much was at stake, not merely the personal ambition of the man who wanted to be bishop. No, there were two irreconcilable opinions in the church which collided, personified by him and by me. He was determined, by any means, to rise to the top in order to destroy the basis of our creed.

DEFENSE COUNSEL

Because he would deprive you of your everlasting hell?

TORNKVIST

It's very easy to speak scornfully of these matters. I say: Beware the man who corrupts God's holy word! Beware the man who presumes to know better than the Holy Scriptures! Beware the man . . .

JUDGE

I don't think we need quite so much theology. The court wants facts.

PROSECUTING ATTORNEY

Exactly! Other facts which indicate that Helmer had written the letter?

TORNKVIST

The style of the letter and its tone point to him and him only.

PROSECUTING ATTORNEY

I remind the court here that experts have also established that the style of the letter compares very well with Bishop Helmer's style of writing.

DEFENSE COUNSEL

I object. No one has established anything at all. Any one who has read one of Bishop Helmer's innumerable articles could, very easily, copy his style.

JUDGE

Objection sustained. Continue!

PROSECUTING ATTORNEY

Dr. Tornkvist, suspicion is one thing; conviction is one thing. But proof is another.

TORNKVIST

He was foolish enough to give me proof. (*Excitement in the court. Helmer lifts his head and looks at Tornkvist with a wrinkled brow. Defense Counsel is tense*)

PROSECUTING ATTORNEY

In what way?

TORNKVIST

He had the impudence . . .

JUDGE

Tell us what he did in fact. It is the court's affair to decide whether or not it was an impudence.

TORNKVIST

He sent me, at the last moment, an invitation to the luncheon he gave in the Bishop's residence immediately after his ordination.

PROSECUTING ATTORNEY

You considered this an act of spite?

TORNKVIST

Of course, it was an obvious act of spite.

DEFENSE COUNSEL

Is the accusation now extended to include offensive luncheon invitations? What has this to do with the case?

TORNKVIST

There was something peculiar about the invitation card. All the others had been sent out many days before and were evidently filled out by his secretary on the office typewriter. I have one of those cards here. *(Takes a card out of his pocket)* And here is the one I received. *(Holds a card in each hand)* He has obviously written this one himself, as a malicious joke, I presume. It is written on another machine, certainly a portable.

DEFENSE COUNSEL

What are you driving at with those card tricks of yours?

TORNKVIST

I noticed that the 'o' in the word 'Tornkvist' had jumped halfway out of line. And I had seen that characteristic little jump before, in another document.

PROSECUTING ATTORNEY

Yes, in the anonymous letter!

The Prosecuting Attorney and the Defense Counsel both leap for the witness box.

JUDGE

To the court's bench, please! *(Prosecuting Attorney hands the cards to the judge. He studies them, the assistant judges looking over his shoulder)* It's true that this card is written on another typewriter; undoubtedly it can be established whether or not it was a portable.

DEFENSE COUNSEL

What on earth does that prove?

PROSECUTING ATTORNEY

That will be shown!

JUDGE

Silence! It is also correct that the 'o' in the word 'Tornkvist' seems to be out of line. Is it requested that these cards be accepted in evidence?

PROSECUTING ATTORNEY

Yes, Your Honor.

DEFENSE COUNSEL

Your Honor, I object. That card is printed. Only the words 'Dr. Tornkvist' are written on a typewriter. It is absurd to maintain on such flimsy evidence that the same machine wrote both the card and the anonymous letter.

JUDGE

The cards are admitted as evidence. But the court is inclined to agree with the Counsel for the Defense. The uneven 'o' cannot be accepted as incontestable evidence.

TORNKVIST

It was evidence enough for me.

JUDGE

That's your affair. Continue.

PROSECUTING ATTORNEY

I would like to put a question to the accused. *(Helmer rises)*

JUDGE

Witness, you may step down for the time being. *(Tornkvist steps out of the witness box and sits)*

PROSECUTING ATTORNEY

Did you personally write that invitation card to Dr. Tornkvist?

HELMER

Yes, but certainly not to spite him . . .

PROSECUTING ATTORNEY

Thank you. Your reasons don't interest me.

JUDGE

They interest the court. Continue.

HELMER

I wrote it after long consideration, and I admit that it was perhaps not polite to send it to him so late. I wrote it because I heartily wished that for once we two could speak out, be reconciled. Because I respected Dr. Tornkvist. Because for me it certainly was not necessary or natural that we be enemies . . . even though we hold

24 — Modern Nordic Plays: Norway

diametrically opposed convictions on the doctrine of eternal damnation. On my part, the invitation was an honest, out-stretched hand.

JUDGE

I see. Proceed, Prosecuting Attorney.

PROSECUTING ATTORNEY

That was very touching, but quite irrelevant. You wrote the card on your little portable typewriter?

HELMER

Yes.

PROSECUTING ATTORNEY

Tornkvist received the card on Saturday, the 26th of November. When did you write it?

HELMER

It must have been on Friday.

PROSECUTING ATTORNEY

Exactly, it must have been on Friday. Let's figure a little further, Bishop. Your ordination took place on Sunday. The same day you were notified of Tornkvist's accusation. On Monday, the 28th of November, the Chief of Police asked to see your typewriter. But, no. It was gone. You couldn't at all remember when you had last seen it. And yet, Bishop, on Friday, the 25th of November, only three short days before, you wrote that card on the self-same machine.

DEFENSE COUNSEL

Your Honor . . . !

JUDGE

Allow the accused to answer the question.

PROSECUTING ATTORNEY

I haven't asked it yet. But I will now: Did you or did

you not *lie* to the police? *(Stir and reaction in the courtroom. The judge bangs his gavel)*

JUDGE *(angrily)*

The Prosecuting Attorney knows very well that the use of such words is not permitted here.

PROSECUTING ATTORNEY

Well, let me ask then: Can your explanation to the police have contained a slight lapse of memory? *(Helmer has received a serious shock. The Defense Counsel is disturbed. Helmer hestitates to answer)* We have time, of course, even though it is not unlimited.

HELMER

I ... what I said to the police was, to the best of my knowledge, true, I had really forgotten on which typewriter I had written that card. You must believe me ...

PROSECUTING ATTORNEY

In every situation you say, 'You must believe me.' But should you not give us some grounds for believing you? We cannot swallow all sorts of rot even though it comes from a bishop.

JUDGE

I will not tolerate that sort of comment! Put your question.

PROSECUTING ATTORNEY

We know that the typewriter was in your office on Friday ... but on Monday ... Whoops! It had vanished. Is it logical to conclude that it disappeared between Friday and Monday?

HELMER

Yes ... yes, it must have.

DEFENSE COUNSEL

Bishop Helmer has expressly stated that he knows nothing about the disappearance of the typewriter.

PROSECUTING ATTORNEY

I'm grateful for my worthy opponent's help. That fact had not escaped my attention. He has most expressly stated it.

HELMER (*almost desperate, yet still obstinate. He is, after all a bishop*)

I beg to be spared the insulting tone of your cross-examination! I have said and I repeat: I have had absolutely nothing to do with those anonymous letters! I demand that you accept my word! I ask, moreover, if I had really wished to strike at Dr. Tornkvist, would I have acted so foolishly? What man in his right mind would have done such a thing?

PROSECUTING ATTORNEY (*rises*)

I am here to prove that you wrote the letter . . . not that you are in your right mind!

JUDGE

Keep to the question!

PROSECUTING ATTORNEY

Gladly, if I can get other answers than declarations of innocence. Let's go back to Sunday noon when Dr. Tornkvist threw his accusation in your face. Didn't he say to you then that today the police have means of establishing on which machine a letter has been written?

HELMER

I . . . I cannot remember.

PROSECUTING ATTORNEY

Oh, yes, think. Try to remember.

HELMER

He did say something of the sort! I didn't pay much attention to it.

PROSECUTING ATTORNEY

I can well believe that. But your typewriter must have paid attention to it! Your little green Romeo down in the church office must have heard his words and thought that now was the best time to disappear!

DEFENSE COUNSEL

Your Honour, I object to this cross-examination.

JUDGE

I don't like it either.

PROSECUTING ATTORNEY

There's a very great deal I don't like! I demand that the bishop begin to understand that he stands before the law. I have the burden of proof in this case against him! And I shall provide that proof, even though the Bishop has wilfully and purposefully suppressed it. Either I shall place that typewriter here before the court, or I shall clearly and decisively convince everyone that if that typewriter no longer exists, it is because it would be a manifest, striking, and irrefutable proof against the accused, Sigurd Helmer!

JUDGE

I forbid such argumentation. *(To Helmer)* But I am in agreement with the Counsel for the Prosecution that your case is weak as long as you do not present that machine here or give a complete explanation as to why, when, and how it disappeared.

HELMER

I cannot.

During the whole of the preceding cross-examination, there have been natural reactions on the part of Leif and Mrs. Helmer. During the last few speeches, Leif writes a few words on a slip of paper. After having made several unsuccessful attempts, he attracts the attention of the Court Clerk. The Clerk goes to him, takes the paper and goes with it to the judges' bench. During the following he gives the judge the slip of paper. The judge reads it.

PROSECUTING ATTORNEY

Well, we aren't going to leave it at that! Your explanation, which you have stubbornly clung to, is that the machine must have been forgotten in some hotel or other, in some private home, or in some pastor's office which you visited during one of your trips.

HELMER

Yes.

PROSECUTING ATTORNEY

This case is now famous throughout the nation. Is it conceivable, in your opinion, that the people whom you visited do not realize that that typewriter is missing? Is it conceivable that it would not have been found long ago and sent to you . . . or to the police?

HELMER

I don't know . . . (*The Judge looks at Leif Helmer*)

PROSECUTING ATTORNEY

Moreover, your explanation doesn't hold water! Because we know that that typewriter had no more than three days in which to disappear. And during those three days you weren't travelling at all!

HELMER

I cannot say more. (*Prosecuting Attorney throws out*

*his hands in disgust, flinging his pencil on his desk. He
sits down)*

JUDGE

I have just received a communication from the accused's son, Leif Helmer, whom I understand is present
in the courtroom?

CLERK

Yes, Your Honor.

JUDGE

Will he please come forward? *(Leif steps up, stands
before the witness box)* Is it true that you have something of significance to state on the exact point with
which the court is now dealing?

LEIF

Yes, Your Honor.

JUDGE

Are there any objections by either party to this witness's being heard? *(Helmer has become very uneasy,
confers with his lawyer.)*

PROSECUTING ATTORNEY

The prosecution has no objection. We have only one
wish and that is to clear up this sorry mess.

DEFENSE COUNSEL

Your Honor, the defense considers this testimony as
quite irrelevant to the case. The accused's son obviously
has had nothing at all to do with the matters related to
this accusation.

PROSECUTING ATTORNEY

How do you know that?

JUDGE

I agree with the Counsel for the Prosecution. Before

the witness has been heard, we know nothing. Does the Counsel for the Defense object to hearing the witness?

PROSECUTING ATTORNEY

If he does, I call the witness in the name of the state.

DEFENSE COUNSEL

We do not object.

JUDGE (*dictation to the court stenographer*)

'Leif Helmer, age 28, son of the accused, appeared as the eighth witness, is familiar with the responsibility of a witness, testified' ... (*To Leif, rapidly*) It is my duty to admonish you to tell the full and whole truth and to keep nothing back. You may refuse to answer a question which exposes you or your nearest of kin to pennalty or loss of public esteem, but if you answer, then your answer must be the truth. Proceed!

LEIF

Well ... er ... I mean ...

JUDGE

Yes? Tell us what you know.

LEIF

Well, I was the one who ... who took the typewriter. (*Violent reaction in the courtroom, several photographers jump up and take pictures of Leif*)

PROSECUTING ATTORNEY

Well, I must say!

JUDGE

I am examining. (*To Leif*) You took it? When?

LEIF

It ... it was Saturday evening, the day before the ordination. I had come home on a short visit ... haven't been home in five years ... and so my mother showed me around the house and office ...

JUDGE

Yes?

LEIF

Well, there was the machine. And so ... I just took it ...

JUDGE

Wasn't that theft?

LEIF

It was, in a way. I had to get some money. I had thought of asking him ... my father ... for some, but then I decided I could avoid that. I figured everyone would believe the typewriter had been lost during the moving.

JUDGE

Continue.

LEIF

Well, so I went into town again, Sunday evening. And at the Seamen's Hotel I met a fellow who wanted a typewriter. I got three hundred crowns for it.

JUDGE

Where is that man now?

LEIF

I don't know.

PROSECUTING ATTORNEY

What's his name?

LEIF

I ... I don't know ... Only that they call him Jens ...

PROSECUTING ATTORNEY

Excellent! There has just been one character I've missed

in this illustrious company up until now ... an Unknown Man! I bid him welcome!

JUDGE

A seaman?

LEIF

Yes. He was leaving the same day.

PROSECUTING ATTORNEY

On an unknown ship, naturally?

LEIF

Oh, no, he's boatswain on the *Ringholm*. Was bound for Australia.

JUDGE

Then the police have the possibility of contacting the ship and locating this Jens?

LEIF

Yes ... but ...

PROSECUTING ATTORNEY

Aha! There's a 'but'. I thought as much.

LEIF

Well, he said he was going to leave the ship at Dover.

PROSECUTING ATTORNEY

And with that he disappears into the Great Unknown. Thank you!

JUDGE

Are you telling the truth?

LEIF

Yes.

JUDGE

Why haven't you told this before?

LEIF

It . . . it was so . . . unpleasant . . . And I knew that this about the anonymous letters was just nonsense . . . that he could never have done that . . . I thought it would turn out all right without my . . .

PROSECUTING ATTORNEY

But then you saw that your father had got himself into deep water, eh?

LEIF

Yes. I had to tell how it was . . .

PROSECUTING ATTORNEY

Did your father ask you to tell us this cock and bull story?

HELMER

I protest! This is disgraceful!

PROSECUTING ATTORNEY (*quickly*)

Why? Would it be so disgraceful if this were the truth? (*Pause*) But the bishop doubts perhaps as much as I do that this is the truth? (*Helmer is silent. The Prosecuting Attorney rises, threatens with his finger*) Answer! Do you or do you not believe that your son has told the truth?

DEFENSE COUNSEL

He can have no opinion on that score!

PROSECUTING ATTORNEY

Perhaps he knows best himself when he can have an opinion. Answer!

HELMER

I don't know . . . I don't know . . .

PROSECUTING ATTORNEY

So you don't know, Bishop! Are you sure about that?

HELMER *(almost inaudibly)*
I don't . . . believe . . . he took the machine.

PROSECUTING ATTORNEY
Then we agree. I don't believe it either!

JUDGE
Is there a request that this witness take the oath?

PROSECUTING ATTORNEY
No. There is a request that he does *not* take the oath!
(To Leif) And I request this for your own sake, young
man. I respect your loyalty to your father, but I am
shocked at your frivolous attitude toward the law.

LEIF
But it's really . . .

PROSECUTING ATTORNEY
Keep quiet! While there is still time!

JUDGE
Any further questions for the witness? *(Silence.)* You
may step down. The oath is waived. New witness!
(Leif, abashed, leaves the courtroom)

PROSECUTING ATTORNEY
Jens Artur Gren.

CLERK *(at the door)*
Jens Artur Gren.

*Gren enters and goes to the witness box. He is a plain,
trustworthy craftsman, between 50 and 60, slightly cor-
pulent and short of breath. Not especially bright. He nods
and bows with respect about the courtroom, especially
to Helmer, who obviously does not recognize him, but looks
quickly about for his glasses in order to see him more
clearly.*

JUDGE *(dictating from a paper the court clerk has given him)*

'Appeared as ninth witness, Jens Artur Gren, repair shop proprietor, 59, familiar with the responsibility of a witness.' *(To Gren, reciting)* It is my duty to admonish you to tell the full and whole truth and to keep nothing back. You may refuse to answer a question which exposes you or your nearest of kin to penalty or loss of public esteem, but if you answer, then your answer must be the truth. You may proceed, Counsel for the Prosecution!

PROSECUTING ATTORNEY

Mr. Gren, have you ever seen this before?

Suddenly pulls the much-talked-of typewriter from under his desk and holds it in his right hand.

GREN

Yes, sir.

PROSECUTING ATTORNEY

I present as evidence in this case, Bishop Helmer's portable typewriter! *(Enormous sensation in the courtroom. Photographers pop flash bulbs, the judge bangs gavel)*

JUDGE

Silence! Or I will clear the courtroom! Silence down there! *(Pause until it becomes dead-quiet)* Continue, please, Prosecuting Attorney.

PROSECUTING ATTORNEY

Fortunately, I did not have to travel all the way to Australia in order to find this machine. But the man who had it actually *is* named Jens . . .

JUDGE

Enough, enough! The court will hear the witness.

PROSECUTING ATTORNEY

You own a little workshop on Kongensgate . . . you repair radios, phonographs . . . and typewriters?

GREN

Yes, sir.

PROSECUTING ATTORNEY

Tell us, in your own words, what happened on the afternoon of the 28th of November.

GREN

Well . . . yes, it might have been about half-past three
when this gentleman comes in and asks me if I can fix
a typewriter. 'That depends,' I says, and when I sees
it, I scratches my head and asks myself what in the
world has happened to it.

PROSECUTING ATTORNEY

You mean that there was something especially queer
about the machine?

GREN *(almost indignant)*

Well, queer, yes, sir! If you could have seen it, you
would've thought there was something queer about it.
*(Prosecuting Attorney beckons Gren out of the witness
box and allows him to demonstrate for the Judge)* It
was a fine machine, see, but somebody had mucked up
the keys something awful. Looked like they'd gone at it
with a file. Four of the keys was broken clean off and
the rest was filed down nearly flat.

PROSECUTING ATTORNEY

And . . . the gentleman . . . did he give any explanation
as to how this had happened?

GREN

That he did. He says it was some kids who got their hands on it ... and, believe you me, there's lots of terrible young'uns nowadays. I got about twenty-five of them running wild in the back yard of my shop all day long ...

PROSECUTING ATTORNEY

Thank you. You believed what the gentleman told you?

GREN

Lord, yes, sir, I did. But then I asks him how in heaven's name I'm supposed to fix it. And he turns as white as a sheet and says, 'Can't you do it while I wait?' So I just sits down then and laughs fit to kill. (*Laughs heartily*) Yes, sir ... well, in the end he gives up and says that if it has to take time, then it'll just have to take time.

PROSECUTING ATTORNEY

What made you bring the typewriter to me?

GREN

Well, sir, you see ... I don't often read the papers, don't think there's much in them. But just yesterday I happen to see something about this business and there's talk about this typewriter. And it says it's the exact same make as this one, you see ... so, well, I think maybe its best I say something about it.

PROSECUTING ATTORNEY

Is the typewriter repaired now?

GREN

Yes, sir. It's got brand-new keys. I finished it just the day before yesterday ... Thursday. I kind'a expected this gentleman would come and fetch it.

PROSECUTING ATTORNEY

He may have been engaged with a very serious matter at that time. Do you see this . . . gentleman anywhere here in the courtroom?

GREN *(turns)*

Yes, sir. Ain't that him sitting over there?

PROSECUTING ATTORNEY

Will the accused please rise? *(Helmer rises)*

GREN *(pleased)*

Yes, sir, that's him. Name's Karlsen.

PROSECUTING ATTORNEY

Is that the name he gave you?

GREN

Yes, sir. Mr. Karlsen, wholesaler. I wrote it down. *(Helmer sinks back into his chair, pale and quite shaken)*

PROSECUTING ATTORNEY

Oh, no, I'm afraid you're going to have to stand a little while longer. *(Helmer rises again)*

JUDGE *(very gravely)*

What have you to say to the testimony from this witness? *(Helmer opens his mouth but cannot speak)* Is it in accordance with the truth?

HELMER

I . . . I . . .

JUDGE *(severely)*

I want your 'yes' or 'no'.

HELMER *(after a long pause, murmurs)*

Yes. *(Reaction in the courtroom)*

JUDGE *(strangely charitable)*

It seems clear, then, that what you stated before was

not correct . . . that you did not know the whereabouts of the typewriter?

HELMER (*murmurs*)

Yes.

PROSECUTING ATTORNEY

Let me ask you . . .

JUDGE (*banging the gavel*)

No. I'm doing the asking. (*Earnestly to Helmer*) I imagine then that you want to change your testimony. The court will hear you. But I warn you again to tell nothing but the whole truth. I ask you: Do you wish to plead guilty to having written the anonymous letter referred to in the accusation?

HELMER (*forcefully*)

No! No! Never! I did not write it. I swear that I didn't write it!

PROSECUTING ATTORNEY

May I continue with my examination?

JUDGE

Just a moment. (*To the witness who still stands in the witness box, understanding little of what is happening*) Jens Artur Gren. Do you swear that you have told the full and whole truth?

GREN

Yes, sir. (*All rise and stand during the administration of the oath*)

JUDGE

Raise your right hand and repeat after me: I do so swear . . .

GREN

I do so swear . . .

25 — Modern Nordic Plays: Norway

JUDGE

 So help me God . . .

GREN

 So help me God . . .

JUDGE

 The almighty and omniscient . . .

GREN

 The almighty and omniscient.

JUDGE

 Thank you. You have finished and may go. *(Gren is shown out)* You may proceed, Prosecuting Attorney.

PROSECUTING ATTORNEY

 Sigurd Helmer! The court has given you an opportunity to make a clean confession. You have refused to do so. I will, therefore, ask you a series of concrete questions. And I would like your answers accurately recorded by the court scribe.

JUDGE

 They shall be so recorded.

PROSECUTING ATTORNEY *(standing erect)*

 Is it not true that you were greatly shaken when Dr. Tornkvist stated his accusation against you?

HELMER

 No, I found it absurd. It hurt me, but did not shake me.

PROSECUTING ATTORNEY

 Is it not also true that you became thoroughly panic-stricken when he informed you that a typewriter could be identified by its type?

HELMER

 No, I paid no attention to his remark.

PROSECUTING ATTORNEY

Is it not also true that the same evening . . . Sunday, the 27th of November . . . that you, unseen, locked yourself in your office and went to work on your typewriter with a coarse file taken from your tool chest?

HELMER

No, that's completely false.

PROSECUTING ATTORNEY

Is it not also true that you found the task unexpectedly difficult? That it might have been done with special tools, but not with your coarse file and in your nervous condition? That several of the keys broke off, that the filing was anything but satisfactory? That you finally, in error and desperation, gave up completely and carefully hid the machine, intending to remove it the next day?

HELMER

That's absolutely false.

PROSECUTING ATTORNEY

Isn't it also true that the next morning you lied to the police and maintained that you had no idea where the machine was?

HELMER

I had absolutely no idea where it was at that time.

PROSECUTING ATTORNEY

Isn't it also true that the moment the police were out of the door, you took the machine, went secretly to town with it, and delivered it – under a false name – for repair at Jens Gren's shop.

HELMER

The last is true. All the rest is false.

PROSECUTING ATTORNEY (*throwing his pencil on his desk, dropping his arms in disgust*)
And you expect us to believe you?

HELMER (*tired and toneless*)
I expect nothing any longer ... (*Drinks from a glass of water*) I expect nothing any longer.

JUDGE (*kindly*)
You are tired perhaps? Do you wish the court to recess for a short time?

HELMER (*in the same tone*)
No, no ... I want ... to tell everything, exactly as it happened ...

PROSECUTING ATTORNEY
That's what we've been asking you to do all along!

JUDGE (*with a reproving gesture toward the Prosecuting Attorney*)
Take all the time you need. You may sit if you like.

HELMER
I can well stand. (*The Judge gives the Prosecuting Attorney a sign that he may continue his cross-examination almost sadly, as if he were tossing Helmer to the lions*)

PROSECUTING ATTORNEY (*ironically to Helmer*)
The floor's all yours!

HELMER
I say and swear before God and mankind: I did not write that letter. (*Prosecuting Attorney shakes his head impatiently*) I repeat that I took the whole matter lightly at first, as a completely exaggerated expression of Dr. Tornkvist's bitterness. I repeat that when the police came to see me I told them the truth. I did not

know where the typewriter was. But immediately afterwards ... I found it ...

PROSECUTING ATTORNEY

Where?

HELMER

In the fireplace. Up the chimney.

PROSECUTING ATTORNEY

Do you usually keep your typewriter up the chimney?

HELMER *(ignoring this)*

It was by chance. I was cold. I lit the fire and it began to smoke. That's how I found it. *(Prosecuting Attorney smiles and shakes his head skeptically)* My first thought was to ring the police, and I had already dialed the number when ...

PROSECUTING ATTORNEY

When you had a second thought?

HELMER

It suddenly struck me that something was amiss ... I put down the receiver and opened the typewriter. And then I saw that someone had destroyed the keys ...

PROSECUTING ATTORNEY *(as Helmer pauses)*

Well ... go on, continue ... don't keep us on tenterhooks.

HELMER

For the first time I understood that I was in danger. Something had happened which I could not explain. There were forces working against me, forces against which I could not protect myself. I suddenly realized that no one would believe me ... someone had trumped up damaging evidence against me.

PROSECUTING ATTORNEY

Someone had 'trumped up' damaging evidence against you? I see!

JUDGE

You didn't dare ring to the police?

HELMER

That's right. I was afraid they wouldn't believe me.

JUDGE

That was foolish of you. The police might have been able to find fingerprints on the typewriter . . . fingerprints of the guilty person.

HELMER

I didn't think of that. I understood that someone had set a trap for me and that I was helplessly caught in it, if I didn't . . .

PROSECUTING ATTORNEY

If you didn't . . . what?

HELMER

If I didn't deprive them of the evidence they had manufactured.

PROSECUTING ATTORNEY

You believed that this was what American gangsters call a 'frame-up'?

HELMER

I believed that.

PROSECUTING ATTORNEY (*sarcastically*)

Well, things begin to brighten up. This all seems remarkably plausible. If you now will just tell us the name of this 'someone', I'll have him charged at once. (*Helmer is silent*) Come now, Bishop. There's no reason for you to shield such a wicked person.

HELMER

I don't . . . I don't know who he is . . .

PROSECUTING ATTORNEY

But you have your suspicions, don't you? *(Helmer is silent)* Is this sort of 'frame-up' usual in church circles?

DEFENSE COUNSEL *(jumping up)*

In your mockery, you say more truth than you realize. We have heard witnesses testify here to the unhealthy atmosphere, the intense spying and gossiping, which prevailed between the rivaling factions during this ecclesiastical election.

PROSECUTING ATTORNEY

Now I *am* interested! Perhaps my worthy opponent will formulate the charge which his client does not dare make himself!

DEFENSE COUNSEL

I accuse no one. But I maintain that there is nothing impossible or illogical in Bishop Helmer's explanation or suppositions.

PROSECUTING ATTORNEY

Your words really provide our church with a splendid testimonial!

DEFENSE COUNSEL

And rightly so! There is nothing more bitter than religious disputes. In order to defend their doctrine of eternal damnation many churchmen have used means which make them deserving of hell . . . if it exists!

JUDGE

I will not tolerate a theological dispute about damnation between the two counsels! Please, continue, Prosecuting Attorney.

DEFENSE COUNSEL *(indignant)*

I state these things in order to throw some light on this case. I want it recorded that the court has denied me the opportunity.

JUDGE *(with a hard blow of the gavel, then, after an ominous, threatening pause)*

The court warns the Counsel for the Defense, and expects his apologies. The court forbids nothing which can throw light on this case. *(In rising indignation)* But we do not intend to waste one second of the court's time in listening to the Defense Counsel's theological opinions. If the accused himself wishes to speak, he has the floor!

DEFENSE COUNSEL

I beg Your Honor's pardon. And I ask my client to give us the background of the bitter struggle of which he has been the innocent victim.

PROSECUTING ATTORNEY

I object to that statement! We're going to have a closer look at this innocence!

JUDGE

Silence! *(To Helmer)* Proceed.

HELMER *(at first hesitantly, but gradually growing stronger and more assured)*

Yes, it's true that a bitter conflict rages inside the church ... even as a very young pastor, I saw the way I should and had to go ... My faith is as firm, as true, and as correct as Dr. Tornkvist's. I consider myself as good, yes, as a better Christian. I ... there was so much in the history of the church which shocked me, which was contrary to my beliefs: the inquisition, the witch hunts, the inexorable terrorizing of mankind. In our

day, there is only one thing remaining of this terror . . . ·
the threat of hell, of an everlasting bodily torture in a
literal sulphur pit. I believe in God and the Scriptures,
but I believe that on this point the Scriptures have
been distorted by man's hand. I do not believe that it
has ever been God's will that mankind should be
frightened into a Christian life. I believe that this literal
hell has been invented by ruthless men seeking power. I
have devoted my life to fighting for a church to which
men come in free, joyous faith . . . not in a sickening
fear of an eternal hell. I have no faith in those who
are pious because of fear, who sign a sort of insurance
policy for eternity by going regularly to God's house . . .
and who, outside, in their deeds, continue their hypoc-
risy, their grasping, and their sins. This point of view
has made me a dangerous and hated man in many powerful circles. But among free men my faith is the signpost
of the future! . . . Therefore they dare not stone me, dare
not cast me out of the church, dare not deny me the
offices for which my abilities qualify me. But the struggle continues, by dark and hidden means. By ambiguous
pastoral letters, by tossed-off insinuations . . . by . . .
(Pauses)

PROSECUTING ATTORNEY

Go on, Bishop. By what? (Helmer is silent) You have
a word on your tongue. I know what it is . . . Spit it
out! (Helmer is silent) The word is 'provocation', isn't
it? What you wished to say, without saying it, is
that these anonymous letters are concocted as a provocation?

HELMER (firmly)
Yes.

PROSECUTING ATTORNEY

But you cannot point to their author? *(Helmer is silent)* Good. To begin with, let me thank you for your sermon ... It is well said that a man ought to write his own testimonial. He's closest to his subject and can do it best. You ask us to consider you an idealist. Someone who bravely 'stood up to Rome' as they say. Others may, however, have a different opinion about your idealism and its motivation.

JUDGE

I will not permit the Prosecuting Attorney to indulge in sarcastic tirades. If you have questions to ask, ask them!

PROSECUTING ATTORNEY

With pleasure, Your Honor. I'm sure the bishop will reply to them with his usual honesty. Therefore: Isn't it true that you, after two years as a seamen's pastor, demanded a better post?

HELMER *(bewildered)*

Demanded? I sought a call.

PROSECUTING ATTORNEY

Isn't it true that you suddenly adopted a strong liberal line of thought?

HELMER

It may have seemed sudden ...

PROSECUTING ATTORNEY

Didn't you do so because the only possibility you had to get ahead quickly in your career lay in that direction?

HELMER

I don't understand ...

PROSECUTING ATTORNEY

Let me quote from your article. 'The Way of Faith' of the 14th of February, 1936: 'Now, as then, the orthodox legions, in spite of their bitter internal jealousies, stand firmly united against all who are not incorporated in their circle. By a shrewd use of business acumen, they monopolize all clerical appointments.' *(Helmer throws out his arms)* Under such circumstances, it would be to your advantage to be broadminded, wouldn't it? So you followed the liberal line because there you had few, if any, competitors, didn't you?

HELMER *(indignantly)*

I followed my own convictions!

PROSECUTING ATTORNEY

The facts we have about you tell of a rapid career and an untiring worldly industriousness. All of your advancements have been sensational.

HELMER

I have been a controversial figure, I know . . .

PROSECUTING ATTORNEY

And your opponents have usually been left lying on the battlefield! Do you deny that you have, in your writings and speeches, fought to reach the top?

HELMER

No! It is every man's duty to arrive there where his talents can best be used.

PROSECUTING ATTORNEY

In the service of God?

HELMER

Yes . . . in the service of God!

PROSECUTING ATTORNEY

Would it be untrue and unfair if someone considered your whole life as one vain, ambitious chase after publicity and fat offices? *(Defense Counsel reacts; the judge stops him with a gesture)*

HELMER *(bitterly, but quite calmly)*

I believe it would be.

PROSECUTING ATTORNEY

Would it be untrue to say that in your fight you have used harsh and ruthless means?

HELMER

I believe it would be.

PROSECUTING ATTORNEY

Would you call your disposition as a pastor humble, self-sacrificing, and merciful?

HELMER

The Lord also has need of warriors!

PROSECUTING ATTORNEY

He certainly does, and he must be very proud of them.

JUDGE

I must stop this sort of questioning. If the Prosecuting Attorney wishes to continue, he must hold himself strictly to the facts in the case.

PROSECUTING ATTORNEY

Certainly, Your Honor. The newest fact is that Bishop Helmer has formulated a suspicion. Someone has laid a trap for him. Someone has provoked him. Who? *(Helmer is silent)* You have a suspicion. Against whom? *(Helmer is silent)*

DEFENSE COUNSEL (*desperate; no other defense can be found*)

I, too, must ask you to reply, openly and honorably: Whom do you suspect?

HELMER (*quietly*)

It was natural for me to think of Dr. Tornkvist. (*Reaction in the courtroom, talk, murmuring. Dr. Tornkvist rises and stands, white with fury, staring at Helmer*)

TORNKVIST

I expected this last baseness!

JUDGE

Silence! You may speak later.

PROSECUTING ATTORNEY

I was expecting it too. In this, the accused has crowned a deed which I can truthfully call a piece of cowardly villainy!

DEFENSE COUNSEL (*aggressively*)

You can spare us your big words! Let Dr. Tornkvist himself reply to the charge.

TORNKVIST (*goes to the witness box*)

. Yes, I shall reply. And I reply that the very thought of such an act on my part is an insult. I dismiss it with the contempt it deserves.

DEFENSE COUNSEL

And I ask you! Isn't it true that your attitude toward Bishop Helmer was so hostile, so rancorous, that you were capable of anything?

TORNKVIST

Of much. But not of anything. Not of this.

JUDGE

I admonish the Defense Counsel to weigh his words. The

witness is under the protection of the court. I will not
tolerate any unsubstantiated insinuations.

DEFENSE COUNSEL
Some things are done so cleverly that it is hard to sub-
stantiate them. I will, however, try, Your Honor.
I ask that Gunnar Berg be summoned as witness.

JUDGE
Summon Gunnar Berg.

CLERK *(at the door)*
Gunnar Berg. *(Excitement in the courtroom. Gunnar
Berg enters and goes to the witness box. Tornkvist returns to his chair. Berg is an elderly, intelligent, and
alert man, considerate and trustworthy)*

JUDGE *(reading from a paper handed him by the Court
Clerk)*
'Appeared as tenth witness, Gunnar Sigvard Berg, 57,
building superintendent, familiar with the responsibility of a witness, testified . . .' *(To Berg)* It is my duty
to admonish you to tell the full and whole truth and
to keep nothing back. You may further refuse to answer
a question which exposes you or your nearest of kin to
penalty or loss of public esteem, but if you answer,
then your answer must be the truth. Proceed, Counsel
for the Defense!

DEFENSE COUNSEL
You are the superintendent of the Theological Faculty
Building and have been there how long?

BERG
Nineteen years next summer.

DEFENSE COUNSEL
Until quite recently . . . until Sigurd Helmer's ordination

as Bishop of Elveness . . . he was a professor on the faculty and had his office there, just as did Instructor Tornkvist?

BERG

That's correct. Their offices were on the same corridor.

DEFENSE COUNSEL

What was the relationship between these two men?

BERG (*with the reluctance of a decent man*)

Do I have to answer that?

JUDGE

Yes.

BERG

Well, they were like cat and dog.

PROSECUTING ATTORNEY (*with an ingratiating smile*)

Who was the cat and who was the dog?

BERG

Dr. Tornkvist was the cat.

JUDGE

I dislike the witness being forced to make evaluations . . . either zoological or psychological.

DEFENSE COUNSEL

The witness's answer is very interesting. Do you mean to say that you considered Dr. Tornkvist to be the more cunning?

BERG

I must admit that I did.

DEFENSE COUNSEL

And Helmer?

BERG

Oh, he was like a big dog . . . growling but kind.

PROSECUTING ATTORNEY *(regretting his little witticism)*
> The court is always right ... let the witness keep to the facts!

DEFENSE COUNSEL
> Did you, as other witnesses have testified, have the impression that these two spied on each other?

BERG
> Your Honor, I beg to be excused from answering that because I have nothing concrete to base my answer on. But there was a dangerous and unpleasant atmosphere.

DEFENSE COUNSEL
> We must go into more detail. Did these two visit each other in their respective offices?

BERG *(laughs)*
> Never! During the last months I don't think they even looked at each other.

DEFENSE COUNSEL
> Therefore, you have never, at any time, seen Dr. Tornkvist in Professor Helmer's office?

BERG
> Oh, yes. Yes ... that's the whole point ...

JUDGE *(interested)*
> What do you mean?

BERG
> It was so very strange. I've thought the whole time that it was strange. It didn't fit together somehow ...

DEFENSE COUNSEL
> What didn't fit together?

BERG
> Well, it was in August. I remember that it was during

the days when we were all betting on who would get to be bishop. One of the windows was broken in Professor Helmer's office and I was in there fixing it . . . he was at a meeting . . . And then, suddenly the door opened, and Dr. Tornkvist came in . . . *(There is great excitement in the courtroom)* He didn't see me at first. He went over to Professor Helmer's desk and opened the lid. Then he turned and saw that I was over by the window . . .

DEFENSE COUNSEL

And then?

BERG

Then he smiled, a little queerly, I thought, and he said, 'Is Professor Helmer out?' That seemed odd, because he knew very well that Professor Helmer was at that meeting the whole day. Then he said, 'I was just returning this typewriter. Mine has gone to pieces, so I borrowed his for a moment.' Then he put the machine on the desk and left.

DEFENSE COUNSEL

Could you recognize that typewriter if you saw it?

BERG

I could. Only Professor Helmer had that kind. It was very modern and handy.

DEFENSE COUNSEL

Is it the one standing on the Prosecuting Attorney's table? *(Prosecuting Attorney is not happy, but he lifts the typewriter with both hands and holds it out)*

BERG

Exactly! That's it!

DEFENSE COUNSEL

Your witness, Prosecuting Attorney.

PROSECUTING ATTORNEY

Thank you very much! What did you mean when you said that Dr. Tornkvist looked queer? Did he seem to feel guilty?

BERG

I... I can't say that exactly.

PROSECUTING ATTORNEY

If a man is working and his typewriter breaks down, isn't it quite natural for him to try and borrow another?

BERG

Yes, as far as that goes ...

PROSECUTING ATTORNEY

Thank you.

DEFENSE COUNSEL

Do you believe, Mr. Berg, that Dr. Tornkvist would have gone to Helmer and asked to have borrowed his typewriter?

BERG *(laughs)*

No, never! He would rather have chiselled his words on stone!

DEFENSE COUNSEL

Thank you!

JUDGE

Are there any further questions? *(Both lawyers shake their heads)* Do you swear that you have told the full and whole truth and have kept nothing back?

BERG *(who knows the formula)*

I do so swear, so help me God, the almighty and omniscient.

JUDGE

Good. You may step down. *(Berg leaves the courtroom)*

DEFENSE COUNSEL

Dr. Tornkvist! *(Tornkvist has already entered the witness box)* I want to ask you several concrete questions. And I request that your answers be noted verbatim by the court scribe.

JUDGE

They shall be so recorded.

DEFENSE COUNSEL *(standing very erect)*

Is it not true that, at the time ... in the month of August ... you neither spoke to nor greeted Professor Helmer?

TORNKVIST

That's true.

DEFENSE COUNSEL

Isn't it also true that on a certain day you went into his office and found it unoccupied?

TORNKVIST

That's true.

DEFENSE COUNSEL

Isn't it also true that you took his typewriter, carried it to your own office, and wrote on it?

TORNKVIST

That's true.

DEFENSE COUNSEL

Isn't it also true that shortly thereafter you took the machine back to Professor Helmer's office?

TORNKVIST

That's true.

DEFENSE COUNSEL

Isn't it also true that in the meantime, you wrote on Professor Helmer's typewriter, the anonymous letter which forms the basis of the charge against him?

TORNKVIST

. That's not true! That's absolutely not true!

DEFENSE COUNSEL

Can you give us some grounds for accepting your categorical denial?

PROSECUTING ATTORNEY

Dr. Tornkvist need not trouble himself with that. I undertake to show the absurdity of the Defense Counsel's insinuations. It will give me great pleasure to prick the little balloon of lethal gas he has just sent up! (*Walks forward*) Let us say, for the sake of argument, that this unfounded nonsense were possible. That Dr. Tornkvist could have written an anonymous letter against himself, a letter which, in fact, would have the effect of losing him his election to the bishopric. Let us assume that. But, Honorable Judges, there is one thing that he could not have done. He could not, between Friday, the 25th, and Monday, the 28th of November, have broken into the office of the Bishop of Elveness and there manufactured evidence by filing the keys off Bishop Helmer's typewriter, and thereafter hidden it in the chimney pipe.

DEFENSE COUNSEL

Oh, no? Couldn't he have done that? We know that he was in Elveness. He appeared there on Sunday, the 27th, when he confronted Bishop Helmer with his accusation!

TORNKVIST
> I arrived there Sunday morning on the 10:45 train . . . in the company of Bishop Steen. I went directly to the church and sat in the front pew during the whole of the consecration service. I went from the church directly to Helmer.

DEFENSE COUNSEL
> Yes, but afterwards? Afterwards?

TORNKVIST
> I was not alone at any time. I left the bishop's house in the company of his daughter, Agnes. We went together. She is now my wife! *(Sensation in the courtroom)*

JUDGE
> Silence!

PROSECUTING ATTORNEY *(with his fist pointed at Defense Counsel)*
> Your evidence collapses. It collapses like a house of cards. And we are amazed at such a desperate and filthy attempt at defense.

DEFENSE COUNSEL
> I object, Your Honor!

JUDGE *(bangs his gavel)*
> I will not permit invective. Silence! *(Dead silence. Helmer is bowed down with his head in his hands)* The cross-examination is closed. The Prosecuting Attorney may begin his summing-up.

PROSECUTING ATTORNEY *(pompously rising to his feet)*
> Honorable Judges! It is a heavy duty for me to demand dishonor and punishment for this once highly-respected man of the church. To demand that he be dismissed

from his office. To demand that he be defrocked. I shall be brief. It is not my custom to kick a man when he is down. I shall not give voice to the bitter words which his own conscience will speak to him much, much more clearly than I can ... (*The curtain falls as he continues to speak*)

ACT THREE

The Bishop's Residence. It is the same evening. The drawing room is dimly lit and as the curtain rises, Bishop Helmer is standing at the window, staring out into the darkness with his forehead against the window pane. His hands are stretched out to the sides of the window frame ... (But if this illusion of one upon the Cross seems intentional, it must be omitted).

After a moment, the door on the left opens and Leif enters with his coat on, carrying a small traveling bag. He stops and looks at his father. It seems as if his first inclination is to steal across the room and disappear. Instead, he coughs intentionally, and Helmer turns.

HELMER (*his face marked by the day's purgatory, by hopelessness and despair, yet quite controlled*)
    So ... it's you, Leif?

LEIF
    Yes.

HELMER
    Are you leaving?

LEIF

Yes. The *Bermuda* sails early tomorrow . . .

HELMER

Have a good voyage.

LEIF

Thanks.

HELMER *(with great effort, trying to make conversation)*
And what's your destination this time?

LEIF

Rio.

HELMER

Rio? Well, well . . .

LEIF

Er . . . goodbye, father.

HELMER

Goodbye, Leif. *(He almost says 'my boy' and almost weeps. Leif walks slowly toward the door)* Thanks for . . . what you did today . . .

LEIF *(stops, looks at him)*
I only made matters worse for you . . .

HELMER *(smiles bitterly)*
A little, more or less . . . you tried to help . . .

LEIF

It . . . it was stupid of me . . .

HELMER *(quietly)*
Why did you do it, my boy?

LEIF *(looking down)*
I . . . I don't know, father. I had to, somehow . . . I couldn't bear for you to suffer so . . .

HELMER

It's odd . . . To you I'm only . . . a stranger. (*Leif bows his head and is silent*) Isn't that true?

LEIF (*very quietly*)

I thought so . . .

HELMER (*thoughtfully, looking back over the years*)

We two have really never talked together . . .

LEIF

No.

HELMER

It's been my fault. There's so much one never has time for.

LEIF

It isn't that. It was something else . . . you . . . you never needed me somehow, never needed anyone.

HELMER

Before today?

LEIF

Yes, before today . . . You were always so confident. Got everything you wanted. Always won. Always had so many words . . . (*Pause*) Forgive me.

HELMER

No, no, boy. Get it off your chest!

LEIF

It's so . . . so hard to explain . . . and it's so foolish to speak about it now . . . I'm leaving and . . . and you have enough hell . . . trouble, I mean . . .

HELMER (*in deep thought*)

So many words, you said. So many empty phrases perhaps?

LEIF

Not exactly empty, maybe. So many big words. It . . . it was as if you knocked people out cold with them, and they lay there while you went on . . .

HELMER *(laughs a little bitterly)*

In power and glory . . .

LEIF *(forcefully)*

In power and glory, yes! It was as if it was nothing I understood . . . Had nothing to do with . . . Didn't want . . . *(Stops abruptly)*

HELMER

Didn't want . . .?

LEIF *(suddenly, like a cry)*

Didn't want to know about! Didn't want to be related to! *(Pause. Helmer looks at him. Leif's face is defiant, open and unhappy. Helmer takes a few steps, turns)*

HELMER *(coldly matter-of-fact)*

The power and glory are over . . .

LEIF

Yes, father. That's just it . . .

HELMER

They have hurled me down, dragged me through the mud. I am disgraced. My name is a term of abuse.

LEIF

Yes.

HELMER *(through clenched teeth, coldly, turns from him)*

Don't think I'll reproach you if you take another name. I would consider that quite natural.

LEIF *(sure and calm again)*

Lots of times people have asked me if I were the son

of the famous, the much talked-about Helmer. When I could manage it, I said no. But from today, father, from today, I am going to answer: Yes, he's my father!

HELMER *(turns again, looks inquiringly at him, whispers)*
He's ... he's ... my ... father?

LEIF *(gripped)*
Yes! It struck me today in court. It was like when a fog suddenly lifts at sea. He's my father. He's a man, a living, unhappy human being who is in trouble and needs me ... *(An embarrassed pause, bows his head, picks up his bag)* I have to go ... the train ...

HELMER *(stands motionless, looking at Leif. His face betrays nothing, but he finally says, almost automatically)*
Have a good voyage ... to Rio.

LEIF
Thanks, father.

HELMER
Write often to your mother. She will need it now.

LEIF
May ... I write to you, too, father?

HELMER
To me? Will you? Will you really do that?

LEIF
Yes, father. *(Hesitantly extends his hand)*

HELMER *(almost throwing himself at it)*
It's been many years since we have shaken hands, my boy!

LEIF *(trying to joke)*
Let's do it more often! *(Laughs)*

HELMER *(laughs too, slapping Leif on the shoulder)*
Let's do that, my boy. Let's do that!

LEIF *(with strained easiness)*
Well, goodbye, then. *(Walks quickly to the door, turns)*
If ... if it gets difficult with money, my pay's not so
bad on the *Bermuda*. *(Exit quickly. Helmer stands looking after him, deeply astonished. Walks slowly to the
table and sits gazing straight ahead)*

MRS. HELMER *(comes in through the door to the left, sees
him).*
Are you sitting in here all by yourself? *(Goes to him,
sits on the arm of his chair, puts her arm around his
shoulder, caresses his cheek and then looks at her hand)*
Are you crying?

HELMER *(with an affectionate smile)*
More from happiness than from sorrow, I think. In the
midst of my defeat I have gained a son.

MRS. HELMER
Yes.

HELMER
That doesn't surprise you?

MRS. HELMER
No.

HELMER *(thoughtfully)*
When I was respected and honored by all, he detested
me, hated me almost. And now ... now he gives me
his hand. Can you understand that?

MRS. HELMER
Yes, I can understand that, Sigurd. There was One who
walked this earth and met many kinds of hatred because He confounded the learned, hypnotized the masses,

made Himself prominent, rose up, was called King. But when men saw Him on the way to Golgotha, then they *loved* Him. It was then there arose true, deep respect in every soul. Even Caiaphas bowed his head. There is a special glory that surrounds a suffering, forsaken man, Sigurd.

HELMER

You mustn't compare me to Christ!

MRS. HELMER

What's the point of Jesus if mankind isn't to compare themselves to Him? For me He's not called Christ. That cold name gives Him an aura of power which makes Him small in my eyes. I call Him Jesus, a human being and a man, who bore the cross without whimpering, through ignominy and dishonor . . . and thereby won the world's love and esteem.

HELMER

I see what you're getting at. *(Rises, straightens up)* And I shall take what comes!

MRS. HELMER

That was what Leif felt. That's why you've gained a son.

HELMER *(looking about)*

We didn't enjoy the Bishop's Residence very long.

MRS. HELMER

We'll say farewell to it without any bitterness. To the vainglory and the congregational intrigues. We'll turn the page and read on.

HELMER *(will not be comforted)*

But the shame, Margrethe . . . the dishonor!

MRS. HELMER

You're not dishonored in my eyes. Are you in yours?

HELMER

No! Because I am innocent. Whatever they say, I'm innocent.

MRS. HELMER

So was Jesus. You're in good company.

HELMER

My whole life in ruins! My future laid waste!

MRS. HELMER

No, Sigurd. 'The future' and 'happiness' ought to mean
the same thing for people. And you know very well
that you never found happiness on that Jacob's ladder
you so wanted to climb to the top. You were happy
once, long ago, in that little church squeezed in between
two harbor warehouses like a piece of cheese.

HELMER (looking at her, remembering)

That little church . . .

MRS. HELMER

We are longing for a harbor, we two. The man in you
longs for something you can get your hands on. A harbor where Leif could drop his anchor and be proud
of his father.

HELMER (smiles in spite of himself, walks about. His face
hardens suddenly and he strikes the table with his fist)

No! There's no way back for me. I won't be driven
out! I won't be chased from my position like a scabby
hound! I am innocent! I'm going to have this affair
cleared up! The guilty party must be made to pay! I . . .

MAID (at the door)

Excuse me, Bishop . . .

HELMER *(angrily)*
> Why didn't you knock?

MAID
> I did knock, Bishop . . . I thought . . .

HELMER
> What is it?

MAID
> It's Mr. Lind, sir.

HELMER *(eagerly)*
> At last! Show him in! *(Mrs. Helmer turns on the ceiling light. The maid goes to the door, stands aside as the Defense Counsel quickly enters like a thundercloud. She then exits, closing the door after her)*

HELMER
> How do you do, Lind? Thanks for coming.

DEFENSE COUNSEL
> Good evening, Bishop. Good evening, madam.

HELMER *(after a pause, during which he looks at the lawyer)*
> Well, Lind . . . it looks bad . . .?

DEFENSE COUNSEL
> That's an inadequate word, Bishop. It looks hopeless, utterly hopeless.

HELMER
> Hopeless . . .?

DEFENSE COUNSEL *(half to himself)*
> In all my long life at the bar, I've never experienced anything so bitter as to sit there in the court and watch the Prosecuting Attorney pull rabbits out of his hat. Sit there . . . beaten . . . fooled by my own client . . .

HELMER

You mustn't say that!

DEFENSE COUNSEL

I know. Forgive me. I realize very well that my bitterness and despair are nothing compared to yours.

HELMER

You mustn't say that I fooled you. I have said it before, and I repeat, I swear it: I am innocent!

DEFENSE COUNSEL

Well, tomorrow you will be innocently condemned.

HELMER (*fighting for self-control*)

You believe that?

DEFENSE COUNSEL

I *know* it. Your whole case rested on one foundation but a powerful foundation. Belief in you as a man. Until today that belief was unshaken. Like a dike, Bishop, against the raging sea ... When a single stone falls from the dike, nothing can any longer hold back the disaster.

HELMER (*startled and bewildered*)

But ... we must be able to do something ... It's completely absurd ... all of it! I didn't do it! (*Pauses, then with hope*) Tomorrow you will make your final plea.

DEFENSE COUNSEL

I'm no magician, Helmer. Oh, yes, I shall fight. My head is at your service to the bitter end. But my heart ...

HELMER

But your heart ...?

DEFENSE COUNSEL

I can't play the hypocrite. Have never been able to. I can

plead and I'm going to plead. But that sacred glow of conviction which made it a matter of course that I took on your case, that . . . (*He doesn't complete his sentence, but makes an unhappy gesture with his hands*)

HELMER (*infinitely saddened*)
You no longer believe in me. Even you no longer believe in me . . .

DEFENSE COUNSEL (*looks unhappily at him. They look each other in the eyes for a moment. Finally, very low and not very convincingly*)
I believe in you, Helmer.

HELMER (*bitterly*)
But just because it's your duty. Your legal duty.

DEFENSE COUNSEL (*hesitates, not trying to answer the query in Helmer's words. He changes to a crisp, business-like tone*)
It's late. There are some points in the pleadings which we must discuss. Where can we work undisturbed?

HELMER (*half-stunned, as after a blow*)
We can go into my study.

DEFENSE COUNSEL
Fine. Will you excuse us, madam? (*Mrs. Helmer nods her head slightly. The two men go out. Mrs. Helmer stands for a moment. She seems to be listening. She walks to the window, looks out, draws the curtains shut, seems to listen again*)

MAID (*entering*)
Pardon me, madam . . . It's Miss Monsen.

MRS. HELMER (*nods as if she expected her*)
She asks for me?

MAID

Yes, she asked expressly for you, madam.

MRS. HELMER

Show her in. (*The maid steps aside, and later exits, shutting the door after her. Miss Monsen comes in and remains standing near the door. There has always been something dispirited and dejected, something helpless about her, but now she is almost beside herself with nervousness and anxiety*)

MRS. HELMER (*has risen, softly and kindly*)

Come here and sit down by me, Miss Monsen. You're cold?

MISS MONSEN (*her teeth are almost chattering*)

I stood out there waiting . . . then I saw the lawyer come in . . . they turned on the light in the study . . . I thought you'd be alone. (*Meanwhile she walks hesitantly across the floor*)

MRS. HELMER

Sit down, please. Put this shawl around you . . . there. (*Miss Monsen sits, stiff and completely petrified. One sees that she has not slept for many nights. Mrs. Helmer waits calmly, looking compassionately at the girl. After a long pause, she speaks quietly*) Dear little friend, don't be afraid. Just tell me everything . . .

MISS MONSEN (*an expression of terror crosses her face. She gasps*)

You . . . you know?

MRS. HELMER (*patting her hand*)

I have understood.

MISS MONSEN (*completely broken, she falls on the sofa, her face hidden in her hands*)

I can't . . . I can't tell it!

27 — Modern Nordic Plays: Norway

MRS. HELMER *(mildly)*

Let me help you ... because I think I know why you did it. You love him, just as I love him ... *(Miss Monsen quickly removes her hands from her face, stares at her in fear, creeping into the corner of the sofa away from Mrs. Helmer. Mrs. Helmer smiles)* You must know that I am not angry at you for that ... You saw how hard he struggled ... How it had become the most important thing in his life to win this battle ...

MISS MONSEN

Yes ... he had to win. He *had* to win! *(Suddenly, loud, a little hysterical)* Everyone had to see that he was the right one! Everyone had to see how good he was and how wicked ... how horribly wicked ... *(Breaks off, hides her face in her hands again)*

MRS. HELMER

He spoke to you often about this?

MISS MONSEN *(becomes more calm, seems to be recalling the past)*

When he walked back and forth in his office, tense and tormented, then I ... I couldn't bear it. I saw so clearly all the good, the great things he wanted to do with his life ... and all the wretched pettiness which stood in his way. And I thought ...

MRS. HELMER

You thought ...?

MISS MONSEN

I *knew* that all he said was true. It was as true as God's own word. And I thought ... night and day ... that everyone must be made to see it. If they only knew, they would no longer doubt. Everyone would understand that it had to be him and no one else.

MRS. HELMER

You were willing to do anything for his sake?

MISS MONSEN (*carried away*)

Yes! (*Pause*) But not for *his* sake only. For all people, for all the others who were as terrified as I had been ... Ever since I was a little girl they've threatened me with hell ... The first thing I can remember is my father reading and reading in his stern voice, about everlasting torture ... I was always afraid ... of everything ... of the dark, of fire ... whatever I did, I felt my father's eyes on me ... always threatening me with punishment ... and damnation ...

MRS. HELMER

You still live at home with your father?

MISS MONSEN (*shuddering*)

Yes. (*Pauses, then more fervent and confident*) But ... when I came to Bishop Helmer, everything changed ... my whole life changed. Because he made me see that all that I was afraid of ... it wasn't true at all. It was just something ugly and bad that people had made up, just something my father said in order to frighten me ... I became so happy ... so terribly happy ... Nothing was bad any more... He had *saved* me. And now, now he would be able to save many many others ... as he had saved me ... if only ... (*Pause*) If only I could make people understand ...

MRS. HELMER

So you wrote down the things he said?

MISS MONSEN

Yes.

MRS. HELMER

In shorthand?

MISS MONSEN

His words burned into me. I could never forget his words!

MRS. HELMER

And so you sent out the anonymous letters?

MISS MONSEN

Yes.

MRS. HELMER

Then you became afraid when there was talk of the type-writer? You tried to file off the keys and then hid the machine?

MISS MONSEN

I had planned to take it and throw it into the river . . . But then . . . (*Bursts into violent crying, falls face down on the sofa again*) Then he found it. Then he found it . .

MRS. HELMER (*letting her cry, rises, goes to the door through which the men exited, listens, returns. Takes Miss Monsen by the shoulders*)

There, there, my little friend . . .

MISS MONSEN (*lifts her face in despair*)

Many many times I've tried to tell it. But I . . . couldn't. I didn't dare!

MRS. HELMER

Because of your father?

MISS MONSEN (*almost a cry of terror*)

Yes! And that first day in the courtroom when they questioned me. I couldn't tell it then . . . before *him* . . . before all those people who were staring at me.

MRS. HELMER

I can understand that.

MISS MONSEN *(calmer, more confident)*
At last I wrote this. *(Takes a letter from her coat pocket and gives it to Mrs. Helmer)*

MRS. HELMER *(looking at the letter)*
To me?

MISS MONSEN
I thought . . . that you might understand . . . that you would tell him . . . so that . . . that he wouldn't . . . be too angry with me. . .

MRS. HELMER *(taking her into her arms, sits beside her)*
And you, my dear, what were you going to do?

MISS MONSEN
I was going to . . . I *had* to . . . *(Voice breaks)* But . . . But I didn't dare. When I stood there beside the river, I didn't dare . . .

MRS. HELMER
It's difficult to die.

MISS MONSEN *(with a curious, sudden matter-of-factness, she seems to be quoting something she had implanted in her mind during many sleepless nights)*
That isn't so hard . . . I'll manage that . . . Because there's no one who will be sad. No one who will miss me . . . and it's impossible for me to go on living. *(The terror and hysteria seize her again)* But . . . but . . .

MRS. HELMER *(gently)*
Yes, my dear?

MISS MONSEN *(in a cry)*
But suppose it's true all the same! What if it's true that I will go to hell!

MRS. HELMER
He *saved* you, you said. You believed so completely and

steadfastly in him that you could do anything for him. Do you doubt him now?

MISS MONSEN

Yes ... because he cannot *know*. No one can really *know!*

MRS. HELMER

But don't you believe that God understands all things?

MISS MONSEN

Not if ... not if there's a hell. Then, I don't believe that anyone understands anything!

MRS. HELMER

But you know one thing. That Jesus lives. That He lives to take our sins upon Himself.

MISS MONSEN

No one will take my sin upon himself! No one! *(Hysterically)* Everyone speaks all the time about Jesus. I don't know if he exists. I don't know anything. I cannot go on living ... and I'm afraid to die! *(Throws herself again into the corner of the sofa and cries hysterically. Mrs. Helmer pats her tenderly on the shoulder, rises, puts the shawl around her, brushes her hand across her own brow in a tired troubled gesture. Then she walks determinedly across the room to the door through which the two men exited, opens it, and calls)*

MRS. HELMER

Sigurd ... come in here, please. *(Goes back and waits in the center of the room)*

HELMER *(entering quickly)*

What is it, Margrethe? ... We're rather busy ...

DEFENSE COUNSEL *(behind him in the doorway)*

Oh, no, Bishop, not really. There's not much more we

can do today. I'll say goodnight. Madam will excuse me? You try to get some sleep ... and we'll meet in court in the morning. (*During this he enters the room, closing his briefcase*)

MRS. HELMER (*calmly*)
Miss Monsen has just told me that she wrote the anonymous letter.

DEFENSE COUNSEL (*not reacting to this*)
Please forgive me, madam, but I cannot discuss it any more ... (*It suddenly registers*) What was that you said?

MRS. HELMER (*calmly*)
Miss Monsen wrote the anonymous letter.

HELMER (*completely astounded*)
Miss Monsen! What on earth!

Takes a step toward the sofa but is stopped by a gesture from Mrs. Helmer. Miss Monsen is dissolved in tears. Mrs. Helmer hands the bishop Miss Monsen's letter.

MRS. HELMER
You had better read this. (*Helmer tears open the envelope while he springs to the table. He unfolds the letter. The Defense Counsel leans over his shoulder. They read. The Defense Counsel straightens up. He stands quite still, deeply moved. Helmer lets the hand holding the letter sink to the table. They are thinking about two different things*)

HELMER (*looking at Miss Monsen, speaking half to himself*)
Poor misguided child! Poor misguided child!

DEFENSE COUNSEL
It's like a miracle! Defeat suddenly turns into victory.

(The full triumph dawns on him) Victory! Do you realize what this means, Bishop? Salvation! Complete vindication!

HELMER *(has been looking at Miss Monsen, turns)*
Complete vindication . . .?

DEFENSE COUNSEL
And what a vindication! They shall swallow every single one of their words . . . the prosecuting attorney, the newspapers . . . at last! We'll brand this accusation as vile, malicious *persecution* so that it will echo throughout the land. It's all over, Bishop!

HELMER *(the triumph beginning to dawn on him)*
It's over . . .! The whole horrible nightmare is finished!

DEFENSE COUNSEL
And what a finish!

HELMER
To be able to carry my head high again! To be able to look them straight in the eye and say. What did I tell you? I said I was innocent but no one would believe me . . . no one . . .

DEFENSE COUNSEL
You can now sit secure in you bishop's chair, Helmer! No hell-fire preacher can overthrow you now. Good Lord, people will be coming in droves from far and wide to hear your sermons.

HELMER *(with sudden strong joy)*
From defeat to triumph! *(It seems as if all other thoughts have been obliterated. Mrs. Helmer watches his expression attentively)*

DEFENSE COUNSEL *(has picked up the letter and rereads it, saying half to himself)*
Absolutely clear ... can't be disputed ... never in my whole career have I experienced anything like it ...

MRS. HELMER *(steps calmly forward and speaks quietly)*
This woman sinned through self-effacing love and deep fidelity.

DEFENSE COUNSEL *(at first disoriented)*
I beg your pardon? Well, well, her motive will be an excellent extenuating circumstance. I shall defend her myself.

MRS. HELMER *(as before)*
What she wrote in the letter were Sigurd's own thoughts.

HELMER *(struck)*
My own thoughts ...

DEFENSE COUNSEL *(to him)*
Now, now, you mustn't worry yourself about that. It's the deed that counts, the accomplished deed.

MRS. HELMER *(thoughtfully)*
It's the deed that counts ...

DEFENSE COUNSEL
Good heavens, yes, madam. Otherwise where would we all end? All day we think highly disparaging thoughts about a lot of people. Should that be punishable?

MRS. HELMER
Then what the Scriptures say about sinful thoughts and desires is not true?

DEFENSE COUNSEL *(begins to realize that matters are taking a dangerous turn)*
What the Scriptures say is irrelevant to the law. The

law punishes the deed. That's what one's held responsible for.

MRS. HELMER *(firmly and calmly)*
She cannot bear the responsibility.

DEFENSE COUNSEL
She cannot, you say? But she must!

MRS. HELMER
She's too frail to bear it.

DEFENSE COUNSEL
Too frail? *(Glances at Miss Monsen. Human compassion returns to his voice, but . . .)* Don't forget, madam, that the court will show greater leniency toward her than toward your husband. A short imprisonment . . . perhaps even a suspended sentence . . . the sensation around her will soon die down . . .

MRS. HELMER
If she must bear the responsibility, then everything in her life will collapse in ruins.

DEFENSE COUNSEL
Aren't we being a little melodramatic now, madam? What will collapse in ruins?

MRS. HELMER
Her trust in God. All that will remain will be the fear of hell.

DEFENSE COUNSEL
I'd like to understand you, but I don't. Perhaps it's because I have only one religion, and that's justice. There is but one, just human law: guilt shall be atoned!

MRS. HELMER
That's true. But by whom?

DEFENSE COUNSEL
By whom? By the guilty party! If society allows an innocent man to be condemned then a terrible outrage is
perpetrated: a judicial murder!

MRS. HELMER
The whole faith and hope of mankind is built upon
a judicial murder.

DEFENSE COUNSEL
You mean . . .?

MRS. HELMER
The death of Jesus.

HELMER (*struck, half to himself*)
The death of Jesus . . . never has man suffered as He . . .

DEFENSE COUNSEL (*to Mrs. Helmer*)
I grant you that. But . . . (*Suddenly bitter*) It's completely impossible for me to understand what that has to do
with a criminal case in the year 1955.

MRS. HELMER
You see no analogy?

DEFENSE COUNSEL (*after a short pause*)
As a human being I see it. As a lawyer, I refuse to see
it.

MRS. HELMER (*to Helmer*)
And you . . .?

HELMER (*bows his head, quietly*)
I see it.

DEFENSE COUNSEL
I beg that we look at this realistically! Are you seriously
proposing a miscarriage of justice because the truth will

perhaps cost a little stenographer some temporary un-
pleasantness?

MRS. HELMER

It will cost her the peace of her soul. And it will cost
her her life!

DEFENSE COUNSEL *(looks at her sharply)*
Neither you nor I know that!

MRS. HELMER

Yes, *I* know!

DEFENSE COUNSEL *(walking excitedly back and forth)*
It's simply incomprehensible to me! Here, suddenly a
thousand possibilities for a brilliant career open up for
your husband. Instead of the direst misery, he gets,
quite deservedly, publicity, good will, and an honorable
rehabilitation ... a shining example both in criminal
and church history. And then you come and plead against
him!

MRS. HELMER

No, Mr. Lind. *For* him. To my dying breath *for* him.

DEFENSE COUNSEL

But can't you see that it's absurd for a man to take the
blame for someone else? Such a thing is simply not
done!

MRS. HELMER

And yet Jesus thought that one ought to do just that.
That's why He did it. Therefore each Sunday, every pastor
preaches that men must do as Jesus did. The whole of
Christianity is built upon this continuous appeal to mankind.

DEFENSE COUNSEL

There's a difference between Christianity and practical life!

MRS. HELMER

Yes, there certainly is. But some clergymen have thought perhaps that there ought not be such a difference. Do you believe there are such clergymen, Sigurd?

HELMER *(standing, pale and moved, in the center of the stage, his hands gripping the back of a chair)*

Yes, Margrethe, I believe there are. I know that there are many, many pastors who quite glibly preach Jesus's example on Sundays ... but who never think that there may come a gray, dreary weekday when they will be asked to follow that example. *(Pauses. His voice rises)* And yet, it is true. That is a law, Lind, just as strict as your criminal law ... An officer may grow old in times of peace, proud of his uniform and rank. But if the situation arises wherein his life is demanded, then it's his duty to give it. The captain prefers to steer his ship in fair weather. But if disaster strikes, then it's his duty to let all others live, while he goes down with his ship. That's the law.

DEFENSE COUNSEL *(realizing that this is seriously meant)*

Is it possible that you don't realize that a crushing avalanche will bury you if you are found guilty? You will stand there stripped of honor and power, stripped of mantle and collar, stripped of a future and a livelihood! You will be cursed and ridiculed, spat upon, a poor thing without honor, on whom no one will have pity! Do you really understand, Bishop, what is at stake?

HELMER *(cannot prevent a shudder)*
Yes.

DEFENSE COUNSEL
And do you also see what awaits you if you only stretch out your hand? Tenfold greater power and esteem, tenfold greater respect for your ideas and ideals. Do you see that?

HELMER
Yes, I see that.

DEFENSE COUNSEL
Then what is your answer? *(There is a pause. Helmer walks slowly to the window, opens it, stands for a moment, taking in a deep breath. He then shuts the window. The others, with the exception of the weeping Miss Monsen, who lies with her face in the sofa cushion, follow him intently with their eyes. Helmer turns, passes Miss Monsen, lays a hand for a moment on her head, smiling tenderly, then walks back to the chair by which he stood)*

HELMER *(firmly)*
I answer: What is a man profited, if he gain the whole world and lose his own soul? *(The Defense Counsel throws up his hands in resignation. Mrs. Helmer's face lights up with an intense happiness)* It has taken me a life-time to see this. A life which I believed was rich, but which was wasted. I see it now. 'I am the way, the truth, and the life.' *(Takes Miss Monsen's confession from the table, crumples it absent-mindedly while he speaks)* If He, on the way to Golgotha, had met a weak woman who offered to bear the cross for Him . . . then he would surely have smiled and said: Go home, woman, who has sinned in love. Let Him carry the cross

who has the strength to bear it. *(Pause. All are silent, each reacting in his own way. Miss Monsen has lifted her head at his last words. She looks with infinite admiration and love. The Defense Counsel looks at him with dawning veneration)* What has been said here must remain between us. I bind you, Lind, by your oath of silence, as I am bound by mine.

DEFENSE COUNSEL

Whether or not you can bind me to silence . . . that can be debated. But it is your life and your happiness that are at stake. I shall be silent. If you can afford to lose everything, than I can afford to lose a case. And this evening I have won much. New faith in mankind . . . It isn't often that I ask a man to let me shake his hand . . . *(He grips Helmer's hand, deeply moved, turns again, struggling to be businesslike)* And so we'll meet in court at ten in the morning. *(Bows to Mrs. Helmer and quickly exits. Helmer stands in the middle of the room. Mrs. Helmer looks at him with love and pride).*

Curtain